**ADVENTURE
ATHLETES**

Runners and Walkers

Keeping pace with the world's best

Steven Boga

STACKPOLE
BOOKS

Published by
STACKPOLE BOOKS
Cameron and Kelker Streets
P.O. Box 1831
Harrisburg, PA 17105

Printed in the United States of America

Cover design by Caroline Miller with Pam LaBarre

Maps by Chris Jung

First Edition
10 9 8 7 6 5 4 3 2 1

Library of Congress Cataloging-in-Publication Data

Boga, Steven, 1947–
    Runners and walkers : keeping pace with the world's best / Steven
Boga. – 1st ed.
        p.   cm. – (Adventure athletes)
    Includes bibliographical references (p.   ).
    ISBN 0-8117-2414-X : $14.95
    1. Runners (Sports) – Biography.   I. Title   II. Series.
GV1061.14.B64   1993
796.42'092'2 – dc20
    [B]   92-34536
                                                              CIP

Most of us lead lives inferior to ourselves.
——William James

Contents

Preface vii

PROFILES

Frank Shorter: Running for His Life 3

Ann Trason: The Camaraderie of the Long-Distance Runner 24

David Horton: Trail Tough 41

Viisha Sedlak: Walk, Don't Run 65

Tom Crawford: Born to Finish 84

Ruth Anderson: Master of Running 104

Steven Newman: Worldwalker 120

Joan Benoit: Crossroads 143

RESOURCES

Tips to Improve Your Running 162

Safety 175

Running into the Past 185

Pedestrian Oddities 198

Quotations and Inspirations 204

Glossary 216

Organizations 233

Bibliography 237

Shoe Manufacturers 243

Preface

Whatever you can do, or
dream you can, begin it.
Boldness has genius,
power, and magic in it.
————Goethe

Running, and its noble cousin walking, is the most basic, natural form of exercise—and maybe the best. Humans were born to be pedestrians. Our ancestors ran for food, for survival. Today, most children are walking by their first birthday and soon thereafter become adept sprinters. As we age, we tend to favor longer distances. Those who regard the current running-walking boom as nothing more than a fad, along the lines of the hula hoop or the pogo stick, fail to recognize what a primal activity it is for our species.

Though we look with awe upon the blazing speed of the cheetah, the leaping ability of the kangaroo, the underwater antics of the dolphin, and the gymnastic agility of the gibbon, no animal in the kingdom can match the human animal's all-around athletic skills. Picture a mammal decathlon, with events in sprinting, endurance running, long jumping, high jumping, gymnastics, swimming, and deep diving. The other animals would win most of the individual events, but a fit human would capture the "all-around" title. And in one event—long-distance running—the human would outperform all other animals of comparable size, as well as many quite a bit larger.

There are plenty of examples that attest to the human's remarkable powers of endurance. As zoologist David Carrier of the University of Michigan reported in a 1985 issue of *Current Anthropology*, "Bushmen are reported to run down duiker, steenbok and gemsbok during the rainy season, and wildebeest and zebra during the hot dry season. Tarahumara Indians chase deer through the mountains of

Northern Mexico, until the animals collapse from exhaustion, and then throttle them by hand. Paiutes and Navajo of the American Southwest are reported to have hunted pronghorn antelope (one of the fastest of all mammals) with the same technique. Furthermore, aborigines of northwestern Australia are known to hunt kangaroo successfully this way."

It's not just primitive people who have demonstrated this dominance. In the April 3, 1978, issue of *Sports Illustrated*, an Oregon runner named Michael Baughman recounted his experience running down a deer, which turned out to be surprisingly easy.

But since we no longer have to chase down our meals, why be a pedestrian if we don't have to? Here are a few of the many reasons why working the leg muscles is good for you:

- Running and walking help you lose weight, and that's important as there's a lot of weight out there to lose. For simplicity's sake, consider the example of a man who is heavy but not gaining weight—that is, caloric intake equals outgo. Now he decides to begin an exercise program. For every mile he runs or walks, he will burn an additional 100 to 120 calories, depending on his body weight (and to a very small extent, his pace). If he logs, say, twenty miles per week, and changes no other eating or exercise habits, he can expect to lose a pound of body weight approximately every ten days. For those used to hearing the mad hype over miracle cures and crash diets ("I lost one hundred pounds eating nothing but Fig Newtons"), such a pace may seem frustratingly slow. But this type of weight loss—with movement a way of life—is healthier and more permanent than any diet can provide. As George Sheehan, America's foremost runner-doctor-philosopher, says, "If you are one of the 50 percent of Americans looking for a magic diet, here it is: It's the low fat, moderate protein, high carbohydrate, and high exercise weight reduction diet."

- Movement is a veritable fountain of youth. Sheehan participated in a study of people age sixty and over that indicated his maximum oxygen capacity had declined only 15 percent in the forty years since he first started competing in cross-country running. Says he, "Exercise can lower our rate of aging to about 5 percent per decade, maybe as low as 2 percent if weight is maintained."

- Movement prolongs life (the death of runner Jim Fixx notwithstanding). According to a theoretical model developed by the RAND Corporation, each mile walked or run by a normally sedentary person gives an additional twenty-one minutes of life. The evidence is overwhelming that sedentary people are more susceptible to heart disease than are active people. One oft-cited study showed that the conductors on British double-decker buses, who did a lot of stair climbing, lived longer than the drivers, who mostly sat all day. A wealth of studies confirms that finding. One such study, which followed 16,936 Harvard alumni from 1962 to 1978, found that those who exercised regularly had one-half the death rate from heart disease of those who did not.

- Movement gives you time to yourself, time to gather your thoughts, to reflect, to plan. We all need time away from the jangle of everyday life. What better way to attain it than to wander, stroll, jog, trot, amble, or power-walk down a country lane? For Joan Benoit, the effect is downright therapeutic. "I'm not at peace with myself if I don't run," she says.
- Movement helps satisfy our exploratory urges. Whether you're in a foreign country or close to home, what better way to see new places than by foot?
- Movement is sensual. You can feel the wind fluttering across your skin, taste the tangy morning air, tune in to new sights and sounds — plus, the exercise-accelerated blood coursing through your vessels will heighten those very senses.
- Movement gives you a natural high. Exercise triggers the brain to release endorphins, natural painkilling chemicals that have been compared to morphine.
- Movement makes you feel better. Mood-assessment tests given to both active and sedentary people indicate that the former are more cheerful and vigorous. This is not just a psychological phenomenon, though there is something to that, too. Exercise actually increases the number of microscopic energy factories, called mitochondria, in your muscle cells. It also bumps up the number and density of capillaries that transport oxygen to those cells. The more easily your mitochondria obtain oxygen, the more energetic you will feel.
- Movement builds your self-esteem. By setting goals and meeting those goals — no matter how modest — you garner a sense of accomplishment that makes you feel better about yourself.
- Movement is good for others around you and, by extension, society as a whole. There exists in most of us a need to test ourselves — against nature, others, ourselves — and movement gives us a socially

acceptable way to do that. Says George Leonard, "Wholehearted participation in sports allows us to become heroes without going to war, to take risks without breaking the law, to press our limits without imposing on others. And running, perhaps above all other sports, offers us the ultimate challenge. There is no way around it: a timed run of a known length provides an unarguable measure of form, physical condition, and willpower."

- Movement doesn't show favorites for the wrong reasons. When you pull up the sweats and lace on the waffle-soled shoes, wealth, beauty, station, and ethnicity count for nothing. What you put into the activity is what you get out. As Sheehan says, "It is effort that brings us to greatness and the fusion of what we are with what we can be."

- Movement takes less time than you think. According to Dr. Kenneth Cooper, the godfather of aerobics, twenty minutes a day three times a week (1/168th or .6 percent of your week) is sufficient for aerobic fitness. He says that if you are exercising longer than that, you are doing it for reasons other than fitness. And even doing less than that can have a positive impact. Recent studies have shown that health benefits are most dramatic for those who merely climb out of the very lowest (couch potato) fitness category.

A newspaper headline recently caught my eye: TEENS GETTING LAZIER. The 1991 article said that only 37 percent of students in grades nine through twelve participated three or more times a week in vigorous physical exercise (defined as at least twenty minutes of "hard exercise"), compared with almost 62 percent in 1984.

The following week I read more disquieting news: "Of the forty-seven fifth-graders at Valley View Elementary School in Canyon Country, California, not one was able to get a minimum passing score on the state's mandatory fitness test for children their age. . . . Only one of the seventy-nine fifth-graders at James Foster Elementary School in Saugus, California, was able to pass the same test."

It seems the exercise boom has passed by a lot of people. Despite the proliferation of new-age endurance events, like marathons, triathlons, and walkathons, an awful lot of Americans are still sitting on the sidelines. Many of those around us – fortunately it's not us – are sliding into sedentary obesity. The statistics are most dramatic – and dire – among the young. The rise in obesity among teenagers is shocking. In a society that would seem to be capable of assuring that life is getting better for most people, just the opposite often seems to be true.

If pedestrianism is so natural for humans and offers copious benefits, why do most people fail to get off their collective butts?

It's easy to blame TV, the breakup of the family, the financial necessity for both parents to work. But after months of research, the headline that keeps flashing in my brain is simply this: PEOPLE GET-TING LAZIER. The eight men and women—runners and walkers—whose lives are profiled in this book are the antithesis of lazy. They have consistently declined the opportunity to stay at home. For them, sport is a way of life—as is the adventure that goes along with it. There surely has been risk involved—even the threat of death—but so what? I know every one of them would answer, "What better way to die?"

The life of an adventure athlete makes for a fascinating study, but in order to benefit personally from the "movement movement" you don't have to emulate a Steven Newman who solo-walked around the world, or a David Horton who ran-walked the 2,144-mile Appalachian Trail. The go-for-the-burn eighties have given way to the tempered nineties in which moderate exercise is in, less is more, pace is less important than participation.

In other words, as long as you get up and do something, you don't have to do any more than you want to—unless, of course, you want to.

PROFILES

FRANK SHORTER

Running for His Life

What's the secret? Yogurt? Vitamins? Maybe. I don't know. But I'll tell you one thing. You don't run 26 miles at five minutes a mile on good looks and a secret recipe.

——Frank Shorter

Twenty-five miles into his first Olympic marathon—Munich, 1972—Frank Shorter was experiencing runner's euphoria. He wondered how many Olympic athletes got to enjoy themselves, really enjoy themselves, before their race was over? That was the nice thing about the marathon: it was so long that if you had a big lead (his was two minutes) near the end of the race (he had a mile to go), you could actually reflect on how much fun you were having before it was all over.

He did some mental arithmetic, calculating that he could probably run the last mile in seven minutes and still win the race. In other words, unless something catastrophic happened, unless he completely died, he would be the first American marathoner since 1908 to win an Olympic gold medal.

As he turned to go into the tunnel that burrowed beneath the stands and emptied out into Olympic Stadium, he eased the pace ever so slightly. Though he had been operating near his anaerobic threshold for more than two hours, it seemed like thirty minutes; when he was in shape, he found, internal time telescoped to about one-fourth real time; that helped him minimize stress levels.

Entering the dark tunnel, he was met by a blast of cool, damp air that tasted delicious and smelled familiar. It unlocked the vaults of his memory bank, carrying him back in time to the backwards relay, the Bemis-Forslund Pie Race, running to and from school in white canvas Keds . . .

Shorter's first competitive contact with the sport destined to be the centerpiece of his life was inauspicious in the extreme. In 1955 his third-grade gym teacher announced that Shorter would be running the backwards relay in the intramural race the next day. Unfortunately, that didn't mean Frank would be running the opposite way around the track. It meant he would actually be running backward: back first, looking over his shoulder. He was visibly upset.

"Mr. Bolechowski," he implored, "I try so hard when I run backwards that I fall down. I'd rather run one of the forward relays."

Mr. Bolechowski, who also coached football, knew a thing or two about quelling rebellion. "You'll run the backwards relay," he said firmly.

So next day Frank began the backwards relay — and promptly fell down and broke his wrist. Rather than sour Shorter on running, the experience taught him a valuable lesson. "I learned the importance of control," he says.

Like lots of other American kids, Frank's first athletic passion was baseball. An outfielder and first baseman, he was the home-run champion of the Middletown (Massachusetts) Little League. "My hero was Mickey Mantle," he says. "Later, my heroes were ski racers. It would be a long time before any runners made the list."

As a sixth grader, Frank's favorite game was a form of open-field tag. Though he wasn't especially fast, he could always outlast the other kids. It was fun being the best at something, but he could not yet see any practical value in it.

The following year, his mother sent him off to a proper Episcopalian boarding school, a huge Gothic cathedral on the Upper West Side of Manhattan called the Choir School of the Cathedral of St. John the Divine. Frank was a singer but also a player, as he soon showed. The grand athletic event of the year was called Field Day, the winner of which was given an award for "best all-around boy." Frank coveted that award.

Field Day was a pentathlon, consisting of a sprint, distance race, shot put, broad jump, and swim. Despite mediocrity in most of the sports, Frank dominated the running events and won the overall championship, beating older eighth-graders. His prophetic prize: a book titled *Famous American Athletes of Today*.

Driven by those same competitive urges, Frank did well in school, including choir. "Position in the choir was determined by how well you

Frank Shorter's three ingredients for success

1. Truly love the biomechanical motion of the activity at which you want to excel.

2. Remember that consistent training will outperform intense, intermittent training every time.

3. Never discourage any rumor that pertains to you and your performance.

---

sang," he recalls. "Moving up in ranking meant as much to me as my Field Day victory."

Frank returned to Middletown to attend a public junior high school. In gym class, he was reunited with Mr. Bolechowski, of the backwards relay. The seasonal sport at that time was football, which Frank shunned; he asked to run laps instead. "I did it partly to avoid football, partly to get in shape for skiing, partly for the fun of it," Shorter says. "I never counted the laps—I just ran until the bell rang. No one ever bugged me about it, and no one ever joined me."

For most kids, running laps is hellish punishment; for thirteen-year-old Frank Shorter, it was a release from the punishment of blocking and tackling or, more to the point, of being blocked and tackled. It was also a means of getting in shape for skiing. "I watched the 1960 Olympics on television, but it was the winter games that really got me. When I pictured myself winning an Olympic race, it was always a ski race. I knew all about Jean-Claude Killy and nothing about Abebe Bikila."

In the tenth grade, Shorter left home to attend Mount Hermon, a prep school in northwestern Massachusetts where running enjoyed the prestige usually reserved for football and basketball. The school had long sponsored a foot race, the Bemis-Forslund Pie Race, an annual community affair that was older than the Boston Marathon. Dating from 1891, it is a combination road and cross-country race, 4.55 miles around the Mount Hermon campus. Apple pies are awarded to males who finish under thirty-three minutes and females who finish under forty minutes. Shorter had never even seen a road race, but he was confident that if he paced himself, he could go the distance. "I didn't even let myself think about the pie," he says.

At the starting line, Shorter looked absurdly skinny and unprepossessing in his sweatshirt, baggy gym shorts, and white Keds. Anyone who did notice him would never have seen him as a competitive force.

Nevertheless, a couple of miles into the race, he was in respectable position near the middle of the pack of a hundred runners. He finished thirty-fourth in a time of 29:22, earning a pie, which he took back and shared with his buddies.

But it was the following year's race that really stirred his juices. "I began to pass people on the downhills. I kept my pace on the flats and passed some more. Then, with about a third of a mile to go, winding down a hill, I saw that there were only a half-dozen runners ahead of me. As I approached the line, on my way to finishing second, I thought, 'So this is what a race is like. Maybe I do have some talent.'" (The following year, 1964, Shorter won the Bemis-Forslund Pie Race; in 1979 he set the course record, 20:54.)

He watched the 1964 Olympics on a small black-and-white television at the school recreation center, and this time the summer games caught his attention. He was especially moved by the gutsy distance victories of Americans Bob Schul in the 5,000-meter run and Billy Mills in the 10,000. The Olympic distance coach was Bob Giegengack, from Yale, a fact Shorter would recall when applying to colleges.

Coach Giegengack was a neat fit in Shorter's life. His coaching style encouraged variety and allowed the runners to set incremental goals in interesting ways. "He believed in mixing hard and easy days," Shorter explains. "Three times a week, there were critical hard days – two intervals and one long run. It was a highly individualized system. We never knew exactly what we were going to do until the day of the workout. We'd talk with Gieg, tell him how we felt, how the long Sunday run had gone, then he would give us the workout. After we did the workout, we'd go back and talk with him again. If we were able to do it as scripted, we got positive reinforcement; if not – say we were having a terrible day – then we could scale it down. For example, if I was supposed to run twelve quarters in sixty-five seconds each, and I did eight and now I'm running sixty-seven, Gieg would say, 'Okay, run eight 220s at thirty-three.' His system let us quantify our training and be honest about our effort. Even today, it's the way I train."

During Shorter's stay at Yale, Giegengack often told his runners,

"Look, you're going to be professionals in your chosen field. My obligation is to give you the means to coach yourself, so that if any of you want to continue with running — I'm sure you won't, but if you do — you'll have the means." To this day, Shorter has had no coach since Giegengack.

Frank's first three years of pre-med studies at Yale were highlighted more by academic success than track accomplishments. Training was his personal reward for studying hard, but studying hard interfered with training hard. Competitively, he was, in his own words, "a fairly steady distance runner, good for dual-meet points, good for the anchor mile on a distance medley relay, improving my times from Mount Hermon, and on occasion scoring well in a conference meet."

The summer after his junior year, he ran, almost as a lark, the 1968 U.S. Olympic Trials Marathon, in Alamosa, Colorado. He borrowed shoes that were a half-size too small, causing him to drop out with bleeding feet after a few miles. As always, Shorter went to school on the experience. "I was in ninth place when I quit," he recalls. "If not for the tight shoes, I definitely would have finished, though probably no better than twentieth. I learned that there were people better than me — but only a few and only a little better. Those people were running twice a day, about twenty miles total, while I was running seven or eight."

He also learned that he didn't like the marathon very much. "It seemed an awfully long way to run. I saw it the same way everyone else did — a possible way to make the Olympic team."

During his senior year at Yale, he raised his game to a new level, finishing nineteenth in the National Collegiate Athletic Association (NCAA) cross-country meet and earning All-American honors, a rare feat for an Ivy Leaguer. In track, he won both the one-mile and two-mile races at the Harvard-Princeton-Yale meet, then finished second in the indoor NCAA two-mile race, lowering his personal record (PR) to 8:45.2.

One afternoon before a spring practice, Shorter approached Giegengack. "Level with me," he said. "Just how good do you think I could be?"

The coach, who had often been critical of his charge's work habits, didn't hesitate. "Very good — especially in the marathon. If you work at it, you could make the Olympic team, probably even win a medal."

Those words had the effect of a performance-enhancing drug. "I simply wasn't willing to put in the time unless I had a good chance of success." So great was his respect for Giegengack that he now fully believed he had that chance. With a juiced-up training regime and buoyed confidence, Shorter closed out his college career by winning the NCAA six-mile race (29:00.2) and finishing fourth at three miles (13:43.4).

After college, relieved of academic stress, Shorter became intent on discovering his full potential as a distance runner. "I zeroed in on running, made it so nothing else mattered. One thing I've always liked about running: you can't hide anything from yourself. The watch never lies, so you always know how good you are. On the other hand, it's easy to have the feeling, 'If I had only worked harder, I could have been . . .' I didn't want to quit and say for the rest of my life, 'Well, maybe I could have been.'"

He dropped out of the University of New Mexico medical school because there was not enough time to train and study medicine. For the next couple of years, he was a "running bum," living an itinerant life, crashing at friends' homes from Florida to Colorado to California. He got married and his wife traveled right along with him. He earned little money, apparently thriving on the opportunity to excel at running.

Shorter eventually enrolled in law school at the University of Florida, skipping the semesters that interfered with his Olympic training buildup but staying with it to acquire his law degree. In Florida, he trained with Jack Bacheler, the top distance runner in the United States. Bacheler was running about 150 miles a week, and he convinced Shorter that he too could take on a high-mileage program and avoid injury.

Bacheler became a sort of guru for Shorter. At six-foot-seven, he was an easy guy to look up to. He taught Shorter the nuances of the running game, including how to handle abuse from nonrunners. Says Shorter, "Back in 1970, runners were still freaks, and it was not uncommon for people to yell or throw things from their cars. It never seemed to bother Jack, and he would glide along, head up, not changing expression. Except one evening, that is, when several of us were running at dusk, and something—maybe an egg—came flying at us from a passing car. The car had to stop at the next red light, and when Jack saw that, something snapped and he took off after them. There were

four or five of us, and we followed him like sheep. We didn't know
what he was going to do, we just knew we were going to do it with
him. Well, he ran to the back of the car, up onto the trunk, over the
roof, and down the hood without saying a word. We followed him in
single file, like steeplechase runners taking a water jump. It must have
been deafening inside the car, but the people were so stunned that
they didn't even come after us."

Shorter's new high-mileage program brought results. In the summer of 1970, he won the 10,000-meter run in Leningrad at the U.S-
U.S.S.R track meet. His time of 28:22.8 was an astonishing 27.4 seconds ahead of his buddy Kenny Moore, who finished second. *Sports
Illustrated* heralded the victory by putting Frank on the cover. Prodded
by Moore, Shorter ran his first serious marathon in the summer of
1971. He finished second to Moore, and they both earned spots on the
U.S. Pan-American Team.

The Pan-American Games in 1971 were held in Cali, Colombia—
elevation 4,000 feet. The air was not only thin but hot (ninety degrees
at the start of the marathon), conditions that Shorter believed favored
him. His thin frame wicked heat effectively, and his mountain training
at Boulder and Taos figured to help, too.

Six miles into the marathon, Shorter was hit with the intestinal
ailment popularly known as *turista*. When he dropped out at fourteen
miles to find a ditch and relieve himself, he was in the lead pack, with
Kenny Moore and two Colombians. "Bye, Kenny, see you later," he said,
hoping it was true.

Thirty seconds later, he was back on the road, churning out the
miles at a 5:05 pace. He was content to chip away at the Gang of
Three's lead. Running ten-seconds-per-mile faster than the leaders, he
was back in their shadow three miles after his rest stop. So light was
Shorter's step and so great their concentration on one another that
none of them realized Frank was there until he announced in a sing-
song voice, "Yoo hoo, I'm back."

Though levity in the face of competitive tension was an instinctive
response for Shorter, it was also an effective psychological ploy. The
Colombians soon fell back, Moore dropped out altogether with heat
prostration, and Shorter won the Pan-Am marathon by a whopping
four minutes.

In December 1971, Shorter won Japan's Fukuoka Marathon (he
would win it four years in a row), one of the most prestigious mara-

thons in the world. Encouraged by his performance, he decided to get serious about training for the Olympics in both the 10,000-meter run and the marathon. The impressive track results at the 1968 Olympics in Mexico City (elevation 7,440 feet) had convinced him that altitude provided greater return for a given training effort. Wanting every edge, he moved to Vail, Colorado, so that he could train in a mountain valley above 8,000 feet. Two other Olympic hopefuls, Bacheler and Jeff Galloway, made the move, too. Says Shorter, "The three of us and our wives (Jeff was single then) set up shop in a house owned by Robert Lange, the man who pioneered the plastic ski boot. We had use of a pool, sauna, and weight room. Vail is a fairly flat valley, which was perfect because we wanted the effects of being at high altitude without having to do a lot of hill work. We wanted to run high mileage, which is done more easily on flat terrain.

"We had two months. Vail was our laboratory, and we were the guinea pigs. We ran two or three times a day, one hundred seventy miles or so each week, which is probably equal to two hundred miles at sea level. All we did was run, eat, and sleep. I slept ten hours at night and napped in the afternoon."

Whether it was genetics, high mileage, or world-class camaraderie and shared perseverance, all three men made the Olympic team.

On the day of the 1972 Olympic marathon, Shorter felt sleepy. Some might have attributed it to the two liters of beer he drank the night before, but he knew better. "Lethargy is good," he liked to say. "It's a way to minimize movement, muster resources, almost as if the mind and body were conspiring to lower the metabolic rate—just before going all out."

He hadn't run that morning—the marathon would be enough. In the afternoon, he jogged a slow mile on the warmup track adjacent to the stadium, then went inside and lubricated his feet with Vaseline. He taped them, which helped to compensate for his weak, congenitally flat metatarsal arch; then he taped his nipples to prevent bleeding. Slowly, he changed into his racing shoes and went outside.

The last few minutes before the gun are the worst for most marathoners, Shorter included. Until the start of the race, he had a tendency to badger himself with the question "What more can I do?" He had to remind himself of what Gieg had taught him: "If the race is on Saturday, you are ready by Thursday, even before. Nothing you do the last couple of days is going to make any difference. In fact, at the highest level, nothing you do the last couple of weeks is going to make a difference."

Shorter paced about the infield, sizing up the competition, looking for weaknesses in posture, face, movement. Mostly, he wanted a standard of comparison for possible use later in the race. He believed that if there were ten contenders in a marathon, only three, on average, would have a good day. Personally, he felt ready to do well even if it weren't his best day. That was what the "training effect" was all about. Training gave him the confidence he needed to make the most out of less than his best. Racing didn't hurt either: just seven days earlier he had placed fifth in the Olympic 10,000 in 27:51.4, a new U.S. record. "Even if it's my worst day, I should be top five," he thought. "And if it's a good day, I should crack the top three."

He glanced furtively at the athletes he expected to be in contention, paying particular attention to Mamo Wolde of Ethiopia, the defending champion; Derek Clayton of Australia, the world-record holder (2:08:34); and Ron Hill of Great Britain (2:09:28). Hill in particular caught his eye. He'd apparently sprayed a silver coating (it was reflective titanium) on his shorts, shoes, and singlet, giving him an otherworldly look. Maybe he hoped to be beamed up and over the twenty-six miles. Shorter also noticed that Hill, in a desperate attempt to drop a couple of ounces, had severed the tongues from his shoes.

Shorter thought, "Now there's a guy who has lost sight of what he can do to help himself run faster," and dismissed him as a serious contender.

Next, Shorter mentally reviewed the course. He had trained over most of it during the week, and so his visualization had real texture. "I want to stay relaxed in the beginning," he told himself. "Aggressive but relaxed . . . then be the first one to make a break. I don't know when exactly, but it will be early. Historically, whoever is leading at twenty miles wins the race."

The crouch; the gun; the sprint. Shorter dug hard, knowing that the speed of oxygen delivery was increased by a quick start, knowing also that he wanted the inside position near the front of the pack of seventy-four runners. It paid off: he hugged the inside of the track, alternating between third and fifth place. "Even in a race as long as the marathon, you don't want to waste any steps," he thought.

He settled in and found a comfortable tempo, his rhythm broken only occasionally by the need to avoid getting tangled up with a runner who was slowing ahead. He listened for the first 400-meter time with special interest. "Seventy-four! Good!" he thought. "Just under a five-minute pace." He was equally pleased with the 800 time: 2:26. He placed a lot of importance in those first two splits. On the basis of his time over the first 2 percent of the course, Shorter usually knew just how the day would go. "When I'm under a five-minute pace and feel like I'm just loping along, I know it's going to be a good day."

They ran the first half-mile in the stadium, then up a slight incline, through the tunnel, and out into the streets of Munich. As they turned right and headed toward the Olympic Village, Shorter remained near the front. Then about a mile into the race, the press bus was suddenly clogging the course, forcing the field to swing wide to the left. But Shorter, spotting a gap between the bus and a fence, tried to squeeze by on the right. Had it worked, it would have saved him some time. But as he moved for the hole, the bus cut him off, forcing him to stop and retrace his steps. As he doubled back around the rear of the bus, he swore and smacked the side of the vehicle—"just to let them know they had screwed up"—before accelerating to regain his position near the front of the pack.

Marathon runners at the Munich Olympics were permitted to take fluids only at the designated water stations. Runners supplied each station with personalized bottles of whatever fad beverage they were imbibing that day. Shorter's special drink was defizzed cola. He wanted it for the caffeine, sugar, and water, but had removed the carbonation to avoid stomach cramping.

As he neared the first aid station at 10,000 meters—in eighth place, eight seconds behind Clayton and Hill—he was really looking forward to that defizzed cola. He quickly spotted his numbered squeeze bottle on a table surrounded by dozens of other bottles, but just as he was about to reach down and grab it, the child-sized hand of an African runner plucked it off the table. "Hey!" Shorter cried, with ineffectual indignation. Then, in the heat of the moment, he reached down and grabbed the next bottle he saw. It was Kenny Moore's bottle.

Shorter knew he had erred; but how to correct it? The dilemma was this: If he drank from the bottle, he would be depriving Kenny; if he handed Kenny his bottle, it could be seen as improper aid, and both of them could be disqualified. Shorter, having heard of disqualifications over such seemingly minor matters, couldn't take the chance. He threw Kenny's bottle to the ground, then ran up to the runner who had taken his bottle, grabbed that, yelling "That's my bottle!" and threw that one down, too.

Moore sidled up to Shorter and said, "I'll thank you to leave my bottle alone next time." Then he flashed him a knowing smile.

The pack moved swiftly through fifteen kilometers, a little more than nine miles. But as they ran down the side of a canal in front of the Nymphenburg Castle, the pace inexplicably slowed. Shorter found himself overtaking the leader, Derek Clayton. He glanced around, wondering what was going to happen next. Then it hit him: it was time for him to make something happen. So he darted ahead, daring the field to go with him. No one did. The field believed the unsung American would fall back.

But Shorter had no intention of rejoining the pack. He concentrated on relaxing and on sprinting from his shoulders. It was more efficient to focus on pushing at the shoulders than pulling at the arms, and the faster the shoulders, the quicker the legs. With everything in sync, he proceeded to gobble up the next nine miles at a 4:42 pace, extending his lead. "Yes, running out front fits my personality," he thought. "There are undeniable psychological advantages. I like being able to say, 'If I can keep going at this effort, anyone who is going to catch me will have to put in even more effort—and I don't think they can.'"

At the twenty-five kilometer aid station, his wife, Louise, was waiting for him. "They're not there!" she yelled, meaning the two squeeze bottles of defizzed cola with number 1014 on them. Shorter, believing that this was the most important aid station, had provided two bottles instead of his usual one; they were both gone. He shrugged, grabbed plain water instead and went on, vaguely wondering if he had been sabotaged.

Entering the English Garden, near mile eighteen, a photographer hollered to him, "You got a minute lead!" That was good for another energy jolt. And it was news because Shorter had not once looked back, figuring that every time he did, it cost him a couple of yards of his lead.

"Sixty seconds," he thought, "a nice cushion." He did some calculating: "Sixty-second lead, eight miles to go . . . anyone who catches me is going to have to run almost eight seconds per mile faster. If I go 5:05, they need 4:57; even if I run 5:08, they need 5:00 . . ." He knew it would be tough for anyone to run five-minute miles on the winding, gravel path through the Garden. "Of course, the gravel affects me, too," he thought, "but it's a lot easier to deal with problems when you have a one-minute lead."

For Shorter, the remaining question was whether his training and conditioning had been sufficient to allow him to sprint as he had, then recover and keep going at a slightly slower pace.

He knew he was approaching the hardest part of the race. The English Garden, late in the afternoon, was in dark, leaf-dappled shadow, the path loose gravel. Physiologically, as he neared twenty miles, his glycogen stores were due to run out; the body would have to shift to its reserve tank. At this stage, known as the collapse point or "wall," the body would begin to burn fat, a less efficient fuel.

Alert to the fact that the shortest distance between two points is a straight line, Shorter was careful to run the tangents of every curve. "Put out as much effort as possible now," he told himself, "because when I pop out of the park, there'll be five miles to go—about the length of a short morning run—and while the others are still struggling on the gravel, I'll be cruising on smooth road and able to lengthen my lead even more."

Shorter glided through the park, appearing at times barely to brush the ground. His confidence was bolstered by his intimacy with the last five miles of the course. He had run it frequently in workouts, "just in case I happened to be in a position where it mattered."

As his body began to wear down, his mind picked up the slack and drove him on. "Have to run the next couple of minutes as fast as possible," said his inner voice. "Those guys on the gravel won't be able to run as fast as I can, and I have to take advantage of that. Push the pace, keep up the pressure. When the others come out of the park, I want to be out of their sight. I want them to think the race is for second place."

Shorter moved out from under the cover of the English Garden and into the open streets of Munich. Despite the pep talk from his mind, his body was starting to buckle, which in turn caused his spirits to sag. Doldrums were inevitable in the marathon—"bad patches," the English called them. Shorter talked himself through it: "Okay, you've been here before . . . you know what's going on . . . past twenty miles everybody feels bad, everybody slows down. You just need to slow down . . . less. Do whatever it takes. But make it to the finish line. Can't die out here."

Though Shorter slowed only a few seconds per mile, he felt for a time as though he were running through molasses. Then someone called out that he had a ninety-second lead, and the molasses magically evaporated. If he just maintained his present effort, he would win the race. The notion was exhilarating; on the other hand, could he do it?

Like most marathoners, Shorter mentally divided the big race into several shorter races: it helped him dole out his effort evenly. Besides, the alternative—visualizing the entire race—was just too overwhelming. His immediate goal, then, was not the finish line but a television tower about two and a half miles down the road. His search for that tower became almost a mantra: "Looking for that big tower . . . holding form . . . keeping up the effort . . . looking for the tower . . . five kilometers . . . the tower? . . . four kilometers . . . the tower!"

Shorter did some more calculating. He figured he could probably run the last two miles at a 5:40 pace and win the race. His internal clock, a finely tuned instrument, told him he was running 5:10. "I have a cushion," he thought. "No sense in trying to run three or four seconds faster and risk blowing up."

Now he was thinking about Olympic Stadium. Not the finish line, just the stadium. "Just let me see the stadium. Where is it? Let me see it . . . the stadium . . . the stadium . . . ah, the stadium!"

Shorter held form and moved beyond pain—familiar territory for him. When he turned to enter the stadium tunnel, he had a fluid, hypnotic rhythm and more than a two-minute lead. Midway through the tunnel, he heard the muffled cheer of the crowd. "Probably the high jump," he thought. "Wonder who won it . . ."

A moment later, he emerged from darkness into preternatural light. It was like a glorious rebirth—followed quickly by a rebirth trauma. For though the stands were filled to the rafters, the multitudes were mute; an eerie silence prevailed. Where was the wild cheering? As he started down the straightaway, USA singlet hanging loosely on his frail-looking body, his first thought was, "Gimme a break, folks. I know I'm an American, but consider my . . . effort. Okay, I wasn't supposed to win this thing, but someone say something."

As if in response, some fans started whistling, Europe's version of booing. A man in the stands cupped his hand to his mouth and called to him in English, "Don't worry, Frank. It's okay."

"Of course it's okay," he thought, bemused. "I'm winning."

In the ABC broadcasting booth that day was Eric Segal, the author of *Love Story*. A marathoner himself, he had once been Shorter's classics professor at Yale. Earlier in the race, as Shorter had opened up his lead, Segal had been an unabashed cheerleader. Eighty million Americans, sharing a collective swelling of interest in the marathon, watched and listened as he rooted Frank toward the finish.

But the first man to come through the tunnel wasn't Frank at all. It was a German man, an imposter, and Segal was outraged. "That's not Frank!" he shouted over the air. "That's not Frank! It's an imposter! Get him out of there! It's not Frank!"

With half a lap to go, Shorter glanced across the infield at the finish line. There was some sort of confusion, but it didn't hold his attention. Instead, he concentrated on holding form; a physiological breakdown here would be disastrous. And it was not unheard of. In fact, the last American to win the Olympic marathon, Johnny Hayes in 1908, had been awarded the victory when an exhausted Italian runner, Dorando Pietri, collapsed a few yards from the finish and had to be dragged across the line.

As Shorter crossed the finish line, he closed his eyes and raised his fists. Emotions flooded the chambers of his soul. "I've done it!" he thought. "All that training, all that work . . ." He felt horrible, he felt wonderful, but mostly, he just felt relief.

As he stood near the finish line, considering his time (2:12:20, a PR by three minutes), and waiting for Moore and Bacheler to finish, he wondered when the joy would start welling up. Someone stuck a microphone in his face and said, "You finished only 8.6 seconds off Bikila's Olympic record. Could you have sprinted at the end and . . ."

"I could have, but with the lead I had that would have been hotdogging. The point was to win the race and that's what I did."

"What do you think of the imposter that came in ahead of you?"

"Imposter?"

Though Shorter had been aware of a loss of thunder, he hadn't realized until then that it had been stolen from him. But even then, he showed no particular ill will toward the intruder. On the other hand, the incident had an enormous impact on millions of viewers. It was, in fact, one of the most emotional moments in the history of sports, containing the key ingredients of high drama: injustice, final justice, the thrill of victory. And with Kenny Moore finishing fourth and Jack Bacheler ninth, the Americans put three Olympic marathoners in the top ten for the first time ever. Such heroics inevitably spurred many of their countrymen and -women to realize the marathon wasn't just for masochists. At least partially in response to Shorter's gold medal, and his silver medal four years later in Montreal, Americans across the country rose from their couches, strapped on running shoes, and began taking the first tentative steps on the road to fitness.

Indeed, Shorter's success in the marathon is now regarded as the primary catalyst for that social paroxysm known as the running boom. Before Shorter, most people didn't know a marathon from a moonwalk. Hell, life was a 100-yard dash—who had time for a marathon? Even those familiar with the distance tended to think of it as wretched excess, associating it with weird diets, brutal pounding in bad weather, shaving the soles of shoes to save weight, blood in the urine, and the "wall."

For Shorter, though, long-distance running has always been movement, glorious movement. It's the wind whistling through his hair, brushing his skin like a caress. "I think my sensual love of running came across to many of the people who saw me race," he says.

Frank Shorter, at forty-four, looks as though he hasn't lost a step. At five-foot-ten and 135 pounds, less than three pounds above his Olympic weight (body fat, though, has soared from 2.2 percent to 6.9 percent), he is still the classic ectomorph: high center of gravity, less than two pounds per inch of height. His full mop of black, curly hair, only lightly salted, and his pellucid skin give him a youthful look. He has large, alert eyes and an aquiline nose. Though his legs are tanned and well-muscled, they are shockingly lean, especially the thighs, which appear only slightly larger than the calves. Marty Liquori's description of Shorter seems apt: "A vertical hyphen."

He resides in Boulder, Colorado, with his second wife and "tons of kids," some his, some hers, and a two-year-old girl, who is their own. The Shorters live in a sprawling two-story house in the shadow of craggy mountains, an area Frank says has the best bicycling in the world.

Shorter is only slightly less busy than God. He has developed a line of running attire that bears his name. He opened a retail store, then a mail-order business, and now is quite successful abroad as well as in the United States. He became National Run For Your Life spokesman for Connecticut Mutual Life Insurance Company. He has done TV talk shows and running commentary for the networks. He signed an unprecedented deal with the AAU (Amateur Athletic Union; now

The Athletics Congress) and Hilton International that permitted him to do promotional work for Hilton and still retain his amateur status. He is a lawyer who rarely practices law ("It's been a hedge against unemployment and comes in handy when I have to read a thirty-page contract"). He went to the mat in support of a trust fund system that allows Olympic-level athletes to be paid aboveboard for their efforts and still retain their amateur status. He was in trouble with the International Amateur Athletic Foundation (IAAF) for a while, but came out of it with his amateur status and business intact.

In between his two daily workouts, Shorter is seated in his den. In sharp contrast to the plush living-room decor upstairs, the den is sparsely decorated with pieces of exercise equipment and a big-screen television. "I'm just an average kind of guy," Shorter is saying (yeah, and Michelle Pfeiffer barks at the moon). "I just happen to be good at running an arbitrary distance. In the physiological tests I went through at the Cooper Clinic, I was very average. I didn't show special strength or VO$_2$ Max" (maximal oxygen consumption rate—the amount of oxygen utilized at peak exercise effort).

Maybe not, but something is certainly operating at an elite level. With the success he's had at distances ranging from two to twenty-six miles, Shorter is arguably the most versatile distance runner since Emil Zatopek, the Czech who won the 5,000, 10,000 and marathon at the 1952 Olympics. "It has more to do with goal setting than physical skills," he says. "I think that's what appealed to the people who watched the Olympics: they could appreciate an ordinary guy who set a long-term goal and went after it. Look at the people who have taken up that banner. Every year thousands train for months to do the New York Marathon. It's really not so different from what I did."

What's different is that he's so darn much better than they are. Though he is past his salad days, Shorter's aerobic fitness is still so heightened that he can run mile after mile at a sub-5:30 pace—all the while eating, drinking, laughing, or carrying on a conversation—without going into oxygen debt. Aerobically, a 5:30 mile is to Shorter as a desultory stroll is to the average American.

As for the physiological tests at the Cooper Clinic, Shorter speaks the truth but not the whole truth. In the seventies, Dr. Kenneth Cooper tested twenty-two elite runners at his clinic in Texas. While Shorter did have the lowest (worst) VO$_2$ Max (72.4 milliliters per kilo-

Despite his demanding schedule, Shorter still finds time for daily runs through the streets of Boulder, Colorado.

gram of body weight per minute), he also had the lowest (best) friction coefficient. That is, he was the most efficient runner of the lot, diverting less energy into the ground and more into forward movement. It was empirical confirmation of what many had long known: Frank Shorter was feathery light on his feet. Moreover, at a cruising speed of twelve miles per hour, Shorter's heartbeat was ten beats slower than that of any tested runner. It wasn't surprising when you considered that his resting pulse was a languid thirty-eight (the average mortal's is seventy).

Shorter is convinced that his greatest strength is consistency of training. "I can train very consistently, and with that comes confidence. You gain a lot of confidence by training well. If you feel you've done more than someone else, you've got a mental advantage over them."

At the root of that consistency is his love for the activity. The man flat-out adores long-distance training. At one point in his life, he missed only six days of running in five years. At Munich, the swimmers he talked to confessed that they were quitting the pool after the Olympics. But Frank ran five miles the morning after the marathon and fifteen the day after that. "It's the movement that grabs me," he says again. "I even love interval training – the variation of effort, the fatigue – it's very sensual. Just this morning, I was doing intervals on the treadmill. I could feel myself sinking, sinking as I approached the anaerobic threshold – it was fun!"

Less fun is the racing itself – especially the marathon. "Sometimes I compete just so I can tell others that's why I'm training. People have this notion that you should train to compete. It's socially unacceptable to be training with no competition in mind.

"I have always enjoyed track more than the marathon. The marathon tears you down, cuts into your training, which is what I really want to do. It takes at least six months to fully recover from a marathon." Then, in what will strike most people as classic understatement: "The marathon is okay for about eighteen miles, then it's really kind of unpleasant. Running that distance is always a battle against slowing down. After twenty miles, everybody slows down – it's just a matter of how much. With that distance, the mental aspects are most important. But you can't get psyched up for it – you have to relax into it."

The ability to relax in the face of competitive pressure is a common attribute of successful athletes. It's closely linked with the ability to adjust to the unexpected, which Shorter has repeatedly demonstrated. At the Munich Olympics, for example, when he was obstructed by the press bus on the course and when he couldn't find his bottles of defizzed cola, he was quickly able to reconcile himself to the situation. "Marathon running is like whitewater paddling," he says. "You're not ever going to be in total control. Things will always pop up that you didn't anticipate. You have a plan, but at some point the situation is going to get unstructured. Still, even though you can't be in total control, you can be more in control than anyone else. The more prepared you are, the better you can deal with the unexpected.

"Psychologists have a term for it – 'reframing.' It's when you hit a wall and then back off to reevaluate and see how you can correctly hit it again. It's the ability to recognize quickly that you have to change what you are doing. The allure of endurance sports is that it's you and your body and you've got control – but only to a certain point."

Early in his running career, when he was Olympics-bound,

Shorter was physically blessed. Despite years of averaging more than 150 miles a week, he suffered no serious injuries. Then, in 1976, he broke a bone in his foot. He won the silver medal in the marathon at the Montreal Olympics on that foot, but it was the beginning of a physical decline. In the 1978 Boston Marathon, he passed the halfway point in about 1:05 and then began experiencing severe ankle pain. Always the finisher, he limped through the second half and, three days later, a surgeon removed bone chips from that ankle. To maintain cardiovascular fitness during rehabilitation, he taped his cast to the pedal of a stationary bicycle and rode furiously. "For the next ten years," he says, "I would spend months getting into top racing shape only to be derailed by one minor injury after another. I began spending more and more time on the bike and haven't been hurt in almost three years."

Today a run and a long bike ride have replaced his two daily running workouts. "I run eight to twelve miles a day and bike twenty to forty. It's the same two to four hours a day I've always put in, but a lot less pounding."

Less pounding, but still plenty of challenge. Shorter has taken up the competitive biathlon—half run, half bike. In his first race, he beat John Howard to win the masters division. Though today he runs in only one marathon per year—the Honolulu—and a few less daunting distances like the Bemis-Forslund Pie Race (22:40 in 1990 for third place), he does at least a dozen serious biathlons. And he is as hungry as ever: "There's no better feeling in sports than doing better than you thought you could . . .

"If I can just improve my biking a little bit more," he says, making a small space with his thumb and forefinger, "I can be top ten."

Two questions remain. He handles them both with the same calm, unsmiling assurance.

"First, the running boom. Was that really a Frank Shorter Production? Take away Shorter, the Olympic medals, would there still have been a running boom?"

"There would have been something," he answers. "The time was right. Medicine was preaching exercise. Maybe the marathon wouldn't have become as big, but running would have taken off anyway."

The second question, about his father, is personal, though I have no idea how personal. While Frank was at Yale, Dr. Samuel Shorter quit his lucrative New York medical practice and moved his wife and

ten kids (Frank is second oldest) to Taos, New Mexico, where he became a missionary doctor, attending mostly to Mexican-Americans
and Indians.

"That move to Taos by your father, was it as saintly as it seemed?"
Without hesitation he says, "It was probably atonement, penance."
"Atonement for——?"
"Lots of abuse, lots of philandering, lots of drunkenness." Pause.
Silence. With no trace of levity, he adds, "It wasn't exactly the Brady
Bunch Goes to New Mexico."

Yet in everything written about Shorter, including his autobiogra-
phy, his father comes across as supportive of his son's running career.
He drove shotgun in Taos, for example, protecting Frank from the local
hoods while he ran (he was on their hit list for interrupting some
pachucos while they tried to stuff a hippie girl into the trunk of a car).

"That was probably more out of hatred of the *pachucos* than support of me," says Shorter. "No, there was no support. My father saw me
race exactly once—in high school—and never again. He didn't even
watch the Olympics. His excuse was that it made him too nervous.
Yeah, I'd call it an excuse. All I can say is that I don't get nervous like
that watching my kids compete."

Needing no prompting, he continues: "Fortunately my mother recognized the abuse and got me into boarding schools by the time I was
ten years old. Although she was too passive to prevent the abuse, she
was smart enough to get me out of there."

"If one is the sort to be abusive, why have ten kids?" I wonder
aloud.

He allows the slightest flicker of a smile to flesh out his lips.
"Maybe that's a form of abuse in itself."

The more I reflect on Frank's revelation, the more it speaks to
me of character and motivation. "Runners are self-battling, inward-
looking loners," says Dr. Bruce Ogilvie, director of the Institute for the
Study of Athletic Motivation. Shorter, often described as tough, serious, analytical, stoical, has often been contrasted with his seemingly
lighthearted contemporary, Bill Rodgers. Richard Benyo, a former editor of *Runner's World*, thought there were at least two Frank Shorters.
"He was incredibly hot and cold," says Benyo. "One time he would be
very giving, answer all your questions, and the next time he would act
like he didn't know you."

But is it any wonder the guy is moody?

A long-distance runner—particularly a marathoner—has to be tough. Not tough like an NFL linebacker; rather he needs, as Joe Henderson says, "a quiet, long-suffering toughness—a survival instinct rather than a killer instinct—directed as much inward as outward. Distance races aren't so much runner-against-runner competitions as bouts of runner-against-self." Shorter wins that battle time and again. And when he runs, he wears an expression that seems to say, "Yeah, it hurts, but I don't care." Now, after disclosures of a harrowing childhood, we know why: before he ever ran his first race, Frank Shorter had an elevated pain threshold.

The traits that show up strongest in endurance runners, says Ogilvie, are aggression, autonomy, and introversion. "Runners prefer turning their aggressive feelings on themselves instead of others," he adds. Good thing for Shorter—and for us. If not for his ability to sublimate aggression into long-distance running, to sweat the meanness out of himself, he might have become just another of life's losers. And we would have been deprived of so many transcendent moments.

ANN TRASON

The Camaraderie of the Long-Distance Runner

See Ann run. And run, and run, and run. See the big smile on her face. She loves to run. That helps explain her success running long distances faster than any woman alive. Faster than 99.9 percent of the men, too. See Ann's backside as she leaves you in the dust.

See Ann Trason resting at an aid station in midrace and you might be tempted to downgrade her ability. Seated at the Robinson Flat medical aid station, at mile 30 of the 1988 Western States 100-mile trail run, she looks more like a wayward teenager than a world-class runner. Wearing a T-shirt, neckerchief, and blue and white painter's hat pulled down low, with dirt-splattered shoes and socks, she looks like a skinny little kid taking a breather from her paper route.

Sitting in a bustling Berkeley cafe nursing a beer, she appears more — well, let's face it — attractive. She wears earrings, and her shoulder-length brown hair, combed if not coifed, is no longer plastered against her forehead. She has an angular, high-cheekboned face with thin, expressive lips that move like Gumby's. She seems shy but has a smile that belies that once she gets to know you. In civilian clothes she looks younger than her thirty-one years, a youthfulness that is compounded by the fact that she is soft-spoken, almost diffident. She explains that she doesn't particularly like talking about herself. "But I believe in doing what I said I would do and I said I'd do this interview," she adds, "so fire away."

"Let's start with *why*."

She takes a pull on her beer and thinks about it. "I always did like to move. When I was little, I remember my parents tied bells around my ankles so they could keep track of me. By the time I was in the sixth grade, the Presidential Fitness Competition was real big. We had to be tested in stupid things like how many sit-ups could we do in one minute and how far could we run in six minutes." Trason's sit-up performance was not the stuff of headlines, but she managed to run nearly a mile in the allotted six minutes. "I finished second in the school," she remembers, "even though I hated running track."

Her father, a sports enthusiast, was delighted with her success. He started dragging Ann out to the track for practice sessions. "Naturally," she says, "anything your parents want you to do, you don't want to do. I thought running track was really boring."

But she kept running, albeit with no particular intensity. A year later, then living near Monterey, California, she contracted mononucleosis and missed an entire year of track. She was surprised to find that she longed for the sport. "It was something to do after school," she says, with something less than a ringing endorsement.

When Trason returned to action, she increased her distances; by high school she was regularly running 10,000 meters. "That's about twenty-five times around a track," she says, rolling her eyes, "which is *really* boring." Still, she was good at it. In her senior year, despite being the second youngest in the race, she finished sixth in The Athletics Congress (TAC) Nationals. The University of New Mexico offered her an athletic scholarship, but before she could benefit from it, a knee injury derailed her. She forfeited her scholarship, had surgery, and enrolled at U.C. Berkeley.

At Berkeley, athletics was relegated to the wings while academics moved to center stage. "I didn't run NCAA events at all," she says, looking like she just tasted something sour. "I hated it. . . . And the coach . . ." On this point she insists on going off the record, officially allowing only that "he was a bad man who was eventually asked to leave the university." With no track or cross-country to divert her, Trason threw herself into her academic passion: biochemistry. She worked hard and ran only once or twice a week. "It was more to release stress than to stay fit. I'd study all evening, then call someone up to go running at midnight."

By the time Trason graduated from the university, her running career was a memory. What for many athletes are the formative years – eighteen to twenty-three – were for Trason the lost years; she seemed destined – content, in fact – to live out her years in athletic anonymity. To this point, her story was that of the typical "also-ran": promising athlete succumbs to debilitating injury, then to the time constraints of adulthood, never to be heard from again.

But a funny thing happened on Trason's march to maturity: she returned to running with far more enthusiasm than she was ever able to muster as a promising youngster. "Out of college, I took a job as a laboratory researcher at a hospital in San Francisco," she explains. "It was pretty boring work and Golden Gate Park was right there, so I started running again. I soon decided I wanted to get competitive, so I entered a triathlon, a half-Ironman." She looks up with an ironic smile. "I don't know how serious triathletes do it. I was getting up to swim at six A.M., running at lunch, then bicycling in the evenings. I was always tired."

In her first triathlon, Trason was two-hundredth out of the water, after which she passed fifty people on the bike, fifty more on the run. She offers a terse analysis of the affair: "It was really tough, but I survived. I finished." Any thoughts of doing another triathlon were put on hold when she was hit by a car while bicycling. She took twenty stitches in her elbow and to this day cannot straighten that arm. "It hurts when I swim," she says. "That's my excuse for not doing another triathlon."

When she saw an ad for a fifty-mile race in *City Sports Magazine*, she thought, "This has got to be better than a triathlon." So she signed up, then visited a sporting goods store to buy shoes and ask questions. "Most important thing in the long races," said her impromptu adviser, "is to learn to walk as well as run." Although she was an ultramarathon rookie, she reacted to that remark as if it were a dare.

The race was the American River 50-Mile Run – Sacramento to Auburn – and though it was April the temperature at the start was ninety-five degrees. An hour into the race, a fellow runner sidled over to her and offered some unsolicited advice. "I don't know who you are," he said, "but maybe you should be carrying a water bottle." Stubborn but not stupid, she recognized her mistake and quickly borrowed one.

She was like a rookie southpaw pitcher: a bit wild but possessing great stuff. Untutored on the finer points of running long distances, she still managed to finish first woman and thirteenth overall, in seven hours, nine minutes. In her first ultramarathon, she had run fifty 8:30

Ann Trason's seven things not to think about while running an ultramarathon

1. Stopping
2. Sitting
3. Lying down
4. What you're going to eat when you're through
5. The parts of your body that hurt
6. How you should have altered your training
7. Running your next ultra

---

miles, a new course record. She was, by God, an ultrarunner. "I did all right in that race," she says in typical Trason humble-speak.

For the first time since high school, Trason began setting serious athletic goals for herself. She decided that in 1985, she would do an ultra, a marathon, the Davis Double (a 200-mile bicycle ride), and a triathlon. She accomplished all but the triathlon. "Problem was," she says with a laugh, "I did the first three in a three-month period, then collapsed. I tried to do a second marathon, but had to drop out because I was ill. I tend to overdo it, then get sick. It's a problem I'm learning to deal with."

That same sort of precipitate behavior cost her valuable trail time the following year. "I toured New Zealand on my bicycle, then began running too far and too fast and reinjured my knee. I had surgery and missed all of 1986. I couldn't run or ride or do anything."

Looking at her impressive record in the 1987 and 1988 seasons, it is tempting to say something like "Trason returned to running with a vengeance." But such terminology runs counter to her nature. She feels no vengeance, she says, and when reporters pose questions like "When did you first get serious about running?" she curls her upper lip and says, "I'm not that serious. It's fun—that's why I do it. When it's not fun anymore, I'll quit."

She favors a line delivered by former world-class quarter-miler Lee Evans: "I love to run just to feel the wind in my hair."

"That's the same way it is for me—" her dark eyes blazing, she is no longer soft-spoken—"and I just like to feel it . . . only longer. My friends tell me I'm not addicted to crack, I'm addicted to endorphins [the morphine-like brain chemical supposedly activated with aerobic activity], but I don't believe that. I really don't feel any different at the end of a run than at the beginning. It's just fun. And now that I run mostly trails, it's even more fun. I especially love training for the Western States 100. I can go to the Sierra and do sixty, eighty, one hundred miles in a weekend, and see what I want to see. It's great being above timberline. I carry a camera in my fanny pack and fill albums with photos of my runs."

Fun, okay; but hard work too, right? In order to ready herself for a steady diet of 50- and 100-mile races, Trason does 120 to 160 miles of road and trail work per week. In order to succeed, she must be a tough taskmaster; she must carefully monitor her sleeping and eating habits; she must say no to even one Twinkie. She laughs, dismissing sacrifices of that sort with the back of her hand; the only deprivations she will acknowledge have to do with friends. "All that time I spend running, I sacrifice friendships. I have a list at home of people I should call or do things with."

But she declines to dwell on the negative. She accepts that everything comes with a price, and her friends will have to wait. In the meantime, she has many miles to go and so little time. "People have told me that if I learned to accept walking, I'd be a better ultrarunner. But I hate walking. If you're really tough and you only have twenty miles to go, you won't walk. Yiannis [Yiannis Kouros, a world-class ultrarunner from Greece] doesn't walk. I want to do a twenty-four-hour run without walking. If Yiannis can do it, I think I can do it. Why not?"

In 1987, Ann Trason returned—with or without vengeance—to the American River 50-Mile Run and set another course record, finishing in 6:23, first female, sixth overall. She also set a course record in the Firetrails 50-Mile Run, finishing third overall in 7:30. But the year was not all tape breaking and course records, for in June she took her first of many shots at the Western States 100, the most infamous of ultras.

The Western States 100. *Amid the majestic pines and jagged cliffs of the Sierra Nevada Mountains this race takes endurance to great heights—and equivalent depths. Along one hundred miles of centuries-old trail laid down by Native Americans, about 350 endurance junkies compete in the eighties' answer to marathon dancing. Squaw Valley to Auburn by rock-strewn trail, the Western States 100 offers more than three vertical miles of up, more than four vertical miles of down.*

Clutching a water bottle in each hand, Trason concentrates on the trail ahead. (Courtesy of Martin Jones)

The trail begins by climbing 3,700 feet over Squaw Peak to Emigrant Gap, snakes through the Granite Chief Wilderness Area, winds up and down several canyons (often in stifling three-digit heat), and twice crosses the American River before emptying out in California Gold Country. Hazards include rattlesnakes, heat stroke, kidney failure, dehydration, broken bones, lacerations, and even a phenomenon called necrosis, a localized death of muscle tissue through sheer exhaustion. A silver belt buckle and a hearty handshake are the rewards for the competitor who finishes in less than twenty-four hours. Any other recompense is strictly personal.

At about mile 30 of the 1988 race, Trason passed Shelby Clifton-Hayden, a former winner of RAAM (the bicycle Race Across AMerica). As *she went by, Trason couldn't resist asking, "Which is harder—RAAM or Western States?"*

"Western States is harder on the feet," Clifton-Hayden said humorlessly.

Ann Trason is especially light on her feet, which is important in 100-mile races, where foot meets earth about 175,000 times. Like most distance runners, she carries no excess weight. At five-foot-four and 105 pounds (110 in the winter), she is reed-thin, with pipe-cleaner limbs and a lean, angular face. It is a body forged by the burning of about two thousand extra calories per day.

"I don't worry about my weight," she says, popping a marinated mushroom into her mouth. "I probably should, but I don't. In high school I underwent tests; they found that I had a huge lung volume, but also 16 percent body fat. They told me I could be a world-class athlete, but that I was, well, fat. You don't tell that to a sixteen-year-old girl. I went home and didn't eat for six months. My weight dropped to eighty-five pounds."

Now she keeps the weight off by keeping the engine revved to high RPM, which could also stand for runs per month. "Training is the best part," she chirps. "I'll run anywhere, but I especially love being above timberline. My training schedule used to be loose, but now Carl [her trainer and husband] makes me tally my weekly mileage. I used to feel bad and not know why. Then we'd figure out that I had run a hundred and sixty miles without realizing it. Now I try to alternate easy and heavy weeks. I'll run a hundred and fifty miles one week, ninety the next. I run mornings and evenings, but I'm just not a morning person." Yes, so lazy is she in the morning that it's all she can do to run the nine miles to work, which she does four days a week. And the other days? "I only did ten miles this morning," she confides, "mostly because I had such a long workout the day before yesterday. I did twenty miles before breakfast; then later did twenty more; then did some plumbing around the house and went out and did fifteen more. I ran seven-minute miles the last nine miles. A workout like that, you feel it the worst two days later."

One of the reasons Trason is able to put in such rigorous daily pounding is that aside from her two knee injuries she has been relatively free of the ailments that often beset ultrarunners. She does have large heel spurs, but with diligent icing they don't bother her. And as long as they don't bother her, she keeps running.

Actually, not much bothers her. Witness her reaction to the usual obstacles to running mega-distances.

Heat: "It doesn't bother me that much."

Altitude: "It doesn't bother me that much. Of course I have to acclimatize, but that's usually no more than a day."

Boredom: "I get bored running track but not running trails." She said that before the Santa Rosa Junior College (SRJC) track run, in which she set a 100-mile world track record of 14:29:44, "I was afraid I'd get bored. But there were so many people out there—runners, officials, lap counters—that it didn't happen. I occupied myself during the four hundred laps trying to learn everyone's name . . . On the other hand, once is enough."

Health: It's said that with ultras, if you start throwing up, it's all over. "I think it's more mental than that. I threw up the last forty miles of Leadville and finished [and set a course record]. You have to have the mental strength to push through it. You're going to feel bad, but the question is, can you put it aside? For me, getting sick is only a problem in one hundred miles and beyond. Anything shorter and I won't have problems. Now if I do get sick, I slow down. In long races, you have to listen very closely to your body.

"I'm doing better with nausea now. I drink more water—lots and lots of water—and a replacement drink called Metabolol, which tastes like a chocolate milkshake. Sounds disgusting, but it sure tastes good at eighty miles. It's a lot better than Gatorade, which I call 'Gatorbarf'."

Loneliness: "First of all, Carl is a good runner and we often train together. He likes to run trails and we're very compatible. Second, every Wednesday I run with a group on Mount Tamalpais. I especially like running in the winter when we have to use our flashlights." Her eyes brighten, as though reflecting the flicker of an old love affair. "I love running when it's raining and we have to use our flashlights."

Leading vs. following: "I hate to admit it, but I like being a follower."

"Why do you hate to admit it?"

"It sounds so . . . weak."

Mile 46. *The Swinging Bridge at Northfork (elevation 2,800 feet) spans the rock-littered American River. It is sensually beautiful here, with the rustic wooden bridge cloaked in green mountain foliage, the scent of pine and laurel, sunlight licking the leaves . . . But just on the other side of the bridge, the trail begins what most runners agree is the toughest ascent on the course, 1.7 miles of heart-thumping switchbacks that rudely dump the runner atop a plateau known as Devil's Thumb, elevation 4,365 feet. That's a*

1,565-foot vertical climb, greater than the height of the Empire State Building. It's not unusual for runners to take an hour to go from bottom to top.

Trason approaches the bridge, running with fluid ease. She seems well-oiled, as though expending less energy than the other runners. Her feet fairly brush the ground. As she nears, we see that she is . . . smiling? She knows the course, knows the intensity of the battle ahead, but for now has eyes only for beauty. She hits the bridge with a rhythmic pad, pad, pad. Sucking on her water bottle, she glances around at nature's offerings. The smile remains.

Trason expresses genuine fondness for the salt-of-the-earth types who do ultras. "They appreciate the outdoors," she says, "and they're not all wrapped up with their Jaguars." There are, however, too few women in the sport — about 10 to 15 percent of most fields — and that is something she would like to see change. "A lot of women are still locked into crewing for their boyfriends," she says sadly.

"Some of the male runners can be pretty macho," she adds. "One told me that because I don't have the male genes, I couldn't run as fast as he could." A devilish smile crosses her face. "I can't wait to see him again. I want to pass him on a hill and ask him how his male genes are doing."

Though she tries to ignore press rumors and scuttlebutt within her sport, and just do her own thing regardless of what others say, she fails. The inner-directed part of her is drawn to a life suggested by the book title *The Loneliness of the Long-Distance Runner*, but the outer-directed part is very much a people person. She listens to what others say and is often moved, even goaded, by it. Like the time she ran the Jackson Five-O, a 50-miler in Dallas, in the winter of 1991. "I finished first woman, second overall, set a new women's world record [5:45:42], but all I heard was how stupid I was to run in Dallas when I could've run five weeks later in Houston and won some money." She was upset but didn't brood. Instead, she returned to Texas for the Houston Marathon 50-Mile, ran 5:40:18 (a new world record), and won ten thousand dollars. "I didn't do it for the money," she says. "I did it to shut people up. But it didn't work. After Houston I kept hearing that the course was 'soft.' You can never please people."

The vindictive smile and the flashing incisors when she speaks of "shutting people up" form one picture, her usual gentle, soft-spoken manner quite another. Her dichotomous nature is perhaps best captured in the famous Cassius Clay verse, "Float like a butterfly, sting like

Ann Trason's ten favorite places to run

1. Mount Tamalpais
2. Point Reyes
3. Big Sur
4. Western States trail
5. Grand Tetons, Wyoming
6. Sawtooth, Idaho
7. Sequoia-Kings Canyon National Parks
8. Yosemite National Park
9. Pyrenees Mountains, France and Spain
10. San Juan Mountains, Colorado

a bee." She is a docile lab researcher with a hidden knockout punch, one whose instinctive reaction to a dare is "Oh yeah?"

"Earlier this year, Carl and I were running in the Berkeley hills. It was raining and I was hating it. I was just whimpering and suddenly—" she looks up, recollected hurt flooding her eyes "—he called me a wimp. A wimp! The Big W! I couldn't believe it. Right then I decided I was going to work to be a better hill climber than he was."

Mile 93. *In the dark, lonely chill of evening, flashlight trembling in her hand, Trason stumbled into an aid station. Seven miles to go but it may as well have been seven hundred. She looked like a war victim and felt even worse. She had passed the last hour a couple of miles down the trail, ignominiously retching her guts out. "I did it so many times it was disgusting," she told the medical person who asked for details. She wasn't sure she was going to die, just that she wanted to. Being this sick was scary. Her mind-body split was a chasm: While her body whimpered "Quit!" her mind was driving her forward like a crazed stage mother.*

The doctors pronounced her dehydrated and offered two choices: hang around and drink fluids for two hours, or take an intravenous saline injection, wait forty minutes, and try to finish the race. But she didn't have two hours to wait, and she hated needles. What she wanted was apple juice. She heard her voice—a sort of croaking sound—ask for it, but the doctors, in their own odd voices, said "No, too sweet. It will make you worse." She tried to take some anyway, but they took it from her as though she were a defiant

*schoolgirl, as though she didn't know what was best for herself. She sought
counsel. Her runner friends urged her to take the IV; the medical people
nodded and urged her to take the IV. She hesitated, but eventually took
the IV.*

*She was in agitated repose a few minutes later when the head doctor
approached and asked for her identifying wrist bracelet. "The IV you took
was against the rules," he said as briskly as a northwest wind. "You're out of
the race." Did not finish. DNF.*

"Oh, I hate not finishing," she says, her carotid artery pulsing
slightly. "I guess I've started about twenty-six ultras and finished about
eighteen. I was so upset after that DNF. I hate DNFs, and that was my
second straight at the Western States. [She had dropped out at the
halfway point in 1987 with knee problems.] Actually, though, it turned
out for the best. Because of that unfinished business, I was determined
to finish a one hundred-miler. I don't like failing, and if I do fail I want
to go back and get it right. So I went to Colorado and ran the Leadville
One Hundred, and did pretty well there."

To say she did pretty well at Leadville is like saying Jesse Owens
did okay in front of Hitler at the 1936 Olympics. Trason not only
finished that steep Rocky Mountain event (elevation: 9,200 feet to
12,600 feet), but also won the women's division—an impressive seventh overall—in 21:40, despite episodes of vomiting during the last
forty miles. She finished almost two hours ahead of the second-place
woman, breaking the course record by more than an hour. It boggles
the mind to imagine how well she might have done had she stayed
healthy.

Her sick stomach kept Trason from eating anything the last forty
miles of that race. "Most of the time during a race, I eat PowerBars for
their complex carbohydrates, vitamins, and no fat. At the beginning of
a race, I'll have half a turkey sandwich because it has lots of salt. Salt is
the big problem. You have to get most of your salts in fluids."

The dietary trend for endurance athletes is away from protein in
general and meat in particular, which is consistent with the changes
Trason has made in her own eating habits. "I don't eat red meat except
after ultras. Only time I crave a hamburger is after an ultra." She
smiles, adding, "That's the day after. Immediately after, all I want is to
be horizontal."

After Leadville, determination still intact, she was off to Europe
and the biggest race of her life: the 100-Kilometer World Champion-

After her victory in the 1989 Western States 100, Ann Trason still had enough energy to do an interview with Frank Shorter. (Courtesy of Dave Gilbert)

ship in Santander, on the north coast of Spain. It was the ninth annual Santander 100-Kilometer, but this 1988 event, with 389 runners from an unprecedented twenty-five nations, was thought by many to be the most significant ultramarathon in history. It certainly was the most significant for Trason; she was going international.

The runners faced daunting conditions as they headed out on a twenty-kilometer, up-and-down, out-and-back segment, followed by twice around an undulating forty-kilometer circuit. An hour after the start the humidity had dropped, supplanted by a baking sun that sapped the runners' strength. Those who made it to the far turn of the forty-kilometer circuit confronted a chilling, heartbreaking twenty-mile-per-hour headwind rushing hellbent from the ocean. By that time, almost half the starters had dropped out and most of the survivors were plodding along like refugees. Not Trason, though; even into the wind she kept a steady pace, gliding over the hills with the stride of Lady Mercury, provoking one veteran British ultrarunner to exclaim, "That's the most beautiful stride I've ever seen. Why, I'd believe in God again if I could run like that!" Showing function as well as form, Trason won the women's division, finishing ahead of all but twenty men in a world-best time of 7:30:49.

The end. *Trason finally found her voice, croaking out a plaintive "What?" Her world had become a black void.*

"That IV you took," the doctor said. "It's against the rules." He showed a distaste for what he was saying, but not nearly enough to suit Trason. Now the doctor was saying something else, but she wasn't able to listen. She said something mildly abusive—she wasn't even sure what—then ripped off her ID bracelet and threw it to the ground. Something, no doubt, about how nice it would be if someone, somewhere, knew the rules.

Trason found new determination after that DNF in the 1988 Western States 100, and for the past four years there has been almost no stopping her. She has arguably had the three best years any ultrarunner has ever had—man or woman. She won the Western States 100 in 1989, 1990, 1991, and 1992, setting a course record each time. She won the Leadville Trail 100 in 1988 and 1990, setting a course record. In all, since that Western States DNF, she has finished twenty-one races—eighteen ultras and three marathons—and won twenty of them. (The only exception: a second-place finish to Eleanor Adams in the Edmund Fitzgerald 100-Kilometer in Duluth, Minnesota, when she had the flu.) In that time, she has set thirteen world track and road records, often breaking her own from the year before, and set a course record in every race but the Fitzgerald. Most incredibly, at least from the perspective of those with male genes, she swept the field outright in four of the races, beating all the men. Before Trason, no woman had ever won a major ultra outright. "At the Sri Chinmoy [TAC 24-Hour National Championship, September 14, 1989], the men were betting heavily that I wouldn't finish. They're nice guys, but it was kind of obnoxious. It motivated me to keep going and beat them all just to shut them up."

Though Trason genuinely likes most people, she has few heroes; however, she sounds positively reverent when she discusses Yiannis Kouros. "They call him the Greek God," she says dreamily. "He's been in the *New York Times*, for running a thousand miles around a one-mile loop in ten days. And he still holds the six-day record. He's crazy."

But her greatest admiration is reserved for the last official finishers in the Western States 100. "I love to go out and greet the thirty-hour finishers," she says, shaking her head with admiration. "They're great! I don't know how they do it. They see two sunrises! There's no way I could run that long.

"That's the thing about ultras—there's so much camaraderie. Just finishing is an accomplishment, and we all share that. I'm not sure a two-twenty marathoner and a three-hour marathoner have much in common, but ultrarunners can talk about what we drank and what we saw out there. It's great."

With a love like that, clearly Trason is not in the sport for the money. That's fortunate because ultrarunning offers little more than loose change. She did win ten thousand dollars for setting a world record at the Houston Ultramarathon 50-Mile in 1991, but that kind of prize money is extremely rare.

"Yiannis gets money," she says evenly, "but he's one of the few. If he wins the Sydney-to-Melbourne race, he gets fifty thousand dollars, while the winning woman gets five thousand dollars. I won the world championship in Spain and got a trophy. The man—Domingo Catalan—won a new car." Her voice is rising now. "I was a visitor in Spain, so I tried to stay cool, but I was pretty upset. There's a one hundred-kilometer race in Washington, D.C., where they give the first North American finisher a trip to Italy and then have a lottery to choose someone else to go—instead of picking the top woman. I called TAC on that one. Their response was: 'You don't like it, write a letter.' I called the directors of the race and they said, 'There are no women who run in our race.' I said, 'What incentive is there for a woman to run?'"

Trason has little tolerance for political games. She recently set three world bests in a single 12-hour track run (50 miles; 100 kilometers; 12 hours), none of which are recognized as American records by TAC because the splits were not officially timed by stopwatch. "My husband kept the times, they were called out to me, and I broke records by nearly twenty minutes. It's ridiculous, but not surprising. I've had my problems with TAC before. I was supposed to race in Belgium the same day as the 1989 Western States," she explains. "It was a big race, excellent competition. No money, but great perks, namely two weeks in Europe for two—paid. I was going to take Carl. It was to be his reward for all the times he's had to watch me throw up. We were really looking forward to it.

"Then a week before the race, TAC officials informed me that because there were South Africans in the Belgium race, I'd be suspended if I competed. It's so hypocritical. If I had it to do over again, I'd probably go to Belgium. According to TAC, we're supposed to care about what's going on in South Africa – well, that's fine, but what about what's going on in the United States? TAC doesn't care at all about the discrimination against women. It doesn't make sense to me."

Politics aside, one might ask why she would rather run in Belgium than the High Sierra. "I felt I needed a break from Western States," she says. "It's ridiculous, the emotional hold that race has on people. I've known runners who finished it one year in twenty-one hours, the following year in twenty-seven hours, and then were depressed for the whole year after that. They couldn't wait to go back and try it again. They were possessed. I didn't want that to happen to me."

And now, after winning it four straight years, what sort of hold does the race have on her? "For me the Western States is what ultras are all about. It's trail, it's in California, it's the best competition, and the best organized."

Trason now has a job working with biology students at a Bay Area community college. She enjoys it more than working with laboratory rats, which she used to do. She wants to return to school someday for her master's degree, which will allow her to teach full-time at a community college. "I guess I'm too lazy to do it now," she says, ever hard on herself. "Something would have to go – either work or running – to make it happen."

There are now more than a handful of 100-milers in the United States every year, and Trason would like to do them all. "If I could afford it I would, but it's expensive. You have to take time off work and fly all over the country, and you can't do it alone; you need a crew. For me the ideal crew is three, but it's hard to ask people – even your good friends – to give up their time. Realistically, I might try to do four hundred-milers next year, the so-called Grand Slam. Helen Klein did three of them when she was sixty-six years old!"

Though Trason loves doing 50- and 100-milers, she has no desire – at least for now – to do another 24-hour race. In fact, except for her attack of hypothermia at the 1992 Jackson Five-O in Dallas, her only recent DNFs have been in 24-hour events. "I enjoy sleeping too much," she says. "I tried a twenty-four-hour race in Portland, but in the middle of it, I just sat down and said, 'We're a bunch of hamster-heads. I don't want to do this anymore.' I quit after thirteen hours; I should've quit after one. Of course, the race director wasn't too happy . . ."

As the number-one woman ultrarunner in America, Trason is frequently pressured by race directors to compete in events she'd rather skip. In 1992 she succumbed to pressure and traveled to Dallas for the Jackson Five-O, in spite of strong reservations against doing it. "I was reeling from the death of my mother and the fire in the Oakland hills that burned three thousand homes and our backyard, and I shouldn't have gone. But the director is really a nice guy . . ." The race took place in a driving, freezing rainstorm, and Ann was victimized by hypothermia, which drove her from the race. "It's hard to say I quit that race," she says. "More like I passed out."

At the other end of the meteorological scale, Trason once considered running the Death Valley 150, a summer non-fun run from Badwater, Death Valley, to the top of Mount Whitney, most of it across blistering desert. "I put in my application for Death Valley," says Trason, "but then I talked to Tom Crawford and Eleanor Adams, and I came to my senses. I thought, 'If I can't even finish a twenty-four-hour race, I'll probably die out there in the desert.' And I know Carl wouldn't help me. When we got married, he had a list of things and that was one of them: 'no race longer than twenty-four hours, otherwise immediate divorce.'" She chuckles. "It was in our vows."

Although Trason often belittles head-to-head competition, adhering to the purist point of view that the real competition is within, she jumps a little when someone suggests that she is the number-two women's ultrarunner in the world. She knows that Birgit Lennartz of Germany is being assigned the top spot, but Trason resists that ranking without coming right out and saying it's false. "She's run a faster one hundred-K time [7:19 to Trason's 7:30], but she never runs any other distance. Her father is her coach and he wrote this hotshot magazine article saying how great she is. I like to be versatile—I run trails, road and track—ah well, I shouldn't complain so much."

When she finished the 1991 Western States (first woman, ninth overall, new course record of 18:29:37), she expected Carl to be there with a big hug. In his first 100-miler, he had finished sixth overall, forty-three minutes ahead of his wife. "I taught him all my secrets," she would say with no bitterness, "and he used them against me." But now, when she needed him, he was not at the finish line and neither was her hug. "I finally found him on a massage table, getting medical attention," she says. "I congratulated him, but he couldn't even lift his head off the table."

Ann is proud of the strides Carl has made as an ultrarunner, proud that he did so well in that race. But her smoldering competitiveness is never far from bursting into flame. "Carl is faster than me," she says, "but I always look better at the end. At Western States, I was gaining on him near the end. I told him that if the race had been one hundred twenty miles, I would've caught him."

Trason radiates a sort of callow youth, but she is wiser than her years. Facing world-class competition will do that to a person. It has honed her judgment, developed her resources, and airlifted her self-confidence. Training for that competition has enabled her to spend countless solitary hours asking and answering the Big Questions. And she has learned an important lesson: the race – that is, the Race – really is against herself. Ultimately, all the effort is not about beating the clock, the course, or the other runners – though she clearly delights in kicking butts, especially those of loudmouthed guys. No, that effort is about pleasing herself, living up to her own lofty standards. "My father thinks I should do marathons because I could make some money," she says, "but then I'd be competing against other people. In hundred-milers I'm competing against myself. You see, when you run a hundred-miler, finishing is always in doubt."

That's because there are so many perfectly good reasons to quit. The mind is dying to run up a white flag. Which raises the question: how do those who are successful deal with the potentially overwhelming mental task of running a hundred miles? Some marathoners and ultrarunners have described the process of mentally breaking up the race into "manageable segments." After her 1990 Western States victory, Frank Shorter put that very question to her: "Do you," he asked, "break up a race like Western States into more manageable segments, say aid station to aid station?"

"Actually," she replied, "I do it tree to tree."

Ann Trason Update. In June 1992, Trason won her fourth straight Western States 100 with her fourth straight course record. Her time of 18:14 broke her old record by fifteen minutes and was good for third place overall.

DAVID HORTON
Trail Tough

I go forth to make new demands on life. I wish to begin this summer well; to do something in it worthy of it and of me; to transcend my daily routine and that of my townsmen.

——Henry David Thoreau

The phone rang at the Horton residence. This time it was for David and not for one of his two teenage kids.

"Professor Horton, this is Scott Grierson," said the voice at the other end. "I hear you're going to try to break the Appalachian Trail speed record."

"Hi. Yes, and I hear the same about you."

Independent of one another, David Horton and Scott Grierson had decided to find out how fast they could do the Appalachian Trail (A.T.), all 2,144 miles of it. Horton had heard of Grierson, had heard on the ultra grapevine that a twenty-four-year-old long-distance hiker was planning to go after the 60½-day A.T. speed record. Grierson had twice before hiked the entire Appalachian Trail, albeit at a comparatively leisurely pace, and Horton thought it would be interesting to speak with Grierson, who lived in Maine. Before he could call, however, Grierson called Horton. An amicable conversation ensued:

"What's your goal?" Grierson asked.

"Fifty-six days. What's yours?"

"Fifty-six days," Grierson replied. "I plan to start on May seventh."

"I teach school, so I'm going to start on May ninth."

"I'm going to hike the trail," put in Grierson. "I'm going to run the levels and downhills, walk the uphills."

"What route are you taking?"

Horton wasn't positive what Grierson meant, but he guessed it

41

was both a test of Horton's integrity and the establishment of basic ground rules for their tacit competition. "I'm going to be true to the white blazes," Horton replied.

"Good. Me too. That's the right way to do it."

This was a reference to the white rectangles, two by six inches, painted onto trees and rocks to define the route. The A.T. is forever changing course, and as crews reroute the trail away from towns and roads and private property, the old, usually shorter route is marked in blue blazes and the new, longer route in white.

Grierson signed off with a cocky but friendly challenge. "Good luck, Professor. I'll wait for you on top of Mount Katahdin with a bottle of champagne."

"I don't drink," Horton said.

"Well then, I'll wait for you with a bottle of Coke."

"Okay. I'll see you there."

Horton's soft-spoken diffidence, bordering on obsequiousness, was quite intentional. He was a competitive person, and though Grierson's final remark had rankled him a little, he knew better than to respond in kind. "I knew from a lifetime of competition never to do anything that would motivate the other person," he says.

The last month before the start of the run was "horrible." The physical reality of what he was about to do set in like concrete. Besides continuing his job as chairman of the Physical Education Department at Liberty University in Lynchburg, Virginia, he faced the logistical nightmare of trying to organize and prepare for a two-month, 2,144-mile ultrarun that no one had ever done before. The final month was a frenzy of activity:

1. He sought sponsors. Believing that he would have to carry a backpack most of the time, he contacted the Kelty company and requested a free one. The folks at Kelty sent him their latest model, the White Cloud, a $450 full-service backpack that weighs only a fraction as much as normal models. It's ivory-white: the innovative light material will not take dye.

Next he contacted Nike, requesting four pairs of his favorite shoe, the Air Pegasus. The company responded with what he thought was a pathetic excuse. "They told me that the Olympics were coming up [the next year] and that all their money was committed." Horton is fairly imbued with Christian courtesy, but even he cannot hide annoyance

David Horton's three hardest sections of the Appalachian Trail

1. White Mountains of New Hampshire — rocks, rocks, and steep, vertical climbs.
2. Maine — rocks, roots, and steep, vertical climbs.
3. Virginia — four H's: heat, hills, humidity, and hard.

with Nike. "Full retail price of the Pegasus is $64.95," he continues. "Wholesale is $32.00 Their price: $25.00. So I was asking for $100 — oh, well, they must get lots of requests. Why should they believe a bum like me could do it?"

Believing at first that he would carry a camera, he wrote to a camera company and asked for a free one. They sent not one but two, which arrived too late, and then followed with a letter saying the cameras were just a loan and would have to be returned. "There really wasn't much sponsorship for this adventure," he admits. "I did get all the Conquest (carbohydrate replacement drink) I wanted — eighty gallons — and crates of MREs (Meals Ready to Eat), which I ended up not using. But that was about it."

2. He recruited helpers. He had long believed that he would have to carry his backpack most, if not all, of the way. That meant shipping food ahead to twenty-two post offices along the way (*Hold for Northbound Hiker* . . .), camping near the trail, eating MREs. All that changed, however, after he put an ad in *Ultrarunning* magazine:

Wanted: People to help carry my backpack, provide aid, comfort and transportation . . .

Horton was deluged with calls from ultra aficionados offering help. He scheduled thirty helpers to do such things as meet him at road crossings and accompany him on short stretches carrying his backpack. Some people volunteered to drive him to a restaurant and motel, or to their own homes in the evenings and then back to the trail early the next morning. He would have to spend only three nights in trail shelters and carry his backpack only one day. "The support was unbelievable," he says warmly. "Ultrarunning is like a cult, a fellowship."

3. He plotted his daily mileage, based on where crossings and helpers would be. As it turned out, he would stay right on schedule for the first twenty-five days.

4. He did research. He read about the Appalachian Trail. He went to slide shows by people with nicknames like "Happy Feet" who had thru-hiked the A.T. He spoke with exercise physiologists who told him it was theoretically impossible to replace glycogen stores fast enough to provide enough fuel to run forty miles a day up and down mountain trails. "I teach a course in exercise physiology," he says. "The books say that after two to three hours of intense exercise, it should take nearly forty-eight hours to replace glycogen stores. Physiologically, then, I had to doubt whether it could be done."

Ultimately, two things convinced him that he had a chance. One was a Biblical passage, Philippians 4:13: "I can do all things through Christ which strengthens me." The other was a rough calculation that he could cover three times the mileage of the average hiker. "I figured the average hiker does ten to fifteen miles a day, so I ought to be able to do thirty-eight, which is what I needed to break the record. For some reason, that made it seem possible."

5. He told his wife. Late in the preparations, after Horton had informed several people he was going to run the A.T., it struck him that he better ask Nancy's permission. (If eighty gallons of Conquest suddenly showed up by surprise at his house, he was a dead man.)

He sat her down in the den and bared his soul. She wasn't the type to rant and rave, but he knew she wouldn't make it easy for him. On the other hand, she had long ago accepted the fact that her husband had a wild side to him. On the other, other hand, all those previous ultramarathons had been 50- and 100-mile runs – nothing like this. She waited impassively until he had finished, then carefully measured her words. "I know you've wanted to do the Appalachian Trail for a long time," she said. "The only thing that bothers me is that you are going to be gone from the kids and me for so long."

He smelled victory. "I know, honey, I thought of that. But by leaving May ninth, I'll be done in time to go on a vacation with y'all before school starts. And I'll be passing right by, so a couple of the nights I can spend at home. And you and the kids can come see me."

She couldn't suppress a chuckle. Her husband was forty-one years old, but at that moment she could clearly see the child inside the man. "Well, you're going to do it anyway," she said. "So I might as well give you my blessings."

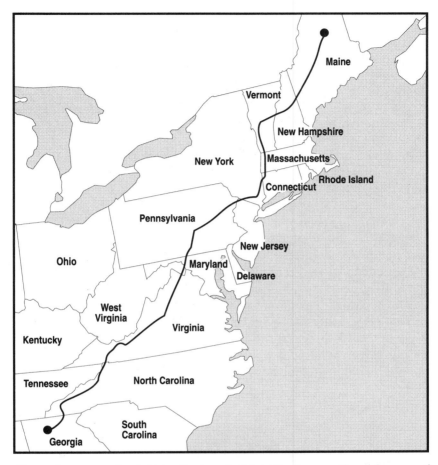

Horton's course — the 2,144-mile Appalachian Trail — runs through some of America's most beautiful uplands.

6. He practiced. In preparation for what would be a 280-mile-a-week event, Horton ran about 100 miles a week, only a slight increase over his usual output. He came to believe that he could not effectively train for a run of such duration and intensity. Instead, he would have to train on the trail. "I came to believe that there was a higher level of fitness to be reached — even for someone who was already fit. Of course, if I was wrong I was in big trouble."

Still married to the idea of carrying a backpack, Horton took a training run on a stretch of the A.T. near his Lynchburg home. "I did sixty miles in two days carrying nineteen pounds on my back, and it liked to kill me. My friend Dennis Herr—Animal we call him—picked me up at the end, and the first thing I said was, 'I quit! I'm not going to do this. I can't do this.'"

"Now, now," said Animal, or words to that effect. An accomplished ultrarunner in his own right, he was intimately familiar with post-ultrarun prouncements. "No, really," Horton continued in full rant, "*I can not do it.* Look, I'm supposed to average almost forty miles a day for almost two months, and I just did thirty miles a day for two days and it liked to kill me. No, no, no. Tomorrow I'll send out letters telling everyone I just wasn't tough enough. It'll be okay."

Animal suggested Horton sleep on it. Sure enough, next morning Horton had a different view. "I still believed I couldn't do it," he says. "I had not even come close to demonstrating that I could do it. But I knew I had to try it. There were too many people counting on me."

Mostly, one senses, it was Horton doing the counting.

7. He did his real job. "I was trying to teach school and give finals and act responsibly as head of the PE Department, but near the end it was very hard to concentrate. There is a gigantic map of the A.T. on my office wall, and I would be talking to a student or a faculty member, all the while looking over their shoulder at that map, miles away . . ."

Horton gave two finals on May 7 before catching the red-eye

David Horton logged steep miles in the Virginia mountains in preparation for his speed-record attempt on the Appalachian Trail.

Amtrak train to Gainesville, Georgia. En route to the train station, he passed a Baptist church with a sign out front that said, "Do you know which direction you're going?"

"Good question," Horton thought. Then tentatively: "I think so."

The train station seemed old, dark and depressing—and nearly deserted until two dozen friends jumped out of the shadows to surprise him. For the next hour (the train was late) everyone surrounded Horton, staring at him, hanging on his every word. "I was very uncomfortable with all the attention," he says. "I am usually outgoing and friendly, but I was so withdrawn that night, so full of self-doubts. I had nothing to say."

His entourage escorted him to the train. As he found a seat in a darkened compartment, his friends waved cheerfully from the platform. But he felt like a ransom victim locked in a dark closet. "That was about as lonely as I've ever felt in my life," he says. "As the train pulled out of the station, I felt like I was going to be gone forever. It felt like I was going off to war."

That night he scribbled the first of his daily entries in his journal.

May 7 1991. *10:44 P.M. Left Lynchburg. I feel lonely. Leaving my friends and family, the darkness seems to envelop me, making me very small.*

Thirty-two hours later, Horton, with two volunteer aides, stood shrouded in mist on Springer Mountain, the southern terminus of the Appalachian Trail. The air was alive with the scent of pine and honeysuckle and mountain laurel, but Horton was too busy dodging doubts to stop and enjoy it. "What am I doing? What am I *trying* to do? Run from here to Maine? It seems so foolish, so crazy."

This is what he wrote in his first trail register: "I can't believe it's humanly possible for someone to run and walk from here to Maine. It seems so idiotic to think one could."

At the end of the day, he again wrote in his journal.

May 9. *Day 1. 37.1 miles. Started on Springer Mountain, Georgia at 6:54 A.M. Foggy at start and all day long. Rained pretty hard in morning—off and on in afternoon. Didn't even feel first 15 miles. Had to make myself run slow. Blood Mountain was much easier than I thought it would be. Toughest section was from Neely Gap to end. Felt a little nauseous at the end. Stopped at 3:36 P.M. Early on in the day I felt very confident—as the day wore on some of my confidence faded. It is going to take a lot of hard work. I'm depending on you, God.*

Horton is a religious man, a born-again Christian, who doesn't seem the slightest bit evangelical except when speaking of the Appalachian Trail. At five-foot-eleven and 155 pounds, he is clean and lean—a man who has run thirty-six thousand miles in the past ten years—with tortoise-shell glasses and a boyish haircut that makes him appear younger than his forty-one years. He regularly attends Sunday services with his family. He is careful about his language and doesn't drink anything stronger than Sprite. He believes in the power of personal prayer, a trusted form of communication he relied on over and over during the A.T. run.

He also talked with Nancy, telephoning her nightly with an emotional editorial on the day's events. She in turn put out newsletters each week to friends and fans, updating them on her husband's progress. Each newsletter finished with two Biblical passages and was signed Runner's Widow.

May 10. *Day 2. 45.3 miles. Cumulative miles 82.4. Start 6:05 A.M. Finished 6:00 P.M. I saw a turkey and a fox, a deer snorted at me. Felt good most of day. Last 8–10 miles got difficult. Felt nauseous for 2–3 hours after run. Rain for half of day. No views of Georgia at all. . . . Lord, you're going to have to deal with this nausea factor if I'm going to make it. Gary and Millie are a Godsend. Their help is super. Didn't see a single hiker last 30 miles. . . . I really haven't thought too much about Maineak. . . . I have to start sleeping better. Woke up at 2:07 A.M. and didn't go back to sleep until 4:45 A.M. Got up at 5:00 A.M.*

Maineak was, of course, Scott Grierson, who had left Springer Mountain two days before Horton. He was from Maine, hence the *nom de trail* Maineak. Since thru-hikers sign in all along the way, it's customary for them to assume catchy trail monikers. The registers are filled with comments from people going by Geek, Stormbringer, Magpie Shuffle, Calorie Monster, The Old Smoked Ham, Second Wind, Half/Fast, Smiles in Our Hearts. Horton was The Runner.

May 11. *Day 3. 38.9 miles. Cumulative miles 121.3. Start 6:30 A.M. Finish 3:25 P.M. Best day yet. Felt good all day. Really no bad times. Overcast most of the day. Heavy shower in the afternoon. No views. Prettiest section of trail was first 13 miles of day. Did 24.2 miles by noon. Ran too hard last 5 miles (49 minutes). I think this is the first day I started getting used to the trail. Started having fun and enjoying it today. I hope and pray to have many more days like today! Thank you, Lord, for a wonderful day!*

David Horton's three most beautiful parts of the Appalachian Trail

1. White Mountains of New Hampshire
2. Roan Mountains of North Carolina and Tennessee
3. Mount Katahdin, Maine – the finish!

"I've wanted to do the whole trail ever since 1987, when *USA Today* did an article on the fiftieth anniversary of the A.T.," says Horton. "But I assumed I would hike it, camping, cooking my own food."

The typical thru-hiker begins in Georgia in the spring and chases the hot weather north, arriving at the northern terminus, Mount Katahdin, five or six months later. (Actually, the typical thru-hiker drops out before Maine, as only about one in ten completes the journey.) Horton, who has trained for years on Virginia sections of the A.T., has met lots of thru-hikers. "First time I met a thru-hiker, I couldn't believe anyone could hike from Georgia to Maine. All the same, I thought it was neat."

Horton knew he couldn't take off five straight months, so he began exploring the possibility of doing it faster. He discovered that the Appalachian Trail Conference does not officially recognize speed records. Thin-lipped spokespersons from the ATC typically respond to speed attempts with terse comments like, "It's not a racetrack." But another group, the Appalachian Long Distance Hikers Association, does keep speed records. According to the association, the unofficial record of 60½ days was set in 1990 by Ward Leonard of Salt Lake City.

May 15. *Day 7. 35.4 miles. Cumulative miles 266.8. Start 6:33 A.M. Finish 3:09 P.M. Right shin very sore all day. Took 6–8 aspirin and 2 Tylenol No. 3. Hot and humid. First day it didn't rain on me. It started raining just after I finished. I got down mentally during the morning but hung in there and felt mentally good after I finished. . . . Next two days may be real interesting as I don't have anyone helping me and I must carry my pack and fix my meals.*

Horton would later identify the eighth day as the worst of the trek. It was, as it turned out, the only day that he had to carry the nineteen-pound backpack instead of the four-pound belly pack. It was also the day that he reached the highest point on the trail, 6,700-foot Clingman's Dome in the Smokey Mountains. A long downhill stretch followed, during which he began to notice a pain in his right shin. At first he ignored it, but the pain persisted.

May 16. *Day 8. 34.8 miles. Cumulative miles 301.6. Walked all day. Rain late in afternoon. Right shin was sore. Tendinitis—shin splints. Downhills really hurt. Mentally down during day. Doyle Carpenter met me about 6 miles from end. Picked my spirits up. I carried my backpack until I met Doyle. Lord, please help my leg get better.*

His prayers were not immediately answered. His right shin grew red, sore to the touch, and swollen about 50 percent larger than normal. "It didn't hurt to run the levels or walk the uphills," he says. "What was excruciating was going downhill. Since I only had thirty-three miles planned for the day, I decided to walk." If it hurt this much after three hundred miles, how was he going to make it for eighteen hundred more?

There were other signs that something was wrong with his body. His fingers and wrists began to swell; he loosened his watch but an hour later had to loosen it again. Most disconcerting of all, he began urinating blood. "It wasn't just traces of blood either," he says. "It was all blood—like I'd cut an artery."

He never told anyone—especially Nancy—about the blood. As an exercise physiologist, he knew that it was caused by severe tissue damage. He had experienced traces of blood in the urine after long training runs, but never anything like this.

At several points on the trail, he thought, "What an unbelievably difficult day! I have no help. I'm by myself. I'm carrying the big backpack, my shin is killing me, I'm urinating blood, my fingers are swollen . . ."

Despite the litany of negatives, he did not seriously contemplate quitting; however, it did cross his mind for the first time that he might not make it. "How humiliating," he thought, "to go back and tell people I wasn't tough enough."

He relied on three antidotes for reducing the swelling in his shin: ice, anti-inflammatory medicine, and prayer. The combination worked for him. Despite a punishing routine that would seem counterproductive to healing, the blood in his urine soon disappeared and his shin pains began to diminish.

May 21. *Day 13. 41.1 miles. Cumulative miles 488.3. Start 5:43 A.M. Finish 5:07 P.M. Beautiful morning. Nice weather all day, 55-degree start. High 70 degrees. Beautiful scenery until got on Whitetop Mountain (2nd highest in Virginia). Made real good time until top of Whitetop. After that trail was trashy. Last 2–3 hours both shins were hurting. Quads felt beat up too. I'm glad tomorrow is a shorter day. Ate at Wendy's. Stayed in Marion, Virginia.*

The Appalachian Trail began as a concept. Benton MacKaye's idea for a long trail along the spine of the eastern mountain ranges first saw print in an obscure architectural journal in 1921. The author, a philosopher and conservationist, envisioned a continuous footpath connecting a series of camps for city dwellers to use for the study and appreciation of nature. The first mile of trail was completed in 1923 in New York. Thousands of volunteers later, the last mile was completed in 1937 on Sugarloaf Mountain, Maine. The camps never came to pass.

The completed Appalachian Trail is the longest continuously marked footpath in the world — 2,144 miles from Springer Mountain, Georgia, to Mount Katahdin, Maine, passing through fourteen states.

In 1984 the Department of the Interior, in an unprecedented move, signed over responsibility for managing the trail's public land to a private organization — the Appalachian Trail Conference, headquartered in Harpers Ferry, West Virginia. The ATC serves as an umbrella organization for thirty-one regional A.T. clubs, whose members volunteer to do the dirty work of maintaining the trail.

Whether or not Benton MacKaye ever envisioned people hiking the entire trail, it was inevitable that a lunatic fringe would push that special envelope. Earl Shaffer became, in 1948, the first successful thru-hiker. Since then more than twenty-two hundred people have hiked the entire trail in one extended summer. Warren Doyle has gone the distance eight times. Greg Key, The Traveler, hiked the A.T. four consecutive times. Grandma Gatewood thru-hiked the A.T. twice, the first time when she was sixty-seven years old; she wore Keds and used a sweater for a sleeping bag. In 1990, a blind man and his seeing-eye dog became thru-hikers.

May 24. *Day 16. 38.5 miles. Cumulative miles 600.2. Start 5:39 A.M. Finish 3:35 P.M. Real nice trail and terrain for first 20 miles. Nasty uphill at 20 miles. Got real hot in the afternoon and slowed down — nasty terrain as well. Right shin better but left shin fairly sore last two hours. Ate at Pizza Hut and then stayed at Woodshole Hostel, an old log house. Spirits very good. Maineak still two days ahead.*

May 26. *Day 18. 39.5 miles. Cumulative miles 681.5. Start 5:23 A.M. Finish 4:27 P.M. Tough day—lots of big climbs and descents. Very hot and humid last two days: 85–90 degrees. My friend Animal met and ran with me the last 13 miles. That lifted my spirits. We ate at the Home Place. Animal talked me into spending the night at home. I had planned on going on up to Catawba shelter to stay close to the trail. Left shin was sore from the start but seemed to ease up in late afternoon. Right shin is about recovered, no pain, a little swelling.*

Horton grew up in northern Arkansas on a farm outside the tiny town of Marshall, miles from nowhere. Such rural remoteness offered plenty of hard work but few competitive sports. "Where I grew up," says Horton, "it was all basketball. The game became a passion. I wasn't tremendously talented, but I had that work ethic and I practiced, practiced, practiced."

One day the assistant coach made a seemingly innocent remark to the head coach: "Horton's not the best athlete," he said, "but no one works harder. Give him a chance and he'll achieve his goal."

When Horton was told what the coach said, he did his best Gomer Pyle imitation: "Gollleee! He said that about me?" And today he admits, "Those words had an unbelievable impact on me. I still think about them."

Horton had more than an overdeveloped work ethic. He also had God-given endurance. After basketball practice, the players had to run laps. While the others grumbled, he cruised. "I could go and go," he says. "I knew I had endurance, but what use was that? It was just a way of getting in shape for basketball."

He was promised a basketball scholarship at the University of Central Arkansas if he made the team. He enrolled, made the team, but the scholarship was not forthcoming. He continued to play, albeit with diminishing enthusiasm. Then one day a guy in his dorm said, "Why don't you run for the dorm in the intramural track meet tomorrow?"

"How far do you have to run?" Horton asked.

"Three miles."

"Three miles! Gollleee! That's a long way."

"I bet you could do it."

Horton's roommate offered to run with him and set a pace that would permit him to finish. "We took off running," Horton remembers, "but everyone else took off faster. They went flying out of there. 'Don't

David Horton's three qualities needed to complete the Appalachian Trail

1. Planning
2. Patience
3. Perseverance

worry about them,' said my friend. 'They'll come back to us.' But after a mile and a half, they weren't coming back. We made the turnaround and there were still lots of runners ahead of us. I thought, 'I'll bet I can catch some of them.' So I took off. I started passing runners and thought, 'This is pretty neat!' Pretty soon I got to the track and there was only one guy ahead of me. I tried to catch him but didn't quite make it."

A second-place finish in a college intramural race might have been both beginning and end of Horton's running career but for the attendance of the track coach that day. After witnessing Horton's gutsy performance, he approached him and said, "If you ever get tired of basketball, come see me. I think you could be a good runner."

What the track coach didn't know was that Horton was already tired of basketball—or at least tired of the duplicity of the basketball coach. Soon after the race, he went to him and demanded the promised scholarship. When the coach refused, he quit basketball.

The track coach put Horton with the sprinters but quickly discovered it was not his niche; a quivering mass of slow-twitch muscle fibers, he clearly belonged with the endurance runners. The day before the first track meet, the coach told Horton, "I'm going to put you in the mile run tomorrow."

"How fast should I run?"

"I dunno. How fast do you think you should run?"

"I dunno."

"How about five minutes? Try to run it in less than five minutes."

"Okay."

Horton finished in 4:59.8. "Gollleee!" he said in his best Arkansas twang. "That's pretty neat."

After that, he raced both one and two miles, favoring the mile because "two miles was just too far."

In the conference track meet, two months after Horton's career began, he finished seventh in the mile, lowering his time to 4:34. The following year, as a sophomore, Horton was number-two man on the cross-country team. But during the final race that year—a five-mile conference championship—Horton up and quit. Just walked off the course and right out of the sport. "I'm still not sure why I quit that race—I guess I just wasn't tough enough. But I quit the team because I had to work and pay my bills." For the next nine years—from age nineteen to twenty-seven—Horton almost never ran anywhere.

Then one day during March 1977, he was in the library putting the finishing touches on his doctorate in physical education when he realized that a walk up the stairs had him sucking air. Only twenty-seven, he had already garnered a few snide remarks about his expanding waistline. And his exercise-physiology professor had lambasted the entire class for what he called the students' disgraceful lack of conditioning. "What kind of example are you setting?" he had asked them.

Horton, for one, was stung by his words. "I had heard that our teacher ran five to ten miles every day," he says. "I couldn't believe it. I simply couldn't believe anyone could run that far. But I decided to give running a try again, so I tried three miles. It liked to kill me."

A few days later, Horton ran another three miles. Then another; then another. One day he went running with his professor. "He left me behind," Horton remembers. "Here I was twenty-seven and he was an old man, in his forties, and I couldn't stay up with him. I couldn't believe it."

Horton had increased his mileage to about thirty-five a week by the time he heard about a race called the Hogeye Marathon. To get a feel for twenty-six miles and 385 yards, he measured the distance in his car. It was like driving to the moon. "Gollleee, I'll never be able to run that far."

There was an alternative: you could run the Hogeye as a four-man relay, each runner responsible for about six and a half miles. "I thought I could handle that. But then I could only find two other guys to run it, so I decided I'd run the first half and the other two guys could split the second half. I finished the first half, but as I slapped hands with my

David Horton's three scariest animals on the Appalachian Trail

1. Rattlesnakes
2. Grouse ("They explode into the air next to you.")
3. Man

partner, I wondered if I might be able to do the whole darn thing." He made it about fourteen miles, then began to alternate walking and running; then he walked; then he stopped moving altogther. In all, he completed more than twenty miles and calls it "the start of my real running."

His next race was a year later, the second annual Hogeye Marathon. This time he ran the whole race, in a time of 3:23:54. "Wow, this is fantastic," he thought. "I couldn't have run any farther or any faster than this."

Little did he know what lay ahead. Sometime later, an older man with whom Horton trained said to him, "Y'know, I hear they have fifty-mile races. Maybe we should try one of those."

"You're crazy. I'm not going to run fifty miles. Nobody could run fifty miles."

"I think we could do it."

Horton wasn't convinced and did not immediately act upon the idea. But after he moved to Lynchburg, Virginia, in late 1978, he began to hear about the John F. Kennedy Fifty Mile Race, the oldest ultramarathon in the United States. And in November 1979, he was at the JFK starting line with 405 other runners. He finished twenty-fourth and was ecstatic. "Wow," he thought, "I finally found something I can do."

He was, he quickly learned, best on descent. While he could hold his own on the flats, he regularly gave up a little ground on uphills in order to gain a lot of ground on downhills. Even over rough, root-laced terrain, his size-12s never seemed at a loss for footholds. While others hunted and pecked for secure places to step, Horton flowed down the sides of mountains like stream water.

Today Horton no longer runs marathons, having discarded the

distance in favor of his real strength and love: ultramarathons. He has run sixty-seven ultras, winning thirty and consistently finishing in the top ten. He even organizes his own annual ultramarathon. His wife, Nancy, named the race the Mountain Masochist. The fifty-miler provides eight thousand vertical feet of climb and six thousand feet of drop. "It's hard," he says, "but it's nothing like the Barkley."

The Barkley Marathon (actually fifty-five miles) in the lush, steep Cumberland Mountains of Tennessee is advertised as "the race that eats its young." Horton simply calls it the hardest footrace in the world. There is evidence of that: in its first four years of existence, no competitor finished. In its fifth year, one man did. Since then, others have finished it, including Horton, who is two for three. "It's a series of steep slopes with no trails," he says, talking rapidly now. "The toughest hill is called 'Hell.' It rises almost fifteen hundred feet in a half-mile. Since the race is three times around a loop, it's said that you go to hell three times. The average gradient of the course is twenty-two percent. There's twenty-seven thousand feet of elevation gain, twenty-seven thousand feet of loss—one thousand feet of change every mile. Man, it's quite a challenge . . ." His eyes are ablaze now with the ardor of the True Believer; little bubbles of saliva form at the corners of his mouth. "Next year I'm going to try to be the first to finish in less than twenty-four hours."

Horton loves the story of killer James Earl Ray, who escaped from Brushy State Prison into those mountains. "The authorities didn't even go after him. 'He'll be back,' they said. Sure enough, he staggered in a couple of days later. 'Prison is better than those mountains,' he told 'em."

May 30. *Day 22. 40.2 miles. Cumulative miles 838.5. Start 5:32 A.M. Finish 5:30 P.M. Longest day and hardest day. 95–98 degrees and very humid, with rocky footing. Priest Ridge and three others tough. Died late in day due to heat. Left shin hurt bad at end and right quad was extremely sore. Excruciating just walking downhill at the end. Ate at Gattis and stayed at Animal's house in Harrisonburg. Extremely beat up and very low. Worried about tomorrow.*

May 31. *Day 23. 36.9 miles. Cumulative miles 875.4. Start 5:45 A.M. Finish 3:40 P.M. In the morning I was still beat up. I said, "Lord, it is up to you. I don't see how I can." He answered my prayer. I ran-walked first 16.4 miles* *in 4:05. I took two Tylenol No. 3 at 8:15 because pain in right thigh was so bad. Finally I decided to walk the rest of the day, and I did and made good progress and my spirits rose again. Still very hot, 92–95 degrees, but a nice breeze blew and it felt better than yesterday. It was good to be finished early. Stayed at Neil and Donna Hayslett house in Massanutten Village. Killed rattlesnake after Pinefield Hut.*

Fully one-fourth of the Appalachian Trail is in Virginia. Although fond of his home state, Horton was eager to move into West Virginia and cross another state off the list. Tomorrow would mark the fourteenth day, the five-hundredth mile, in Virginia. Most of it had been hot and humid, and what's more, the gypsy moth had destroyed a lot of the forest cover, eliminating much-needed shade.

At one of the Virginia trail registers, Maineak left his card and wrote, "Hey Professor Horton, I hear you gained five miles on me. What do you think about all this rain? Good luck, Maineak."

June 3. *Day 26. 43.5 miles. Cumulative miles 1002.0. Start 5:37 A.M. Finish 5:34 P.M. First 20 miles terribly rocky, grown over, straight up and down. After that things went well. Left shin got sore last 3–4 hours. Took Tylenol No. 3 going up Weverton Cliffs, felt weird on top of hill. Saw 5- to 6-foot black snake on top of Weverton. Had a measured mile today in 8:46. Surprised. Spirits were good. Went extra 5.9 miles. Pleased with day. Glad to go over 1000 miles. Saw no hikers today and only 2 or 3 yesterday and none of them thru-hikers. Maineak left his card at Crampton Gap.*

Horton wasn't yet aware of it, but he had just entered a new, improved phase of the run. Ailments subsided and mileage increased. Through the first twenty-five days, he had averaged 38.3 miles per day; during the next eighteen, he would average 44.4 miles per day. In Pennsylvania, by far the rockiest state (sections have been dubbed Rocky I, II, III, IV, and V), he had consecutive days of 52.8 and 51.6 miles.

"I went the first one thousand miles right on schedule. Then I started going farther. I'd find out it was another six miles to the next road crossing and I'd do it. I was sleeping well by then, not worrying about my helpers being where they said they'd be. As soon as my head hit the pillow at night, I was out."

Another benefit of this revival: Horton began gaining on Maineak. Communications were primitive, like those of a nineteenth-century battlefield, but word filtered to each of them of the other's progress.

Horton knew that they had remained exactly even for the first 607 miles. "First thing I'd do at every register is check on what day Maineak had been there. He never put down his arrival time – oh, I wish he had – but eventually I was getting to shelters only one day behind him."

June 7. *Day 30. 41.6 miles. Cumulative miles 1232.3. Start 4:51 A.M. Finish 2:58 P.M. Cool at start 44 degrees. Very rocky day. Bonnie and Harry Boyer and Harry Smith helped me. We had a good time. Saw a rattlesnake but Bonnie would not let me kill it. Saw a blacksnake too. Run was easy overall. Very little effort, never really got very tired. I think I'm getting in very good shape.*

The latest message from Maineak: "Hey Professor Horton, let's rock and roll to the Big K." Mount Katahdin.

June 9. *Day 32. 41.1 miles. Cumulative miles 1273.4. Start 5:13 A.M. Finish 3:54 P.M. Took on Rocky IV. The stretch in here was the worst yet. Could hardly walk, sharp rocks. Glad to get out of Pennsylvania and into New Jersey. Ray Cimera and Dick Hearn helped the last 10 miles. Stayed at Ray's house in Wayne. Hot at end of day. I look forward to fewer rocks. Top of left quad hurt a little but not much. Dick had some Ben & Jerry's ice cream at Delaware Gap and Häagen-Dazs at the end. Good day. I think Maineak is only 1 day ahead. 46.2 miles ahead of schedule.*

June 12. *Day 35. 38.9 miles. Cumulative miles 1401.0. Start 4:47 A.M. Finish 3:22 P.M. First 18–19 miles tough, steep and rocky uphills and down-hills. Then the terrain was a little better rest of day. The first 2 registers I signed into, Maineak had been the previous person on June 11. I thought I might see him at the end of the day but didn't. I saw my first bear. Blazes went right through Bear Mountain Zoo and I had to climb fence to follow the blazes and I saw a bear in the zoo!!!! No help during the day. Went about 2 hours without water and bonked a little. Spirits were a little low in morning but better in afternoon. Left shin still a tad sore. Bottom of right foot has been a little sore since Pennsylvania. Stopped taking my anti-inflammatory medicine yesterday. Stomach has been hurting for a few days. I think I'll see Maineak tomorrow. And I think I'll finish in 18 or 19 days from now. 53 or 54 days (if all goes well).*

June 13. *Day 36. 48.4 miles. Cumulative miles 1449.4. Start 4:41 A.M. Finish 4:52 P.M. "God made a masterpiece when he made today." It was a*

David Horton's three best marked sections of the Appalachian Trail

1. Virginia
2. Georgia
3. New York

---

spectacular day. Could see your breath in the morning. Nice and windy all day, low humidity, temperature 70–75 degrees. . . . Maineak signed register after U.S. 22 for 6/13. At Silver Hill Shelter he signed it 6/14 and someone after him signed 6/14, but today is 6/13. A lady in the post office in Cornwall Bridge said she saw him there late yesterday afternoon. I can't believe he is deliberately deceiving me. 74 miles ahead of schedule.

June 14. *Day 37. 43.3 miles. Cumulative miles 1492.7. Start 4:43 A.M. Finish 5:08 P.M. Nancy Hamilton saw Maineak at Jug End Road at 12:10 P.M. Maineak ate 5 pieces of pizza and a sandwich. She told him I was close. He said he had been playing games with me on previous days. I figure I'm about 15–20 miles behind him. Today was hard and tough. It will take 2–3 days to catch him. He said he only did 30 miles yesterday.*

On the morning of the thirty-ninth day, Horton estimated that he would catch Maineak at 2:00 that afternoon. He caught him at 2:20. "I came up to a shelter and out he stepped, this tall, skinny guy (he had lost twenty-five pounds on the hike) with a bushy beard. He looked like Moses. We both immediately knew who the other was. 'Well, it's about time,' he said. When I asked him how he knew it was me, he said, 'Who else would be catching up to me?'"

They stayed together for the next four miles, until Horton stopped for the day. Horton, pumping Maineak about what lay ahead in Vermont and New Hampshire, found him open and friendly. Open, that is, until talk turned to Maine.

"What about Maine?" Horton asked.

"It's all a warmup for Maine."

"What do you mean by that, Maineak?"

"You'll see."

"What?"

"It's all a warmup for Maine."

For the next five days, Horton caught up to Maineak a little earlier each day. They would travel together for an hour or so, enjoying each other's company, an intimacy forged by the adventure they shared, then Horton would take off running. Maineak, who would average more than sixteen hours a day on the trail (compared to Horton's 11:22), would then pass Horton while he rested.

June 20. *Day 43. 45.1 miles. Cumulative miles 1757.7. Start 4:40 A.M. Finish 4:53 P.M. Warmer today—up to 85–90 degrees. Smart Mountain and Mount Cube section tough. Bonked a little on that. Somehow Maineak got behind me then ran up on me and scared me. . . . Saw a beaver and he slapped his tail on the water 4 times at me. The view of Mount Mossilauke was very imposing. Tomorrow will be an interesting day. 111.3 miles ahead of schedule.*

After the forty-third day, Horton passed Maineak and never saw him again. "It was a little sad," he says. "I missed his company." Even more, he missed the trail he'd left behind. For on Day 44, in the White Mountains, the trail turned steep, rocky, and brutal. Prior to the Whites, Horton had averaged about 3.75 miles per hour; for the final ten days, his averages would be 2.84 miles per hour and 13 hours 37 minutes of trail-time each day.

June 23. *Day 46. 37.2 miles. Cumulative miles 1869.9. Start 4:44 A.M. Finish 6:25 P.M. Very tough last day in the Whites. Super-steep ups and downs and very rocky. Bonked the last 17 miles—drug myself in.*

Though the White Mountains are steep, the entire Appalachian Trail is an unrelenting roller coaster of ups and downs. Every mile sees, on average, an elevation gain of 217 feet and an elevation loss of 217 feet. That translates into a total elevation gain of 465,000 feet and a total elevation loss of 465,000 feet, which is comparable to going to the top of Mt. Everest and back to sea level sixteen times.

June 24. *Day 47. 33.6 miles. Cumulative miles 1903.5. Start 4:39 A.M. Finish 5:48 P.M. Another very tough day—tough ups and downs. Mentally very low. Thought about stopping at 14 and 24. Bonked last 7 miles. Crawled up last vertical mountain. I can't wait to get into better terrain. 99 miles ahead of schedule. Spirits low. 240.5 miles to go 6 days.*

David Horton's three worst marked sections of the Appalachian Trail

1. New Hampshire
2. Maine
3. Connecticut

There would be no better terrain. This was the Maine to which Maineak had cryptically referred. It was beautiful and wild, with a no-frills trail. A high-water crossing over Baker Stream was a "bridge" of two suspended cables, one for your hands, one for your feet, a high-wire act for the body. Not even that was available over fast-flowing Kennebec River, which left Horton two options: wait a half-hour for a motorboat to ferry him across or wade the turgid waters. He chose to wade. But the rocky river bottom was treacherously slick with algae, and the current sucked at his legs, and it struck him just how dangerous it was. Indeed, in 1987 a woman had drowned at that spot when she lost her balance and was swept down river.

The consensus "toughest mile on the A.T." was also in Maine: Mahoosuc Notch, a jumble of fifty-ton slabs of granite overgrown with moss and wizened tree scrubs. One does not run the Notch; one levers up chimneys, duck walks through rock tunnels, and slithers over rounded boulders.

June 25. *Day 48. 38.8 miles. Cumulative miles 1942.3. Start 4:54* A.M. *Finish 6:39* P.M. *Tough day—tough mountains, nice view from Saddleback. Spirits were very low. Really tired of all this. Wanted to quit after each section. Glenn, Doug and Jack helped me. 202 miles to go. Slept on ground on old RR bed.*

He was a man nearing the end of his rope. With painful blisters and infections on his feet, his usually superior physical balance had deserted him and he was falling down often. His emotional balance was shaky, too. "I went into the Whites very up, but from then on I got lower and lower. I would think about home and family and feel sorry for myself. I envied people who led normal lives. What would it be like to sleep in? I wondered. I felt like I was on a perpetual treadmill and had to go, go, go. . . . The last four, five days, I'd think about sad things on purpose so that I would break down and cry. I always felt a lot better after I broke down.

"I got through it by repeating two Bible verses: Philippians 4:13, which says, 'I can do all things through Christ which strengthens me.' And Philippians 4:19: 'But my God shall supply all your needs according to His riches in glory by Christ Jesus.' I said those over and over—I never felt so close to the Lord."

On a couple of the worst days, Horton added a new prayer: "Lord, this is probably the strangest request you're going to hear, but help me be brain-dead today. Help me cover the miles and not know what's happening."

June 26. *Day 49. 36.5 miles. Cumulative miles 1978.8. Start 4:33 A.M. Finish 6:13 P.M. Another very tough day. Saw 4 moose in first 2 hours. One moose with a gigantic rack, black and big. Three major sections with big mountains in each one. The Bigelows were really tough. Wanted to quit after first section. Spirits were better after second section. Bonked on third section because 2 springs were dry. Hot the last two days—90 degrees. Glad*

Fifty-two days after starting from Springer Mountain in Georgia, Horton reached the end of the Appalachian Trail atop Mount Katahdin in Maine. (Courtesy of Everett L. "Red" Boutilier)

to be over tough mountains. I look forward to seeing my baby tomorrow. 165.2 to go and freedom.

Horton concedes one to the members of the ATC, who downgraded his feat to a stunt incompatible with the spirit of the Appalachian Trail. "During the last ten days, I had almost no appreciation for the wonders of nature," he admits. "I began to catch views of Mount Katahdin, but it didn't mean anything to me – except as the end of the ordeal."

June 29. *Day 52. 48.3 miles. Cumulative miles 2110.0. Start 4:51 A.M. Finish 7:44 P.M. Longest day (time). First 14 miles were very slow – 5 hours first section. Toes were extremely sore. Not real motivated, but felt better after Nancy Hamilton started running with me. Saw 2 spectacular views of Mount Katahdin, but it didn't faze me. Toes got sore and sorer. Nice weather 70–75 degrees and clear and low humidity. Looking forward to tomorrow and finishing.*

For the most part, Horton thinks associatively while he runs. That is, he checks in regularly with his body. "You have to monitor it like a car," he says, "constantly checking on the gas gauge, the temperature gauge, and making sure you don't blow it up." But near the end of the run, he thought about everything but his body. "After forty days on the trail, my body was sending me warning signals and I was trying to ignore them."

June 30, 1991. *Day 53. 34.0 miles. Cumulative miles 2144.0. Start 4:32 A.M. Finish 4:35 P.M. Felt horrible first 20 miles to Abol Bridge. Took 6 Tylenol No. 3 today. Could hardly run the first 20 miles, toes were so sore and blistered, and sides of heels were bad. Felt real good going up to Baxter Park. Perfect weather 70 degrees. Light wind and low humidity. Fell 4 times. Real fun climbing Mt. Katahdin and rocks. Finish: 52 days, 9 hours, 41 minutes. No emotions really, just relieved. Tough going off mountain. FREEDOM.*

Horton sits behind his desk at Liberty University talking about that last day on the trail. He is surrounded by bric-a-brac and artifacts from the sport he loves; his tiny office is a monument to ultramarathons. The walls are cluttered with running maps, photos of races, signed posters of Bill Rodgers and others. On a shelf behind him is a huge jar of coins. "All the money I have found throughout my years of running," he explains. On his door are two sayings central to his philosophy of life. One, accompanying a picture of a paraplegic runner wearing two prostheses, says, "What's your excuse for not running?" The other, referring to the Iditarod Trail Sled Dog Races, says, "The best long-distance runners run naked and sleep in the snow."

Horton is saying, "Eight miles from Katahdin, I fell for the fourth time in as many hours. I ripped open my right arm and temporarily lost my mind." In front of his seventeen-year-old son, who had come to run with him, he began screaming and sobbing: "I'm tired of this. I'm tired of falling. I'm tired of stubbing my toes . . ."

"You've got blood on your arm," someone said.

"I don't care about that blood," he screeched. "I couldn't care less.

Now Horton is saying, "First time my wife and son see me run on the A.T. and I cry like a baby. At first I felt bad, looking and acting so pitiful, but now I'm glad it happened. My son, who is a high-school cross-country runner, saw me physically beaten down but still tough enough to keep going. What more important lesson is there than that?"

Postscript. A satisfied Scott Grierson attained his goal of hiking the A.T. in less than fifty-six days by finishing the trip in fifty-five days, twenty hours, and thirty-four minutes.

VIISHA SEDLAK
Walk, Don't Run

> It was a blonde, a blonde to make a bishop kick a hole in a stained glass window.
>
> ——Raymond Chandler

When Viisha Sedlak walks by, heads turn. Six feet tall, with angular features, braided blond hair, and a lithe, willowy frame, she would draw stares if she were merely strolling. But using her world-class racewalking technique, as she does at a pace faster than most people can run, she is a compelling sight indeed. Watching her glide through her warmups before an important 10-kilometer race in Palo Alto, California, I am reminded of Jack Lemmon's description of Marilyn Monroe's sexy strut in the 1959 movie *Some Like It Hot*: "Jell-O on springs." It is, however, a very firm Jell-O.

Seconds before the start of the race, Sedlak, in short black shorts and a white Easy Spirit singlet, is fidgeting, along with fifteen other women, while a race organizer explains rules and tactics: "Take the insides of the turns. Don't make the course any longer than you have to. . . ."

Sedlak is not listening; she has heard it countless times. Her self-talk is louder, more insistent, than the race official's monologue. Her head is bowed (she still towers over the other women), as if in prayer. But she is not praying (she would never abdicate the responsibility); she is putting on her game face. First she focuses on her breathing, making sure it is deep and relaxed. Next she recites her litany of affirmations. "I will finish. I will finish healthy. I will have fun." It is a cool, foggy morning with a chance of becoming hot, but Sedlak vows to block out the weather. "It gets no attention," she tells herself. She also reminds herself not to focus on the clock. In her last few races, needing a sub-fifty-minute 10-kilometer to qualify for the Olympic racewalking trials, she has been obsessed with the clock. Some people can race like that, but it just didn't work for her; not only had she not yet qualified but she'd had no fun.

The official calls "to your marks," and the women step to the starting line. "How perfect I feel," thinks Sedlak. "How glad I am to be here . . . a part of the group . . . yet an individual . . . just relaxed enough . . . eagerly tense . . . a good sign . . ."

"Set . . ."

"Remember, Viisha," the inner voice continues, "whatever you do will be okay. It will be the best you can do."

Sedlak likes to joke that she was born tall. "I have good genes," she says. "I come from a solid line of Czech potato eaters." Her father, a career U.S. Navy man, was a stern disciplinarian who constantly moved the family around the world—to the Philippines, Guam, Okinawa, Trinidad, Panama.

Though she was an active kid, her early childhood was practically devoid of organized sports. "We were always walking, cycling, roller-skating, hula-hooping," she says, "but because we moved so often, usually from one Third-World country to another, we didn't play on any teams. Living on islands, we did learn to swim very young. When we turned three, our father taught us water survival. His technique was to throw us off a sailboat into huge rolling waves. It worked. All four of us kids were regular little seals in the water."

Her father, whom she likens to the iron-fisted Robert Duvall character in the 1979 movie *The Great Santini*, was of the kids-should-be-seen-and-not-heard school of parenting. "The up side is that I learned adaptability and independence," she says. "Everywhere we went, we were a minority, so we were taught to rely on ourselves, to listen to ourselves. In every new country, our father reminded us that we had something to learn there—language, food, whatever. Growing up we ate everything, and I bet that's why I never get sick; I've probably had every bacteria known to man in my body." It seems she also gobbled up languages. Besides English, she can converse in Spanish, French, Portuguese, Italian, Russian, and Swahili, and is learning German.

The downside of her rigid upbringing was a dearth of praise and a sometimes elevated level of domestic tension. "It was not an easy household to grow up in," she says. "Nothing you ever did was good enough. My father was guilty of both physical and psychological abuse, my mother was an alcoholic, and all the kids (one older sister, two younger brothers) had to overcome self-esteem problems. You know, it's amazing how common that is among top athletes. I once went out to dinner with eight of the best racewalkers in the country. Turned out, every one of them had at least one alcoholic parent. Someone asked, 'How many of you competed to find approval?' Everyone raised their hand."

The Sedlak family lived in San Diego for Viisha's high school years, and it was there she began a love affair with gymnastics. "I would get up early and fix my own breakfast, then go to school before anyone else, work out for a couple of hours, shower, go to class, then train again after school, sometimes until eight o'clock. I wasn't overly talented, but I loved the balance beam – the worst event for someone tall. I loved seeing improvement and being around the other girls. I was happy as a clam, probably for the first time in my childhood. It was certainly the first time I showed the ability to focus on something. If I had been a teacher looking at me then, knowing what I do now, I would have seen the perseverance of a dedicated athlete, whatever sport she chose."

Her early track experience demonstrates the impact an absence of such insight can have on a young athlete. In 1964 the longest running event in girls' PE was 600 yards, so the emphasis was on sprinting. Sedlak can still recall her teacher telling her, with grim finality, that she just didn't have the talent to be a runner. Sedlak shakes her head in wonder over that remark. "As a teacher myself, I never discourage anyone. They can be eighty years old and say they want to try for the Olympics, and I'll say, 'Okay, let's see what we can do.' That teacher just didn't have the answers." Sedlak's criticism is clear, concise, without rancor. "I was a natural distance athlete, and if she had known more, she might have told me so. It never occurred to me to question her. I just thought, 'Okay, she's the teacher. . . . I guess she knows.' That was the end of my running for a long time."

Nearing the halfway mark of the Palo Alto 10-kilometer race, Sedlak makes what will be her biggest mistake of the race. She is in a pack of three, with Kim Wilkinson and Francine Bustos, striding faster than she has all year and feeling great. She looks to be the embodiment of grace under pressure. Suddenly Bustos asks her, "What's your plan?"

Despite her affirmations, her visualizations, she doesn't really have a plan. "Fran, I'm just here to walk as fast as I can," she replies.

"I'm aiming for a time of forty-seven-thirty," Bustos says.

"Whoa," Sedlak thinks, "if Fran's planning to walk that fast, what am I doing up here?" It is enough to break her momentum, dropping her behind the two women. Disengaged from her support group, she thinks, "Why did I do that? I was doing fine."

After high school, Sedlak jumped at the chance to leave home and attended the University of California at Santa Barbara for a year. There she discovered a new sport, fencing. "I remember one day facing off against a large, lanky man who was quite a good fencer. I was pretty new to the sport, and I realized that my only hope was to be faster and more aggressive than he was. I won the match, surprising everyone. It was exhilarating to discover that aggressiveness could win the day."

At first she did well in school, too, logging straight A's the first semester. "School was not a problem intellectually," she says. "But it was the sixties and I was starting to rebel against the rigidity, the having to measure up, measure up, measure up. It had been that way at home my whole life, and I was tired of it."

Sedlak's major was political science, and her stated career goal was to join the CIA or the foreign service. "One day I came to realize that those really weren't my goals, but rather socially acceptable ones designed to please my parents. What I really wanted was to breathe and be free and find out who Viisha was."

Where did repressed kids with a drive for self-discovery go in the sixties? San Francisco's Haight-Ashbury district, of course. "I had a friend living in the Haight," she says. "I didn't even know her address, but I went up there and just ran into her on the streets. I moved into her communal household and began a year of basic survival. For money I scrounged pop bottles, cleaned out lab cages, shared food. It was an exciting time, before the Haight turned to heavy drugs. The Grateful Dead practiced across the alley from us, the Jefferson Airplane in the very basement of our building."

A year later Sedlak moved to Los Angeles. Walking along the Sunset Strip one day, she was approached by a man who said, "You should be a model."

"Yeah, yeah," she said, not even breaking pace. She had heard that her whole life, usually followed by "You're so tall." Just once couldn't they say, "You should be a model, you're so beautiful."? She was attractive, of course, with her long, lean body, flowing blonde hair, and carved cheekbones, but she utterly lacked confidence in her looks.

She tried to give him the brush, figuring he was just another street hustler. But he persevered, thrusting a business card into her hand and urging her to call. He said he liked the way she moved, a remark that was a cut above "You're so tall." So one day she called. He was, it turned out, a legitimate fashion designer. She went to work for him, first behind the scenes, then modeling swimwear, eventually becoming a capable Wilhelmina model. "I was never really beautiful," she says. "A lot of the other girls were more beautiful, but I learned how to use makeup, how to move, how to make myself look striking."

Modeling enabled her to travel the world, both on the job and between jobs. She would typically work for a while, go off exploring, then, when she ran out of money, return to modeling. "I had some adventures," she says, "but for ten years I did not exercise."

Bored and feeling the pressure from young, fresh-faced models like Christie Brinkley, she retired at the age of twenty-eight and began bon-vivanting through Europe with her wealthy Swedish boyfriend. She lived the high life, hanging out in hotels, taking most of her meals in restaurants, fairly awash in haute cuisine and the social scene. "Then one day I was trying on clothes in Stockholm," she remembers. "Looking in the mirror, the scales fell from my eyes. There I was – not even thirty – and everything was falling. And not gracefully. I was still thin, but mushy, with, ugh, cellulite."

Her awakening made her question her life. There was a lot of "What am I doing?" and "Where am I going?" She said good-bye to her boyfriend and returned to Hawaii, where she had spent time during her modeling years. "I only knew that I had to do something with my life, my body." At Waikiki one day she tried to jog down the beach. "The operative word is *tried*," she says, "because I couldn't do it. After about two hundred yards, my legs burned, my lungs burned. It was really appalling.

"Call it vanity, all I knew was that I was too young to look old and ugly. I decided to start jogging every day." She laughs self-effacingly. "Well, not the next day. I was too sore from doing two hundred yards. Little by little, though, I increased my distance. Why, I can still remember the first time I ran a mile. It was probably a twelve-minute mile, but I didn't care. I was so proud I was literally hopping up and down. Soon after that , I did two miles."

While still locked in at the two-mile level, her brother Guido suggested they run the Primo Brewery 14-miler.

"Fourteen miles!" she exclaimed. "Guido, I've only done two miles. I can't."

"It's okay," he said. "You can do it. I'll do it with you. We'll jog and walk, jog and walk."

"Okay," she thought, "if my brother thinks I can do it, I guess I can do it."

She did it, driven by the thrill of accomplishment and the thought of free beer waiting at the finish line. After it was over, as Sedlak was downing her second cold beer, a woman approached her and asked, "Are you going to do the Honolulu Marathon?"

"What's a marathon?" Sedlak asked in reply.

One month later she got a detailed, personal answer as she ran the Honolulu 26.2-mile. The race is particularly tough because it takes place in oppressive heat and humidity, a meteorological mix that can suck the vigor out of unwary competitors. Sedlak completed the first twenty miles in a respectable three hours. "But," she says, "my body was in distress; my muscles were spasming." She rested at an aid station wondering how she could finish. Other people were jogging by, laughing, talking, obviously not experiencing the kind of pain that was clawing at her. Watching a woman stretch her hamstrings, she wondered if that would help. She limped over to ask the woman if such stretching would stop the pain. "I guess she thought I was kidding," says Sedlak, "because she just laughed at me."

Though she needed one hour and twenty-six minutes to complete the last six miles, it was worth it. "Crossing that finish line was a turning point in my life, just like it is for so many runners. I mean, you're out there and you have to get in, don't you? Nobody's going to carry you. (She didn't know there was a sag wagon to do just that.) And there are no excuses. It's all up to you. When I finished that race, there was a surge of satisfaction like I've never felt. For a lazy, undisciplined person. . . . well, it was positively life changing."

That night her brother and a friend took her out for a celebratory ice cream, guiding her like an invalid. "One took one arm, one took the other, and they helped me up and down the curbs. My psoas muscles were so sore I couldn't life my legs. That lasted about five days. I wasn't in shape to run a marathon, so I paid the price. But I didn't care."

The muscle soreness passed and so did any traces of *lazy* or *undisciplined*. From that day forth, she committed herself to movement. She was able to work out only three or four times a week because of the demands of her booming new business, training and booking models. But even the business itself furthered her athletic development. "I joined a health club and learned the difference between aerobic and anaerobic. I began doing sessions for the girls on nutrition, physical fitness, posture, body alignment, and body mechanics. I even worked on attitude."

Sedlak was running about twenty miles a week, occasionally racing 5- and 10-kilometer events. A year after completing the Honolulu Marathon, she did it again, improving her time by a full hour to three hours and twenty-six minutes. Such a time, while respectable, did not suggest a potential Olympic contender. "I never dreamed of going to the Olympic trials," she says. "My first competitive goal was an age-group ribbon. That's all."

When it finally happened, it was yet another life-changing event, though not in a way Sedlak could have predicted. "The race organizers made a mistake and didn't announce my name," she recalls. "At first I was mad and hurt. But it made me evaluate why it was important that someone else recognize what I had done. I knew what I had done; shouldn't that have been enough? That night my brother made me a little blue ribbon and brought it over."

Success in her business and athletic life had her feeling better than ever about herself, but her social life didn't always keep pace. Love affairs were often stormy. Her longest live-with relationship – six years – was with a man from Hungary, a former national-class athlete gone to seed. He ridiculed Sedlak's commitment to running and to fitness. "If I took vitamins, he made fun of me," she says. "After a workout, he would try to get me drunk at dinner. When it got too destructive, I left."

She ran some more marathons, which taught her two things about herself: 1) she was more competitive than she ever realized; 2) the marathon was not her best distance. "My competitive side revealed itself. I found out I didn't like being passed in a race, though I loved passing others. That was new for me because I'd always been taught not to be aggressive." She laughs mirthlessly. "Be aggressive around my father and you were dead meat. I was used to backing off and taking abuse. But I found in racing that I didn't want to take abuse. And a foot race is a safe, acceptable environment in which to fight back. There I could surpass myself, come out of myself. . . . I could fly."

She wasn't exactly flying through marathons. She would finish in about three hours, more the passer than the passee but still not fast enough to be taken seriously. "At the end of a marathon I was stronger, both physically and mentally, than when I started," she says. "Then I'd watch people stagger across the finish line, obviously feeling worse than I did, and know that I had more in me."

Rather than try to go faster, she decided to try to go farther. In 1979 she ran a cautious 50-kilometer race. A year later she completed a 50-miler, winning it in a good national time. Good-bye marathons. "I found out I loved ultras, because they are even more mental than marathons. In a fifty-mile race, no matter how much you try to stay at the comfort level, the distance will get you. You really have to dig deep mentally."

There were startling physical benefits as well. "Every year in the mirror I was seeing a little more leanness, a little more muscle development, which translated into a little more ability to hang in there. People underestimate themselves so much," she adds. "We are physically, genetically, designed for endurance. We have this great muscle tissue, a beautiful cooling system. The human body is made to perform, to be active; it thrives on demands, on being challenged. That's why I love the ultras. They always remind me of that fact.

"Our capabilities are huge," she continues, blue eyes flashing, obviously in love with this subject. "The body, when cared for and prepared, handles long distances . . . happily. People say, 'How can you run so far? It's incredible!' Well, it's not incredible, it's how the body is built. If you choose to prepare for it, it's very workable.

"Unfortunately, the mentality is growing that life should be easy. I find life very difficult, though filled with rewards. Endurance events have taught me that there are no free lunches. If you want to cross the finish line, you have to start at the beginning and go the course."

And overcome the obstacles. When Sedlak moved her home base to Boulder, Colorado, she viewed it as a great opportunity to overcome her fear of cold weather. "After living most of my life in the tropics, heat and humidity don't bother me," she says. "Lots of people let it beat them, but I kind of perk up because I know others are bothered by it. On the other hand, cold. . . ."

One morning in Boulder she went out to run in a blizzard, a virtual whiteout. At one point, she stuck her hand in front of her face and couldn't see it. "I almost panicked, but then I realized that I knew where I was, I was dressed warm enough, I was okay. I just kept thinking how much this was helping me. I thought, 'I'll beat every athlete not out here today.'"

Sedlak, pushing hard on a slight incline near the end of the third of four loops, is at a critical stage of the Palo Alto race. If this were a rock climb, it would be called the "crux." The comparison is apt, for Sedlak is threatening to climb out of the comfort zone. She is alone now; her only companion is pain. She knows it is decision time. She can push into that pain, or she can lie back in the safety zone. She calls this moment the "glass wall." Her rational mind is saying, "Don't break through that glass because it will hurt." But another part of her is saying, "C'mon, there it is, you can see the other side."

On this day she breaks through that glass wall. Calling up one of her affirmations—"I am willing to die for this"—she goes for it. The shattering of glass is nearly audible to her. As she powers by the big digital clock that stands like a sentinel at the end of each loop, she keeps her head up but angled away from its face. She still has no idea whether she is close to a pace that will qualify her for the Olympic trials.

For two consecutive years in the early 1980s, according to at least one French ultrarunning magazine, Sedlak was the third best female ultrarunner in the world. "I got bitten by the bug to be first," says Sedlak, "but then I took a realistic look at the times. I was running fifty miles at about a seven-twenty-per-mile pace, but the best woman, Eleanor Adams, was doing sub-seven and getting faster."

But one of the beauties of running is that you can always go in new directions. In 1983 Sedlak ran 844 miles from Denver to Dallas in thirty-two days. She wanted to see how her body and mind would hold up before she committed herself to running the three thousand miles from coast to coast, a longtime dream of hers. Between Denver and Dallas, she was blasted by rain, sleet, and wind, including a five-day deluge. "All you could see was my nose sticking out of a poncho," she says. "It was miserable, but I worked hard to see the bright side." She laughs. "The best part: I got two marriage proposals from truckers."

The cross-country run never happened because "time wasn't available to make it happen. I didn't just want to put a pack on my back and head east. I wanted to race it. The women's record was soft. I was sure I could break it. But I wanted the overall record. I could've done it half-

Viisha Sedlak (number 17) blasts from the starting line in an Olympic Trials qualifying race.

assed, but that wasn't in me. I sometimes regret not going, but I might still do it. I have a lot of life yet. So what if I'm sixty or seventy?"

In both 1984 and 1985 she was invited to La Rochelle, France, to a six-day race billed as the world championship in that event. Though she covered about the same distance both years, 380 miles, the two races were not qualitatively equal. "The second year was hell," she says, "though an interesting hell. I hadn't trained for a six-day race, and I got caught up in the question, 'Can the mind overcome lack of physical conditioning?' Well, I got my answer. You can do it—a six-day race is very mental—but it's not worth the price your body pays. And I don't like to harm my body."

After the second six-day ordeal, Sedlak was in California, weary but unwilling to rest. There was a twenty-four-hour track race that she needed to run for a ranking. It was actually a racewalking event, but she received permission from the organizer to run in it instead of using the racewalk technique. "I had a terrible race, eventually dropping out with hypothermia," she says. "But while I was still in it, I was very impressed with the racewalkers. Two walkers were lapping me while I was running. One of them slowed and talked to me. 'You should learn this sport,' he said. 'It's more efficient for your six-day races.' I could see the logic of it."

Back in Boulder, she called a couple who knew the racewalking technique and asked if they would demonstrate it for her. They got together with her just before a walking race in Boulder and showed her the technique. She proved a quick study. "You're legal now," they told her after she learned the requirements of the technique: at least one foot always touching the ground, weight-bearing leg straight by the time it has moved under the hip. "Why not give it a try?" they asked only moments before the start of the event. "Why not enter the race?"

Sedlak took their advice — and won.

When word of that feat spread, she was contacted by a walking coach. Her running coach became jealous. "Are you going to run or walk?" he asked her, with an edge to his voice. "Run," she said unequivocally. "I have no intention of being a racewalker."

Nothing had changed nine months later when she signed up to run the Honolulu Marathon. But at the pre-race banquet, a friend asked how she was and she told him: "I'm tired. I don't really feel like running tomorrow, but I know I should."

"Too bad you don't know the racewalk technique," said the friend, who was president of a racewalker association. "You could racewalk the marathon, which would be a lot easier on you."

"I know how to racewalk," she said, eyes brightening. "I mean, I did a race and I was legal."

She re-enrolled as a racewalker, then won her division. "It wasn't a great time (five hours)," she says, "but I had run the Honolulu Marathon eight times and always ended up nauseous. Fifteen minutes after walking it, I felt perky. That told me something."

The metamorphosis was complete. She was a racewalker.

Seven years later, she is the best Masters woman racewalker in the world. Among her accomplishments:

• Undefeated in all her national and international competitions for the past six years.
• Double gold medalist in the 1987 World Veterans Games in Melbourne, Australia.
• Triple gold medalist in the 1989 World Veterans Games in Eugene, Oregon.

- Double gold medalist in the 1991 World Veterans Games in Turku, Finland.
- Six-time member of the USA Track and Field Team.
- Competed in the 1988 U.S. Olympic trials at age thirty-nine and finished seventh.
- Recipient of the 1990 and 1991 U.S. Olympic Committee Athletics award for Masters Racewalker of the Year.
- Holder of six World Road & Track racewalk records at 5 kilometers, 10 kilometers, 15 kilometers, and 3,000 meters.

Racewalking, actually a technique rather than a competitive event, is the fastest growing sport in America, according to Sedlak. Membership in her group, the American Racewalk Association, is growing rapidly. And the belated introduction of a women's racewalking event (10 kilometers) in the 1992 Olympics should convert even more to the sport. (Racewalking was also an event in the 1988 U.S. Olympic trials, but not yet an official Olympic sport.)

Nonetheless, racewalking looks odd to many people. The so-called hip drop creates an undulating movement at the waist that conjures up the image of a duck-walking contest, or people trying to learn a dance step during an earthquake. There isn't a serious racewalker who hasn't heard the snickers of the uninitiated. Fear of looking funny undoubtedly inhibits some from ever trying the sport.

Sedlak's job is to get people to overcome these inhibitions. Besides being able to walk a seven-minute, twenty-second mile (to better appreciate this feat, try covering the same distance in say, eleven minutes without running), she is one of the most respected instructors in racewalk technique. She claims she can teach virtually anyone the fundamentals of racewalking in an hour, two at the most. "Legal? Eighty-five percent will be legal after an hour," she says. "Efficient? That takes longer. It took me months just to get the hip drop."

She conducts camps, clinics, lectures, and group walks, selling her services to clients like IBM, GE, the U.S. Navy, BATA France, the Special Olympics, the U.S. Shoe Corporation, and retirement groups. She has an instructional videotape and booklet on the market. In 1988 she founded the American Racewalk Association to certify racewalk instructors and "to standardize the teaching of the sport for correctness and for safety."

"Racewalking is remarkably injury-free," Sedlak says. "It's very hard to injure yourself racewalking. There's almost no impact, the straight legs saves the wear and tear on the hip and knee, and bending the arm ninety degrees takes stress off the back. Usually it's only elite athletes who get hurt because they're the only ones going fast enough to tear something. I've been teaching this sport for seven years, sometimes to hundreds of students at a time, and I've never had an injury with a new walker."

Sedlak's tales of physical therapy via racewalking are persuasive. Having taught the technique to people ranging in age from five to ninety-four, she has witnessed countless cases of people rescued from sloth by racewalking. "One woman had her kneecap removed thirty years ago. She can't health-walk, with its bent knee, but she racewalks with no problem. Another client had a fused spine and couldn't swim, cycle, or walk normally. But she racewalks comfortably.

"The thing about racewalking is that you can modify the speed and intensity for learners, and who cares if they're legal? The important thing is that they're out there, moving. It makes no difference if they're lifting."

Lifting means that, like a common runner, both of the racewalker's feet lose contact with the ground at the same time. It is illegal in competition. While runners engage in what amounts to a series of short jumps, racewalkers must push the pace without the benefit of bounce. There are judges at every race to rule on lifting and on whether a racewalker's plant leg is straight. Sedlak was disqualified for lifting in her first big race, a 1986 TAC (The Athletics Congress) qualifier. So were five others in the top ten, forcing race officials to appoint the national team. (Sedlak, who finished fourth, made the team.) In the 1980 Olympics, seven racewalkers were disqualified in the men's 20-kilometer.

"The lifting rule should be eliminated," says Sedlak with calm conviction. "First of all, you don't gain anything by doing it. It's inefficient to fly too high in the air; you lose power. Second, it's impossible to judge. Top racewalkers are moving their feet about three times per second, so how are you going to tell if both of them are in the air at the same time. Some people say it's the one-foot-on-the-ground rule that defines racewalking, but I think it's the straight-leg rule that's critical. Bending the leg and pushing off with the quads – that allows you to be very explosive. It has to be judged."

Sedlak believes that all elite racewalkers lift at some point, but with only five to eight judges for a 10-kilometer race, much of it goes unseen. Moreover, three judges must cite a walker before he or she can be disqualified. Sometimes judges issue a warning. But Ian What-ley, one of America's best 20-kilometer walkers dismisses that ap-proach. "A warning means, in my opinion, that I am walking perfectly," he says.

Two hundred yards from the finish in Palo Alto, Sedlak is walking perfectly – or so she imagines – as she glides through the final straight-away leading to a rising turn that will bring her near the finish line. For inspiration, she thinks of her favorite clients and of her world-class training partner, twenty-five-year-old Sara Standley, who is already nearing the finish line. She is sure Sara has thought of her too; you use whatever and whomever you can to stay aggressive.

With the clock not yet in view, she still has no idea whether her goal of qualifying for the Olympic trials is attainable. She knows she has walked fast, but is it fast enough? Finally opening herself to clues, she begins to listen to the comments of people who rim the paved path, but all she hears are the standard words of encouragement.

Though it is a tense time and she is in pain, she is thriving on the physical movement. How enjoyable it is to have the mental reserves to demand the maximum from one's body. How wonderful it is to feel healthy. She wonders what her pace is, but only fleetingly. Mostly she just revels in movement for the sake of movement.

As she crests the rise, the clock comes into view. 49:14 . . . 49:15 . . . Instantly she knows she will make it. She will break fifty minutes and qualify for the Olympic trials in New Orleans. Ecstasy powers her across the finish line in 49:20, only four seconds off her personal record.

Sedlak is having a post-race breakfast – Spanish omelet, rye-toast-no-butter, decaffeinated coffee – and holding forth on the differences between racewalking and running. She has let her wavy blond hair down and it flows below her shoulders like a lion's mane. "If you tell children 'walk, don't run,' they will break into racewalking," she is saying. "Adults come to my clinics and struggle and struggle, mostly to let go and overcome how they think their bodies should move. Kids just want to move, and have no preconceived notions.

"Racewalking uses more full-body musculature than running. Ac-cording to a Soviet study, the three best sports for overall body development are gymnastics, wrestling, and racewalking – and racewalking is the only one that is aerobic. My fat ratio dropped from 14 percent to 12 percent in my first year of racewalking. I lost an inch from my waist and three-quarters of an inch from my thighs. And that was starting from a point of fitness. The reason racewalking trimmed me is that the hip flex strengthens the obliques. To do the technique effectively, you have to stay tall. Even when fatigued, walkers work on staying up. The support muscles in the back, the abdominals, and the obliques get toned. Dropping the leg back, keeping contact with the ground as long as possible, then whipping it forward makes the abdominal system very strong.

"Racewalking is also more intellectually challenging than running," she says. "You must stay focused on your technique if you want to stay efficient. In running you can zone out – in fact it's sometimes beneficial – but not in racewalking. If a walker loses his concentration, he's out of the race."

With technique so central to success, good teaching takes on a concomitant importance. But when Sedlak was starting out in the sport, she quickly learned that instruction in the United States was poor. The few qualified teachers showed no interest in a rookie racewalker in her mid-thirties. "No one wanted to help me," she says. "So I wrote to the seven countries I thought had the best programs, which

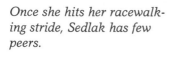

Once she hits her racewalking stride, Sedlak has few peers.

included China and the Soviet Union. I heard from all of them. Many invited me to come to their country and train. Many said that I was the first American they had ever heard from. I thought, 'If we're so poor in this sport, why aren't the coaches doing this research?'"

She went to Mexico City to train under Felix Gomez, who had improved from nineteenth to first in the world in the 20-kilometer walk. "I can't get the hip drop, Felix," she complained one day.

"It will come," he said, as calm as a Zen master.

"How long will it take?"

"Five to seven years."

"Years! But that is so far down the road," she complained. "I would love to win a gold medal."

He raised a hand like a stop sign. "Don't think so far ahead," he said. "Live like a gold medalist now and the medal will come. Train like a gold medalist . . . eat like a gold medalist . . . stand like a gold medalist."

Having never been a gold medalist, she couldn't be sure how one stood. "I faked it," she says. "I figured out he was talking about attitude. I now call the process 'being a champion.' For example, if you're going to pig out at midnight but you're not really hungry, think, 'Would a champion pig out now or would she do some relaxation exercises?' I've gotten used to asking the question: 'What would a champion do?' It's like the concept in the Orient of the 'honored guest.' You should always behave as though you were in the presence of an honored guest—except in this case that honored guest is you."

It requires an interesting mix of skills to excel as a racewalker. Because adherence to technique is so important, the sport rewards people who can walk and think at the same time. Moreover, one must have the self-discipline to persist, to push in a race, even when you really don't want to. Physically, Sedlak says, you must have good aerobic conditioning and flexibility, and strong abdominals, shoulders, back, and arms. "Below the waist, the hamstrings, gluteus, and anterior tibialis are the most important muscles. Emotionally, it's important that you love the sport. You have to be able to find the positive side of a negative experience—and there will be negative experiences. I've seen talented racewalkers drop out of the sport because they couldn't find the positive in a negative, like being disqualified."

Clearly Sedlak loves it. She brings an almost childlike enthusiasm to the sport. "I love biomechanics," she says. "I love looking at a horse or dog that moves well. I guess I've always wanted to be an animal that moves well. When I was an ultrarunner, I worked on my stride. I had a pretty stride." Masters runner Ruth Anderson, who has been to several Veterans Games with Sedlak, agrees, though she is speaking about more than stride when she says, "Viisha always looks good – even when she just finished doing her best."

Breathing, too, is critical in racewalking. In runners,the upper body should be quiet, "along for the ride." That's why distance runners are so small on top. In contrast, walkers tend to have muscular shoulders, arms, and chests. "Walkers have to coordinate the upper and lower body," Sedlak says. "You have strong arm movement, a hip flex, a hip drop, and amid all this elliptical movement, you have a diaphragm going up and down. You have to keep the muscles very relaxed and the torso lifted up, so you don't close off the breathing. There's a lot happening with the body."

And with the mind. Another element critical to Sedlak's success is her ability to imagine, to visualize. It's a skill she has cultivated since childhood. "As a kid I needed imagination to deal with an unpleasant home life and all the new schools I went to. I would visualize getting straight A's and being okay. When I started running, I did the same thing. I would think, 'These people are faster than I am,' then picture myself staying up with them.

"As I became educated in athletics, I learned how to manipulate my fantasies more precisely. Now I will see myself on the road . . . hear the announcer say, 'She's on a world-record pace' . . . see competitors pass me and then deal with that in a positive way . . . see myself pass others, both from the outside looking in and vice versa. I will do this before I go to sleep, in a taxicab, wherever I can."

The only equipment you need to be a racewalker is a good pair of walking shoes. One model, says Sedlak, stands above the rest: the Easy Spirit Mach 1. "Their training flat uses the same shock-absorption system as NASA does. The NFL uses it in their helmets. No other walking shoe comes close. They have eighty-seven sizes, so it's like the shoe is custom-made for you. It's by far the best walking shoe, and I'd have to say that even if they weren't paying me."

Indeed, Sedlak is one of the very few sponsored racewalkers. Easy Spirit pays her to compete, to train in the company's shoes, and to make appearances. That sponsorship and the income she earns speaking and teaching are enough to support her in a modest style. She has her own house and her own business; she is independent, strong, and sexy, the consummate woman of the nineties, yet she lives alone. She has lots of friends, including a few close ones, but she doesn't date, and having children is beginning to look like a lost hope. "I refuse to be with inappropriate men any longer," she says. "I love men. I'd love to live with someone. Sure, I get lonely. We'll be at a race and Sara [training partner Sara Standley] will call home to her husband . . . and I don't have anyone to call. My family has never even seen me race." She pokes her lower lip out in exaggerated sorrow. It's a gesture that says, "Yeah, it bothers me, but not much; not enough to change, anyway."

Sedlak's strength and independence are reminders that a lot of men are intimidated by an attractive, articulate woman, especially if she is faster and taller than they are. She's not afraid to forcefully express a woman's point of view. "Women are told they can't do things, and men are told they're wimps if they don't do things. Men are men if they get out there and master the world, but women aren't supposed to do that. It's changing, but it still exists. Sports has had a lot to do with the changes. For women, the running boom has been huge. A lot of divorces have come out of it. Women have realized, 'If I can run a marathon, I can leave this relationship.'"

The reason for alienation in society, she goes on, is the tendency to separate people into groups: men from women, black from white, Jew from Catholic. "We're all human, after all. Sure, women have breasts and men have . . . smaller breasts, but so what? I'm not allowed to take my shirt off in public, which sucks, but if I want to make a statement about it, I'll get arrested. It's a bad law, but what am I going to do? I don't want to get arrested. But I can make a statement by beating men in sports. Not all men and not all the time, but sometimes. It's my tiny contribution to the cause: providing a little more respect for women and a lessening of that separation."

She tells the story about one man who, before a race in Switzerland in 1991, tried to separate Sedlak from the starting line—apparently for no reason other than that she was a woman. "I was standing at the start of the European Veterans Championships last year with my friend Kathy, when this guy stepped on Kathy's foot and tried to squeeze in between us. We didn't move. I was very relaxed, tired really, after two hard races in Finland. Even after he stepped on *my* foot, I stayed calm. I tried to speak to him in English, French, and Italian but got nothing. It would've been all right if he had just stepped on my foot, but when the starter's gun went off, he pushed me on the arm and slugged me across the chest. I knew he wasn't trying to hurt me, but he was definitely trying to gain an advantage. That made me mad."

And motivated. Setting out after the man like a dog catcher in pursuit of a renegade hound, she was soon in his shadow. "He was fast," she says, "but I wanted him to know that I was going to stay with him." She smiles in happy reflection. "We stayed together. I'd do a little surge, he'd do a little surge. It made the race a lot more fun."

Sedlak eventually passed her nemesis, then another man, then another. Only one man remained ahead of her. "Now I was really into the race," she says, "and I owed it all to the guy who slugged me."

She caught the leader and crossed the finish line, first overall. In the sixty-year history of the European Masters Championships, no woman had ever beaten an entire mixed field. Mr. Unfriendly finished third, two hundred meters behind her.

"I wasn't going to say anything to him," she says. "I didn't want to irritate him further. But people were pretty excited about the woman thing. The guy who finished second smiled and slapped me on the back. Other people were congratulating me. Then the guy who hit me came up, nodded his head, and shook my hand."

That rare case of vengeance-as-motivation aside, beating men offers Sedlak no extra thrill. Her method is to use the other bodies, regardless of gender, to help her do her best in a race. Those behind push her, while those ahead pull her. "I don't personally care whether they're male or female. But in a race, when I pass a man, especially if I'm racewalking and he's running, I sometimes feel the resentment and that bothers me. It would be nice if I didn't have to beat a man to get his respect." She grins. "But someone has to do it, and I'm willing to be the one."

Viisha Sedlak Update. At age forty-three, the oldest competitor at the 1992 U.S. Olympic track-and-field trials, Sedlak finished eleventh — and first Masters woman — in the 10-kilometer racewalk.

TOM CRAWFORD
Born to Finish

When Tom Crawford's wife and crew-chief, Nancy, woke him at 5:30 on the morning of the Death Valley run, he was sleeping the sleep of the tortured. Goons, goblins, and monsters had been flitting across a fiery, desolate moonscape all night. "A restless night in hell," he mumbled, sitting up. As he approached full consciousness, he felt fear claw at his spine.

There were few clues except a rumpled bed that someone had stayed in the room. Supplies, including six ice chests, were already stashed in the support vehicles. In the room Tom had only his clothes—white socks, white shorts, white cotton dress shirt, white hat with a veil, Turntec running shoes—and the duct tape and scissors he needed to wrap his feet.

Two pitchers of water sat on a nightstand. He downed one of the pitchers, like a man intent on winning a chugging contest. Then while he taped his feet, carefully molding the silver duct tape to the contours of his soles, he downed the other one. If running Death Valley is a war, he thought, this phase is the saturation bombing. Fully—if only temporarily—hydrated, feet looking like something from *The Mummy Does the Desert*, Crawford walked out of the room and into the already-rising summer heat of July 1990 to begin a run through hell.

An hour later, at the brackish pond called Badwater, the world's most remote starting line, Crawford and Richard Benyo shook hands, hugged, and wished each other well. Crew members snapped photos.

84

Then the two men toed the starting line, Richard in a tongue-in-cheek sprinter's stance, Tom favoring the miler's crouch. Crew member "Uncle" Billy Owens, dressed in Western garb, fired his .357 Magnum into the desert air, shattering one of nature's great calms, and the runners were off.

While Richard began a brisk walk, Tom took off running down the right side of the ribbon of asphalt that bisected the salt pan. He employed an efficient style, described by Benyo as a "ground-eating shuffle," that kept his feet close to the pavement, thereby conserving energy. But would it conserve enough energy?

It was a point worth pondering, for Crawford and Benyo were attempting to do what no one had ever done before: go on foot from Badwater, Death Valley (282 feet below sea level), to the top of Mount Whitney (14,494 feet above sea level), and back. Their journey would take them from the lowest point in the continental United States, to the highest point, and back. It meant hot-footing it across what some say is the least hospitable piece of real estate on the planet (Death Valley), over a mountain range (the Panamints), through some more desert (Panamint Valley), over another mountain range (Argus Range), through more desert (Owens Valley), then up almost three vertical miles to the storm-battered summit of Mount Whitney. And back. That was the part nobody had ever done before. It all added up to 300 miles and more sweat than most people exude in a lifetime.

Crawford hadn't gone twenty yards before his mind was awash in doubt: "God, I feel so heavy," he thought. "Superhydration has me about one-ninety, twelve pounds over my ideal running weight. I feel like a big oaf . . . plod . . . plod . . . Oh, hell, did I remember to tell the crew to dilute the Exceed? . . . Uh-oh, what's that on my foot? I think it's the tape rolling up . . . and ooh, my hamstring. I'm feeling pains I've never felt before . . . ridiculous . . . My God, can I do this?"

After a couple of eight-minute miles, Crawford began to find a rhythm. Aided by the desert heat (88 degrees at the start) and the sheer repetition of the running motion, his muscles became supple, his joints lubricated, his mind focused.

He was alone now, alone amid the desert's pervasive quiet. There was only the sound of his steady breathing and the pat-pat-pat of his footsteps echoing against the pavement. Benyo was far behind, as expected (his goal was to finish in seven days; Crawford hoped to break five days). The crews had dispersed, some to find refuge in their air-conditioned motel rooms at Furnace Creek and wait their turn, others to set up a mobile aid station two or three miles ahead and wait for their runner.

Although nine hundred species of plants have been identified in Death Valley, no vegetation caught Crawford's eye. Nature's hues ran only from white to brown. Most of the plant life would be found at the higher elevations, for the three thousand square miles of Death Valley National Monument also includes such imposing mountains as Telescope Peak, to the west. Soaring to 11,049 feet, it is often covered in snow. Right now, though, the entire Panamint Range looked brown, bald, and heavily eroded, as though it had been clawed by giant talons.

Crawford, running for his third time across Death Valley, knew that the beginning was comparatively easy. For one thing, he was feeling good—warmed up, not yet beaten down; for another, the sun still lay below the crest of the Funeral Mountains. It was hot but not yet claustrophobic.

Twenty-four minutes into the run, Crawford reached Uncle Billy Owens, his wife's uncle and one of his three crew members (along with his wife, Nancy, and Carol Cognata). Owens had crewed for Crawford before and knew the routine. Conversation was as spare as the landscape.

"Wanna sit down?" Bill asked, shoving a bottle of Calistoga mineral water into his hand.

"Nope."

"Wanna eat?"

Tom shook his head.

"Better slow it down," Bill advised, "or you'll blow it out your ass. You got a long way to go."

"I'm okay."

"You're okay now, but what about four days from now? You'll wish you was dead."

Crawford laughed. "Hell, I'll wish I was dead anyway." Then seriously: "I'm okay."

A minute later, Crawford was again shuffling down the road. He stayed on the right side because the crown of the road resulted in greater weight on his right leg, which would help protect him from a recurrence of plantar fascitis on his left foot, the only debilitating injury he'd ever had. Uncle Billy, sucking on his pipe, watched Crawford move off into the shimmering heat waves. Then he folded up the chair and climbed into his pickup. As he drove past his charge, he

Tom Crawford's ten things to do if you're going to run across Death Valley

1. Talk to someone who has made the run.

2. Visit the desert during July or August before you decide for sure to make the run.

3. Heat train. Teach your body to process up to one quart of liquid every fifteen to twenty minutes (exercising in a sauna at 170 degrees-plus is best).

4. Learn how to tape the bottoms of your feet with duct tape.

5. Have at least three heat-trained people on your crew and two excellent running vehicles.

6. Be prepared for any medical problem – heatstroke, hyperthermia, blisters, nausea, disorientation – that might strike either runners or crew members.

7. Have crew members log your fluid intake and weigh you every three to five miles to make sure you are not getting behind.

8. Have at least four well-stocked ice chests – two for the runner, two for the crew – with twenty gallons of water and twenty gallons of electrolyte drinks.

9. Apply for permits to Mount Whitney and Death Valley two months in advance.

10. Have a separate mountain crew to accompany you up and down the mountain.

---

called out, "I'll have Saltines and a bottle of Exceed (carbo drink) ready for you in three miles."

"No. Calistoga water!" Tom called, but Bill was gone.

A look at a map of Death Valley and it's not hard to see why it doesn't beckon the average bermuda-clad tourist. Place names include Arsenic Spring, Badwater, Coffin Canyon, Deadman Pass, Poison Spring, Rattlesnake Gulch, Starvation Canyon, Suicide Pass, Funeral Mountains, Devil's Cornfield, Dante's View. Then, of course, there's Death Valley itself, named for its impact on some Gold Rushers – most of whom tried to pass through in the winter!

Because it was created by fault action, not river erosion, Death Valley is, in strict scientific terms, not a valley at all but a *graben:* a narrow, elongated trough. It once held an inland sea, but evaporation over the ages has left thick beds of various salts, including sodium, borax, and barite.

On a clear day from Dante's View — 5,475 feet above the floor of Death Valley — you can see the Sierra Nevada Mountains in the far distance. Otherwise the scene is vast desolation. Not many of those nine hundred species of plants are readily apparent from this vantage point, either. What is apparent — and this is key to the mindset of the modern adventurer — is the proximity of the lowest and highest points in the continental United States. In what Benyo calls a "tantalizing perversion of nature," Badwater and Mount Whitney are only 150 road miles apart.

A geographical anomaly, yes, but tantalizing? Only to the Crazed Adventure Runner.

Heading northwest from the man-made oasis of Furnace Creek Ranch, with its graceful date palms and lush, irrigated golf course, Crawford saw nothing but undulating monotony — dirt, dust, sand, and rock — for the next twenty-seven miles. The temperature was now 105 degrees, but Crawford felt fine. He was past the point of believing that his world was imploding. Fully hydrated, he was sweating profusely and urinating frequently, both of which pleased him. There was no sign of blisters, no major aches or pains.

As the sun rose higher, Crawford strove to "dehumanize" himself, to become one with the desert. He pictured himself as a tumbleweed. He ritualistically welcomed the sun, trying to feel genuine affection for it, visualizing its good qualities. But most of all, he tried to quell the shrill little voice inside him trying to be heard: "The sun! Ohhh, shit! I know what that means. I know what can happen out in that desert!"

In that respect, he figured, it was harder for him than for Benyo, who, as a rookie, did not know exactly what awaited him. "Hell," Crawford had told him during one of their training runs, "I know every step of the course. I know how excruciating the pain is going to be."

The mental struggle had been especially intense the last forty-eight hours before the start. For the two years before that, he had been driven by his own original vision; with all the upbeat planning and training, fear simply couldn't find a foothold. But rolling south on Highway 395, partying with his crew just hours before the start of the run, Crawford's jovial countenance was a false front. Inside, he was battling butterflies the size of vampire bats. In a vain attempt to drown them, he drank beer all the way down to Lone Pine.

"It was like knowing that at 6:00 A.M. on July 17, 1989, you were going to be burned on a hot stove," he would later say. "As an event like that approaches, it's natural to start disassociating yourself from your body, to get out of your body."

That raises this question: what manner of man chooses of his own free will to stay in a body that is going to be burned like that?

Tom Crawford (left) and Richard Benyo are smiling because they have not yet started their 300-mile run across Death Valley. (Courtesy of Tom Crawford)

Answer: someone conditioned at an early age to withstand pain; someone like Tom Crawford.

Born March 25, 1946, in Clinton, Oklahoma, Tom was the last of seven children born to Jess and Gladys Crawford. His father was a Baptist minister, a pastor of a country church frequented mostly by farmers. His mom was "chief cook, bottle washer, and friend."

It could be said that the watershed event in Tom's life occurred before he was even born, when his older sister fell off a chair and bruised her knee. The injury developed into osteomyelitis. For the next seven years, his sister was in and out of hospitals, enduring nearly forty operations on her legs. "Seeing my sister go through all that and then go on to educate herself, mother four children, and become a healthy, vibrant woman, it taught me, simply, that you never give up," Tom says. "My father had to deal with everything from the insurance companies who ran scared from the medical bills to the doctors who wanted to amputate my sister's leg. But he never gave up; no one in my family ever did."

As a boy, Tom played lots of organized sports and a few not so organized. "Early on, I played Pop Warner Football and Little League Baseball. Then in high school, I swam, played football and baseball, and wrestled." The wrestling coach first introduced Tom to running. "Coach made us run three to six miles every morning before school. And that was back in the days when you weren't supposed to drink water because you would get a sideache."

One day Tom had a dispute with the baseball coach. He threw down his glove and walked over to the track coach, telling him he'd like to be a runner. The coach sent him out to run a timed mile. Tom responded with a 5:12 effort; not spectacular, even for Clinton, Oklahoma, but not bad. Next day, when Tom patched things up with the baseball coach, he effectively postponed his running career for about a decade.

Meanwhile, Tom and some buddies were secretly engaging in a daredevil sport of their own creation. During the winter, when the Oklahoma rivers swelled to flood stage, Tom and his boldest friends would leap off cliffs into an icy river and do a freestyle bodysurf and dog paddle through five, ten, fifteen miles of white, rolling water. "It wasn't exactly a swim, more of a survival paddle," he says. "We just tried to keep our heads above water. It's a wonder none of us was killed. It was dangerous and stupid, but what a high!" Even as a kid, Tom was the one most likely to push the limits. "I always wanted to extend the river," he admits. "I wanted to see how far I could go. I took it up to about seventeen miles."

When Tom was seventeen, his mother died of a heart attack. Eight months later, his sixty-year-old father died, also of a massive heart attack. "Never sick a day in his life," Tom says. "He was six-foot-one and a hundred and seventy-five pounds, not an ounce of fat on him. Though not an athlete, he was an active man. He'd had a physical two days earlier, and they told him he was the picture of health."

Soon after, in 1964, Tom left home. He intended to start college, but the Vietnam War was gearing up and he decided to join the Navy. "I never saw a ship and only wore the U.S. Navy uniform once," he says. He was channeled into an experimental Special Forces unit, where he was put through a wide spectrum of survival schools. "There were fifty-five of us from all branches of the service," he says. "They put us through jump school, rescue school, jungle survival, water survival, Arctic survival."

Crawford went the distance, learning volumes along the way. Mostly he learned that he could do much, much more than he ever thought possible. He found out that he could suffer for prolonged periods of time. The first such lesson was a by-product of a fifty-mile run with combat boots and a forty-pound pack. "Then we did a twenty-five-mile belly crawl, again in complete combat gear. That was about twelve hours of crawling through mud, stickers, and crap," he says. "On the one hand, I thought it was crazy; on the other hand, it kinda turned me on. I wanted to know, can I do it? Hell, I'd get so psyched up—the military has a way of doing that to you—I thought I could do anything."

After the military, Crawford went to college in California, Oregon, and Louisiana. While acquiring a bachelor of science degree and two master's degrees, he briefly let his body go to seed. Much of his hard-earned military muscle was usurped by fat as he ballooned to 250 pounds on his six-foot-two frame.

Then one day he began running again. "There's no question I was motivated by my parents' dying of heart attacks," he says. "I simply decided I wasn't going to let it happen to me."

"Did you break down?" The German tourist was leaning out the window of his rental car. He wore a silly straw hat on his head and a solicitous look on his face.

Crawford slowed only slightly from his twelve-minute-per-mile "slog." He looked sideways at the man, then a faint smile crossed his face. "Not yet," he replied. "But thanks."

It was not the first time someone had stopped and asked if he needed help. For most visitors to the valley, car trouble or mental illness were the only conceivable answers to the question that always bubbled to their lips when they saw someone like Crawford slogging through the desert: *"What the hell is that guy doing?"*

Frank Shorter's victory in the 1972 Olympic marathon is often credited with igniting the running boom, but Tom Crawford was running long distances before Shorter's gold medal fired the masses. "In fact," he says, "I was running ultras before I knew they were called ultras. I would look at some mountains, wonder what was on the other side, and just take off running to find out. I'd run for thirty or forty miles, just going from town to town."

Being a pioneer inevitably puts one out of step with the masses. Accordingly, Crawford suffered the slings and arrows reserved for those who cannot or will not wait for others. "I had people throw rocks, beer bottles at me," he says. "One guy actually got out of his car and sicced his dogs on me. Another time, four guys in a car decided they were going to take shots at me with their gun. They thought it was real cute. I headed up a hill and hid behind a log until they got tired and left. Crazy stuff like that would happen." He arches his eyebrows and laughs. "On the plus side, girls would sometimes wave and honk their horns."

Crawford quickly learned that he could run long distances. He wasn't going to win many marathons (personal record: 2:50), but he would always be one of the top finishers in a longer race. So he began to use marathons as training runs for the ultras. He would measure off 26.2 miles on a road and set out Mason jars of iced tea every three miles. "Of course, they weren't too icy by the time I got to 'em." he says. "Sweet, though. I'd add two cups of sugar to each quart. But, y'know, in my glycogen-depleted state, I couldn't taste the sugar. It didn't even taste sweet. That told me I was doing the right thing."

In 1971 sports nutrition was in its infancy. With few experts to turn to, Crawford relied heavily on trial-and-error. In his quest to find foods easy to digest during extensive exercise, he even experimented with baby food. "Back then," he says, "there was no such thing as electrolyte-replacement drinks. Electrolytes – what were they? I'd chip off a piece of salt from a salt lick and carry that. That was my electrolytes. Later I discovered that caffeine before a race could help burn fatty acids, which retarded the burning of glycogen for a couple of miles. After that, I was showing up at races shaking from a caffeine rush." He shrugs. "Still, it allowed me to push back the wall a couple of miles. Instead of carbo-loading, I was caffeine-loading."

As Crawford padded past the sun-soaked little community of Stovepipe Wells, no band played, no crowd cheered. In fact, no representatives from the animal kingdom were outside at all. No people, no jackrabbits, no lizards, no birds. That was because the afternoon sun bore down with the savage intensity of a nuclear holocaust. The mercury swelled up near 126 degrees, in the shade – a qualifier that made Crawford harrumph. Where he was headed, shade was about as prevalent as water buffalo. A more meaningful measurement of human discomfort in Death Valley was "ground temperature," and that figure hovered around 190. No wonder the region's Indians called Death Valley *Tomesha*, "ground on fire."

Just how hot is a summer afternoon in Death Valley? Worst case: 134.6 degrees, on July 10, 1913, second hottest shade temperature ever reported on the planet. The high in July and August: typically in the 120s.

Big numbers to be sure, but how hot is that really? To most people who reach for a cold drink and settle in front of an air conditioner long before the temperature reaches triple digits, figures like "125-degree shade" and "190-degree ground" have about as much meaning as plate tectonics. "It's so hot," Nancy Crawford says, attempting to put it in human terms, "that when that wind hits you, it's like opening the door to the oven and leaning down to check on the roast . . . whoosh."

"So hot," says Gary Morris, an erstwhile Death Valley runner, "that if you took a piece of bread out of its wrapper, by the time you handed it to someone else it was toasted."

"So hot," adds Tom, warming to the task, "that you can put out a green banana and watch it ripen to black mush in about an hour."

"So hot," says Benyo, "that I watched a guy fry a egg on the hood of his car – at ten in the morning."

"So hot," says Bruce Maxwell, who four times rambled across Death Valley, "that I went from a size-nine shoe to a size twelve. Instead of the asphalt being so sticky that it came off on my shoes, my shoes came off on the asphalt."

What, then, will this bizarre climate do to the human body?

Says a Furnace Creek ranger: "It will make road kill of you pretty darn quick if you aren't prepared."

"Everything dries," wrote J. Ross Browne, author in 1868 of the first U.S. mineral resource report. "Wagons dry; men dry; chickens dry; there is no juice left in anything, living or dead, by the close of summer."

How then does one run across a surface no more receptive to human footsteps than a sizzling griddle? For most people who have tried it, the answer is "poorly." More people have summited Mount

*Crawford "died" more than once between Mount Whitney and Badwater.
(Courtesy of Tom Crawford)*

Everest than have successfully run across Death Valley. Because of the loosely structured nature of Death Valley events, it's impossible to keep track of all the failed attempts, but there have surely been many. People have also tried to roller-skate it, skateboard it, wheelchair it. One guy tried to ride a camel across a fifty-mile stretch of Death Valley. The camel did his job, but the rider passed out and had to be resuscitated. Benyo, former executive editor of *Runner's World* magazine, has reported that "between 1974 and 1986, a steady trickle of thrillseeking runners mounted seventy attempts on the Badwater-to-Whitney course. Four succeeded." Of course, the percentages may even be worse than that, as many failures decline to alert the media. Clearly, though, lots of ill-prepared adventurers make macho, madcap forays into the Valley of Death every year. Most get only a few miles, then slink home to lick their wounds. Some die. A doctor in Lone Pine sent Crawford a sobering videotape made by a man who walked alone onto the desert salt pan. He had a video camera, three quarts of water, and nary a clue of what he was up against. "He died two hundred yards from where he started," Crawford says. "He went out ten miles, came back nearly ten miles, and videotaped himself dying. When he fell, the camera kept going until the battery went dead. You need a few beers to watch that tape."

It is to the few who have succeeded that we turn for advice on how to cross the desert. Al Arnold, who in 1977 at the age of fifty became the first man to solo the Badwater-to-Whitney run, trained for the heat by pedaling a stationary bike in a sauna four hours a day. The sauna has since become a standard training venue for aspiring Death Valley pedestrians. Both Benyo and Crawford have used it extensively, lifting weights and riding a bike in a box that they regularly crank up to 190 degrees.

Max Telford, a New Zealander who in 1982 broke the Badwater-to-Whitney record by nineteen hours, kept spare shoes in a support vehicle refrigerator and changed into a cold pair every two hours. Bruce Maxwell found that his feet stayed cooler if he ran on the white line instead of the darker asphalt.

Most Death Valley runners agree that the mental struggle is even more difficult than the physical one. But strategies for winning that battle are as disparate as the climates of Badwater and Mount Whitney. Some people pray, some meditate, others hum Broadway show tunes or play with numbers—as in, how far have I come? how far do I have to go? Crawford, who concentrates heavily on mental preparation, believes that aspect is underemphasized by a lot of macho types who go to Death Valley thinking they're going to "kick Mother Nature in the ass."

Said Gary Morris, after completion of the Badwater-to-Whitney course, "You have to move very softly and Zen-like. You must be content to be exactly where you are at any given point."

From Stovepipe Wells to the top of Towne Pass is a seventeen-mile ascent — sea level to 4,956 feet — on a serpentine road. While the first part is rolling hills, the last five miles is nearly a 10 percent grade. While gravity and a northerly crosswind were formidable adversaries, the diminishing heat more than made up for them. As the sun slowly dipped behind the mountains, it created little oases of shade that made Crawford's body go "oooh" and "aaah."

Finally, he lost the sun for good. Even when he topped a rise, he couldn't catch it anymore, and his relief was palpable. He could feel himself relax a little. He even permitted himself a moment's appreciation of the golden sky and the indigo mountains. As he climbed, the relatively cooler air revived him. By the time he topped out at Towne Pass, it was a mere ninety degrees in the shade — with plenty of shade.

While the wind buffeted him, Tom sat and drank, and re-taped his feet. He gazed down upon the unique desolation through which he had passed. In the dusk, the mountains appeared a benign blue and the salt deposits suggested ocean breakers. He was now officially out of Death Valley, out of the worst of the heat, but he was careful not to gloat. He chose his words carefully, avoiding the word "beat," as in "I beat the desert." He knew that nobody beats Death Valley. At best, you merge with it, cooperate with it, take what it gives you, and pass through with a minimum of scars. "See you in a few days," he shouted with a salute. Then he turned and padded on down the road.

The Crawford house is sixty miles north of San Francisco, amid the oak-dotted hills of Northern California. Tom answers the door with a robust, friendly hello and a firm handshake. He's a likable man, the type who makes friends easily. A big-boned six-foot-two and 195 pounds ("one-eighty when I'm in shape"), his is not the typical morphology of an ultrarunner. His hair is fairly short and slicked down, which, along with his ruddy, square-jawed good looks, conjures up a turn-of-the-century, bare-knuckled boxer.

Nancy and seventeen-year-old daughter Amanda are there, too. Adventure sports can be hard on families. These sports are risky and require long hours of training, hours that subtract from the time an athlete can spend with loved ones. And one person's passion can be a partner's nightmare. The best response most adventure athletes can expect from their partners is grudging tolerance.

Not so with Tom and Nancy Crawford. There is nothing the least bit grudging about Nancy's tolerance of Tom's Death Valley runs. An ultrarunner in her own right (thirty ultras, two Western States 100s), she shares his fascination with challenge, if not with the mystique of Death Valley. "People think running ultras is aberrant behavior," she says. "I don't think it's aberrant at all. In our case, we had bought our home, had our child, nailed down our careers. It was natural that we ask, 'What else is there to conquer?'"

Tom has thought of something else—even beyond running Death Valley. He wants Nancy to head the crew on his next Great Adventure, targeted for the summer of 1993. He plans to complete the longest triathlon in history: swim Lake Mead (about eight miles), bike through the desert to Death Valley (274 miles), then run through Death Valley to the top of Mount Whitney (ho-hum, 150 miles). "The main motive is that I love doing what nobody has ever done before. There are so few physical challenges left that haven't been done, but this is one. If I finish, I'll automatically have the world record—that's kinda fun."

For twenty years, running has offered the Crawfords challenge, competition and camaraderie—and, yes, fun. They nostalgically recall the seventies, the glory years, when a "fun run" would be followed by a potluck meal, often at the Crawford house, and two hundred people would show up. "Back then," he says, "I thought everyone on the face of the earth would become a runner. The big thing in medicine was exercise, exercise, exercise. Grandmothers were putting on running shoes and hitting the road."

Why then, despite a plethora of true believers, has the prophecy not come to pass?

He ponders that, but only for a moment: "Because running ain't easy."

Tom tried not to think of the whole race; instead, he broke the route to Whitney into six manageable sections. His next goal was to reach Panamint Springs, mile 70, where he planned to take his first extended rest. Although it was mostly downhill from Towne Pass to

Panamint, it was no cakerun. Going uphill taxes the lungs, the Achilles tendons, and the hamstrings; running downhill stresses the ankle, knee, and hip joints, as well as the quads and hamstrings. If you run hard, the pounding beats you up all over; if you try to brake, your quads take the brunt of it. There is also an emotional toll with running downhill: you never have as much fun as you thought you would.

"Only a half-marathon to Panamint," Crawford calculated, using the unit of measurement that had the most meaning for him. "But the wind has really sucked me dry . . . Don't know if I can make it without rest . . . If I have to walk the downhill part, I'd be better off stopping for a while . . ."

He fell into his patented "slog," a slow, steady swivel of the hips, a waddle, really, that fell midway between a walk and a jog. Crawford believed it was magic for conserving energy; so what if he looked like a large albino duck.

It was dark now, so he hugged the white line in the middle of the road, more for companionship than visibility. Though there was no moon, the starlight reflected off the bald, beige land, lending sufficient light and an other-worldly cast to the topography.

Running down the middle of the road sounds dangerous, but Crawford didn't figure to die in an auto accident. If a car did come, he'd hear it and see it for miles. There were, however, a plethora of other worries. Like a profound fatigue that was producing increasingly bizarre hallucinations. At first, the images were friendly; some Joshua trees suggested crowds of people gathering to wish him well. But then he began to see rattlesnakes lying near a creosote bush, giant tortoises near some rocks. There was a panther, there was a mustachioed mugger. It was frightening, but the worst part came when he began to doubt his ability to evaluate his own condition.

When he reached Nancy, he had the emotional resiliency of a child. He collapsed into a chair and groaned, "I'm not doing this right."

"Yes you are," Nancy said in consolation. "You're doing fine. Here." She held out a bottle of Exceed.

"I think I'm going to have to stop before Panamint. No, I don't want Exceed. My stomach's upset. Let me have a Calistoga."

"I think you can make it. Tom, take the Exceed—you know you can't do this run on water alone."

Crawford took the Exceed and made it to Panamint. In fact, he didn't stop until he was almost two miles past Panamint. Around midnight, Nancy set up a cot out in the desert. Tom fell onto it and

Nancy pulled off his shoes. He felt like a punchdrunk fighter going into the fifteenth round. Trouble was, this was at least a sixty-rounder. With that thought, his head hit the pillow and he slept for two rock-solid hours.

The sun exploded over the Panamint Mountains like the return of an enemy. Already the pavement felt like lava. Crawford's thoughts had taken a dip for the worse; he dwelled in a malevolent funk. "Even with the mountains, daylight comes so early here," he thought, "too early." His attempts to welcome the sun, to become one with the desert, were halfhearted and futile. He was entering a mental depression as deep as Owens Valley, which lay dead ahead.

Owens Valley is always the emotional nadir of the run. Lacking the character of Death Valley, it is grotesquely ugly. The draining of Owens Lake by the Los Angeles water grab has left little behind but bleached, cracked soil and swirling sand devils. It reminded Crawford of geological leftovers. And though the course itself was a gentle descent and the temperature a modest 105, his mind and body had been bullied by twenty-four hours of nearly constant movement through extreme conditions. He had stomach cramps and diarrhea; every joint in his body ached; his eyes burned. All he could do was try not to think about it.

Instead, he focused on his newest goal: reach the tiny mining town of Keeler and crash for about five hours. He could see the town shimmering on the horizon, just as it had been for the past hour.

"God, you see Keeler forever out here," he thought. "If I can just get there without a rest, then it's only a little more than a half-marathon to Lone Pine . . . then another half-marathon to Whitney Portal and road's end . . . then eleven miles of steep trail to the top of Mount Whitney. If I crump before Keeler, I'll regret it. I have to keep on going . . . just keep on going . . ."

Despite such steely resolve, Crawford did not make it to Keeler on schedule. "I thought I was doing eight-minute miles; turned out they were seventeen-minute miles," he says. "Everything was coming unglued for me, both physically and mentally. I now had Carol waiting for me every two miles. When I finally got to her, I was sure I'd gone at least six miles. I almost bit her head off. 'Goddamn it, check your odometer,' I screamed. 'You trying to kill me out here?' She didn't take it personally; she knew I was falling apart."

Carol marked his crump spot with a pile of rocks by the side of the road, dumped him in the car, and raced ninety miles per hour into

Lone Pine to an air-conditioned motel room. His crew taped the curtains to the wall for maximum darkness, and Nancy placed two dresser drawers under Tom's legs to elevate his feet. Having pushed himself to his exhaustion threshold, he was asleep as his head hit the pillow.

The last three miles of the road to Whitney Portal is nothing but steep switchbacks. Cars typically use a slow second gear. Crawford was employing the pedestrian equivalent: run a little; walk a lot; above all, keep moving. It struck him how much easier it was going up at night. He wasn't always tempted to lift his head to see where he was going. In fact, the only way he knew it was uphill was by the effort.

Sound foreshadowed feeling as a warm wind howled eerily through the canyons before reaching him. Through the black of night, he saw the lights of a car descending from Whitney Portal. They seemed to be emanating from some sky lab, or from a spaceship. "My God! I've got to go up there?" he thought.

He silently recited a poem he had composed before his second Death Valley run:

> Do not run with pride
> For with it comes nothing but shame
> But run with lowliness
> For with it comes wisdom and strength
> Run with a balance
> For without it one will surely falter
> Draw each breath gingerly
> Take each step softly
> Swing each arm evenly
> But move slowly and silently within the surrounding warmth,
>   heat and wind
> For with this lowliness
> The wisdom will surely come
> With the balance and strength
> The summit beckons
> Come forth
> Come forth

Up he went to Whitney Portal (elevation 8,600 feet), where he met Nancy at 2:30 in the morning. Crawford was feeling surprisingly spunky. In anticipation of climbing Whitney, he was psyched up. Part of him wanted to grab a flashlight and start right up the mountain. He finally opted to grab a couple hours of sleep and begin at first light. "I was intimidated by my two previous experiences on Whitney," he says. "I had seen some hellacious weather on that mountain."

Next morning, however, the weather was benign. Crawford wore a knapsack filled with two water bottles, a survival kit, two space blankets, PowerBars, a small flashlight, tights, stocking cap, and gloves. Crew member Carol Cognata had started up the trail the day before and was supposed to meet him about nine miles out. She would then accompany him the final two miles to the top, caring for him if needed, going for emergency help if needed.

Unfortunately, Carol had started late and quit early. When Crawford came upon her the next morning, she was breaking camp only four miles up the trail. They hiked together for about a mile before he reluctantly told her, "Carol, I've got to go on ahead."

"I felt bad," Crawford says. "She had trained for that climb and was really looking forward to it. But I think she understood. After all, I had come a hundred and forty miles and was racing the clock."

So steep and rugged are the last three miles to the summit of Whitney that Crawford could average only one mile per hour. As he neared the summit, he began to feel increasingly negative effects from the rapid change in altitude. "Weary, wheezy, and whoozy," he would call it. The desert phase of the course, with its world-class heat, always gets the media attention, but Crawford believes that the mountain is the toughest part of the course. First, it is a formidable climb—about six thousand vertical feet in eleven miles. (Of every 250 people who start from Whitney Portal, only two make it to the top in the same day.) Second, says Crawford, "you've already come a hundred and thirty-eight miles before you start up." In addition, the three elements most likely to contribute to altitude sickness are present: rapid ascent, fatigue, and insufficient liquids. Finally, Mount Whitney is the site of frequent summer thunderstorms. In July 1990, a hiker was killed and twelve others injured when lightning hit the peak. Even in the absence of storms, night temperatures in the survival hut at the summit often drop below freezing. In 1986 Crawford and Mike Witwer, after trudging through massive snow fields, reached the top of Whitney after dark. With no sleeping bag and no feasible way down till morning, they spent the night huddled together in the stone hut, while outside the winds howled and the wind chill plummeted to zero.

This time the weather held. It was clear, cold, and windy as he struggled to the top around midday. The combination of fatigue and thin air had him mired in confusion. He was so disoriented that when he signed in, he couldn't do the simple math necessary to calculate his total running time from Badwater to Whitney. He finally wrote his finishing time on several parts of his body; he would figure out the total later.

He drank some water, but the disorientation persisted. He decided to start back. After enduring for more than fifty-five hours to reach the top of Mount Whitney, he would spend only five minutes at the summit. But as he started down, he headed in the wrong direction, recovering only after a needless descent into a steep canyon. Bushwacking back to the summit cost him twenty minutes, during which time he grew alert enough to recall an impressive array of curse words.

A couple of miles below the summit, Crawford came upon Carol struggling doggedly up the mountain. Crawford always gave his crew members presents; he had planned to give Carol her gift, a necklace, at the top of the mountain. Instead, sensing that she needed a lift, he gave it to her there on the trail. "She cried, and we had a tender moment," he says.

Six miles below Whitney Portal, Crawford crumped big time. He was happy to be safely off the mountain, but physically he had deteriorated from hulk to husk. He had shin splints, his quads hurt to the touch, and he was desperate for sleep.

Too stiff to get into the car, he announced, "I'll ride out here," before flopping onto the hood.

"People will think I shot you," Nancy said.

"People? What people?" His speech had a muffled quality, the last words before sleep.

So as Crawford lay sprawled across the car like a trophy deer, Nancy drove carefully toward Lone Pine, until she spotted Benyo gamefully trudging up toward Whitney Portal.

Nancy carefully stopped the car, Crawford carefully slid off the hood, and the two men carefully embraced like two reunited brothers who had been separated as children.

"What was your one-way time?" Benyo asked.

"Fifty-five hours, eight minutes," Nancy answered for her husband, for he still could not do the calculation.

"Wow, you beat your 1987 time! That's terrific." Though Benyo was genuinely happy for Crawford, he wished that he too were more than half finished.

One hundred and ninety miles into the run, Nancy and Tom Crawford were comparing urine samples. It was all in the name of science, an attempt to assess Tom's condition.

"I think you need to stay put for a while," Nancy said, looking at the blood in his urine.

He staggered over to look at himself in the car mirror. His face was stubbled and sunburned, his eyes bloodshot and dilated. He went back to Nancy and nodded. "Shut it down. We're going to be here for a while."

He would later acknowledge the warning signs. An hour earlier, fighting panic, he had decided the necessary antidote was to brush his teeth.

"Brush your teeth?" Uncle Billy had responded. "I don't have a damn toothbrush."

"Well, the next crew out here, you tell 'em I want a toothbrush."

Crawford rested there for an hour and a half, soaking his size-fourteen (usually size-eleven) feet in tea and watching a storm engulf Mount Whitney that he knew threatened Benyo. He drank copious amounts of water and Exceed, ate watermelon, and sucked on salt scraped from crackers. His urine changed incrementally from the color of tomato juice to the color of pink lemonade. But for Nancy the real clue that he was doing better was the resuscitation of his sense of humor.

"I'm horny," he said, with an R-rated smirk, "let's make love."

She laughed and told him to take a hike, which he did, but at a pace that was painfully slow: six miles in the next seven and a half hours.

On July 22, after five days, six hours, thirty-four minutes, Tom crossed the finish line. He was dried out, beaten up, broken down. His fingers looked like sausages; his feet were swollen. His eyes felt like a gravel quarry; his psychological calorie count read zero. Signaling to Nancy that he needed a moment alone, he continued walking out onto the crusty salt flats, his shoulders slumped, his water bottle dangling from his hand. It was the ultrarunner's peculiar version of a victory lap. There was no exultation, no joy. Only relief.

Tom is an emotional man, and feelings now bubbled freely within him, spilling over into tears that evaporated before they left his eyes. Moments later, when he returned to his entourage, he said to them, "If I ever mention that I want to run Death Valley again, just shoot me, okay?"

Two years later, in the summer of 1991, he and Benyo ran it again.

RUTH ANDERSON

Master of Running

You just wake up one
morning, and you got it!
——Moms Mabley

Squaw Valley, California, 4:45 A.M.: Milling about on the edge of the pack of four hundred-plus runners is Ruth Anderson, a tall, lean woman with boyishly cut platinum hair and a dazzling smile. At fifty-six, the oldest female entrant in the 1986 race, she is a bouncy, vibrant woman who appears ten years younger than her age. She is back for her fourth try at the Western States 100-mile, a run many call "the toughest endurance event in the world."

Anderson wears Nike running shoes, red shorts, a windbreaker, and a fanny pack (filled with four pint bottles of water, granola bars, M & M's, peanuts, ankle tape, Vaseline, and ChapStick). Unlike most of the other runners, she does no stretches, as though she prefers to save herself for the run itself. Instead she greets old friends, laughing and chatting about past runs. Considering the physical and psychological ordeal she faces, she appears extraordinarily centered—excited but not uptight, intense but not demonic. She has, of course, been here before and that helps.

In a race in which the real measure of success is whether or not one has the stuff to finish before the official thirty-hour cutoff, Anderson is only one for three. But no other woman her age is even in the running.

The classic late bloomer, she never even ran around the block until she was forty-three years old. As a girl in Nebraska, she played field hockey and was a state-ranked junior tennis player. But one of the first things she learned after coming west to enroll at Stanford University was to forget about a tennis career. In California she was just another player.

She studied math and science, ultimately taking a job as a radio-chemist at the Lawrence Livermore Radiation Lab, southeast of San Francisco. Her work consisted of analyzing the gamma radiation given off by various substances, which involved her in everything from environmental-impact microanalysis to evaluation of underground nuclear explosions. She found the work interesting, but she clearly would rather talk about running.

"I've always had an appreciation for sports," she says, "but for twenty years I limited my participation to light tennis and swimming. Then in 1972 they closed the lab pool for the winter and two lady co-workers urged me to run with them during lunch hour.

"I'll never forget that first run – eight minutes for a little more than a mile. I've never smoked, but I coughed all afternoon, like I'd never really breathed before. I thought I was dying. I said to myself: 'They'll never get me out there again.' But two days later I was at it again, and in two weeks they had me up to two miles. Two months after that, I entered a novice two-mile race and made it in fifteen and a half minutes. I was hooked."

Those noon runs along the country roads of Livermore soon became a fixture in Anderson's life. After six months she had increased her distance to forty miles a week. When she ran twenty miles in two and a half hours, she became convinced that she could run a marathon. So she entered one in Napa, and not only finished in less than four hours but won the women's division in her age group. She still remembers in vivid detail the breathtaking beauty of the Napa Valley, crosshatched in grape vines; the thrill of victory; the joy of sharing the experience with new and old friends. Her winning prize – a bottle of wine – is still displayed, as one displays the first dollar earned.

Anderson soon discovered that the women's marathon record for women over forty was 3:29:07. That became her goal. Two months later, she entered her second marathon, the 1973 Fiesta Bowl in Phoenix, Arizona. As she recalls the race, flashing perfect white teeth and pale blue eyes, her face radiates the excitement she felt. "At ten miles I was four minutes under a 3:30 pace . . . at twenty miles, seven minutes under. . . . I knew then I could do it. The realization was thrilling."

She finished in 3:26:07, a new world's record for women over forty. Three years later, she lowered the mark to 3:10:10. And in 1978, at the age of forty-nine, she ran a 3:04 marathon – a seven-minute-mile pace. By 1982 she held more age-group records for long-distance running – everything from fifty to one hundred miles – than any woman in the United States. In all she has started eighty-seven marathons – and finished every one.

Ever since 490 B.C., when Pheidippides supposedly ran twenty-odd miles to deliver the message of a Greek victory over the Persians in the battle of Marathon, then fell dead, the marathon has been regarded as the ultimate test of endurance. But no more. Anderson herself has run farther than that – in ultraruns – forty-three times. In 1975 she ran a fifty-kilometer race in four hours, seventeen minutes. In 1978 she ran one hundred miles on a track in a world age-group record 16:50:47. She was the first woman accepted in the London-to-Brighton 54-Miler, finishing it in 7:46:16. In 1980 she ran in the National 50-Mile Championships in Houston, cutting fifteen minutes off her best time and setting another world record for fifty-year-old women.

But all that was merely a warmup for the ultimate ultra, the Western States Endurance Run, one hundred arduous trail miles from Squaw Valley to Auburn, sometimes through snow drifts and rivers, a punishing combination of 17,040 feet of uphill and 21,970 feet of downhill.

SQUAW VALLEY, 4:59 A.M.: At the start of the Western States, you can't help but notice the lighting. On the eastern horizon, there is a faint pre-dawn glow, a subtle wash of pinks and blues; but as you near the starting line, that is overpowered by camera flashes and the abrasive glare of ABC's floodlights. Adding to this eerie effect, almost all the runners carry flashlights.

You also notice how old the runners are. Most are well past their salad days. The race program reports that seven of the male entrants are in their sixties and that the average Western States runner is over thirty-six years old. In 1985 three of the top ten finishers were in their forties, and one, Doug Latimer, was forty-eight.

War whoops greet the gun that sounds the start of the race. At the head of the pack, movement is swift and sure. The best runners will finish in 16 to 18 hours. But back in the middle of the pack

Ruth Anderson's four greatest career highlights

1. 1979 London-to-Brighton 54-Miler — "I broke the gender barrier and had a decent time; I was third woman, in 7:46."

2. 1983 Western States — "through twenty-three miles of snow."

3. 1986 Western States — "First year they extended the course, taking out an easy section and replacing it with a longer, harder section. I finished in 28:56."

4. 1986 twenty-four-hour run at Santa Rosa Junior College track — "I went one hundred ten and one-quarter miles and set five single age-group records along the way."

that Anderson calls home, movement is fitful — walk, slow, stop, walk again. It is suggestive of a post-game throng leaving a crowded stadium.

After a time, however, the crowd disperses and Anderson finds her niche, widening her stride and settling into a pace best described as a brisk walk. She is content with that for now, as the first 4.7 miles of the course is a steep 3,700-foot climb to Emigrant Gap, and she worries about burning out too early.

Although the temperature that day in Auburn, in the foothills of the Sierra, will reach ninety degrees (and one hundred in the canyons of the run), it is — at 5:30 A.M. — cool and breezy. Many runners, thinking only of the afternoon heat, are shivering in shorts and a singlet or T-shirt. Anderson, increasing her pace to a trot, zips up her windbreaker, thankful that she remembered to bring it.

The Western States Endurance Run covers the same trail long used as the course for the Western States 100-Mile Ride. Also known as the Tevis Cup, this world-famous horse race was started by Wendell Robie, a lumberman, banker, and outdoorsman. In 1973 Robie received a call from the head of the Marine Corps training unit at Fort Wayne requesting permission to have twenty of his top Marine trainees try to cover the hundred miles on foot in forty-eight hours, commencing the day before the Tevis Ride.

Of the twenty Marines who started, only two finished.

Sitting in the audience at the Tevis banquet when the Marines stood and received applause from the riders was Gordy Ainsleigh, a twenty-two-year-old woodcutter, who had ridden in the Tevis Cup twice, running with his horse as much as riding it. Ainsleigh was convinced he could best the Marines, so the following year he left his horse at home and ran the Tevis Cup on foot. He completed the distance in twenty-three hours, forty-two minutes, beating many of the horses to the finish line.

By 1977 word of Ainsleigh's feat had spread through the ultra-running community. Fourteen runners applied to run the Tevis Cup, marking the official beginning of the Western States Endurance Run. Only three finished.

Since then, participation and interest in the Western States has swelled with the running boom. The 1986 field of more than four hundred included men and women from forty-one states and four foreign countries. Despite stringent requirements (entrants must pass a physical exam and have run a fifty-mile race in less than ten hours), more than 800 men and women have applied to run in each of the last few years. The field is reduced by lottery, though race management reserves the right to "admit participants who have contributed significantly to the event, or whose participation will significantly enhance the competition" – say, for example, Ruth Anderson.

In 1980 two male friends in their sixties talked Anderson into running the Western States with them, then dropped out a week before the race with injuries, leaving her to run it without them. About fifty miles into the course, she slipped in heavy snow and fell against a pine tree, wrenching her back and temporarily ending her quest.

She returned the next year. On the day of the race, the temperature in Auburn soared to 101. There was a shortage of water, air, everything but heat. Anderson had trouble keeping down fluids and at the sixty-mile mark began vomiting. When the medics weighed her, they discovered she had lost more than the permitted 7 percent of her 124 pounds. She was declared dehydrated and yanked from the race.

She was back in 1983. The evening before that race, after Anderson had been signed in, weighed, and briefed, she and her daughter decided to walk the first couple of miles of the course. It was almost dusk and no one else was around. An explosion suddenly ripped the stillness of the forest. "It sounded like an avalanche," Anderson remem-

Ruth Anderson knows how to use a little high stepping on Western States climbs. (Courtesy of Hughes Photography)

bers. "A gigantic rotten log had broken loose and was rolling down the mountain right at us! . . . Terrified, we started running downhill. The log hit a tree and broke in two, which gave it backspin. . . . When it finally came to a stop it was about ten feet away from us!" Anderson was so shaken she almost didn't run the next day, but then her irrepressible optimism kicked in. "I thought, 'Hey, it didn't get me, so it must be a good omen.'"

Next morning before the race, she was telling anyone who would listen, "Just as you guys are about to turn the first mile there at the bridge, take a look at that gigantic log. It was intended for me, but it didn't get me!"

That year she confronted conditions that almost made her wish the log had gotten her. Twenty-three miles of trail were covered with snow. "I fell down about a million times," she remembers, "but I paced myself, held the nausea to a minimum, and made it in less than thirty hours to earn my plaque."

In addition to winning a plaque for finishing the race in less than thirty hours, a Western States runner can win a silver belt buckle by finishing in less than twenty-four hours. Anderson has long coveted that silver belt buckle. "It certainly is the running goal that has loomed largest for me," she admits with her ready smile. "Sure, I'm proud of a plaque for finishing that rascal, but, darn it, I've really wanted to get under twenty-four hours and win that silver belt buckle."

Mile 30, 12:10 P.M.: Ruth Anderson lopes into Robinson Flat, six minutes under a twenty-four-hour pace and feeling fine. The first major checkpoint of the run, it suggests a war camp: panting, perspiring, even wounded people litter the area in partial states of undress, taking nourishment and receiving medical aid. About twenty runners have already dropped out. A runner who took a bad fall has been helicoptered out with a broken rib and a punctured lung.

The doctors are required to weigh Anderson. She is ushered to the medical area, where she removes her fanny pack and steps on the scale. "One-twenty-two. Minus two pounds." She is pleased, for if she had lost too much weight, they would have wanted to take her pulse and blood pressure, and she really didn't have the time.

Just then Anderson's volunteer support crew—two friends from San Diego—rush up to her full of solicitous inquiries. She is fine, she tells them, feeling pretty strong, but her feet are wet and she has a slight muscle spasm in her right calf from fording frigid streams. While she sits and has a deviled-egg sandwich and coffee, they change her wet shoes and socks. The sun by now is high in a cloudless sky, and Anderson hastily removes her long-sleeved shirt and puts on a singlet and scarf. After another moment of deep breathing, she straps on her fanny pack and waves good-bye to her friends, regaining the trail to Deep Canyon and immediately looking forward to her daughter Rachel's aid station at Dusty Corners. Time of pit stop: eleven minutes.

Ruth Anderson has long been one of the moving forces in the effort to secure equal rights for women runners—especially Masters (over-forty) women runners. Although she insists she is not a political person, her commitment to the movement is undeniable. "The excitement of being part of the emergence of Masters women in long-distance running," she says effusively, "was like being an explorer landing in fascinating new territory. When I began in the sport, there was age-group competition for men, but not for women. Men over forty had been enjoying ten-year and even five-year divisions in major races for years, but what about women? We don't stay thirty-nine forever. For so long I heard the argument that there weren't enough over-forty women to merit separate divisions. . . . Well, we showed that to be false.

"I was motivated by the obvious injustices in women's running that needed correcting, particularly in Masters. The pervasive attitude among the AAU committee members was that only potential Olympians deserved an opportunity to compete and that women were fragile things that shouldn't be allowed to run distances longer than a mile. Nonsense! Women have been running marathons for years. How can you tell a woman who's been doing something for years that she's too fragile to be 'recognized' for doing it?"

Anderson continued to hammer at Amateur Athletic Union members, arguing that they needed a women's long-distance chairwoman at the national level. Partly through her efforts, the first Women's National AAU Marathon Championship was held in 1974. In 1975 the AAU recognized "Masters Women" as a championship category. That same year, Ruth attended the first brainstorming session for the purpose of getting a women's marathon into the Olympics. She continued to lead that crusade, which finally succeeded in 1984.

Anderson herself has broken the sex barrier in several races, most notably the highly traditional London-to-Brighton 54-Miler. "I had long dreamed of doing that double marathon," she says, "but in the twenty-nine-year history of that race they had never permitted a woman to run. I resolved to change that. Being my usual persistent self, I kept writing letters to the British Road Runners Club, which sponsors the event. I finally convinced them to open it up."

In 1980 Anderson and four other women joined 136 men in that race. Afterward, reporters flocked to Anderson, who, with her usual bubbly charm, regaled them with stories. When asked if she were glad the race was over, she told them, "Something anticipated with such ardor is always over too soon."

Mile 56, 7:20 P.M.: Stumbling into the Michigan Bluff checkpoint area, Anderson is fifty-five minutes over a twenty-four-hour pace and feeling terrible. She is sick to her stomach, a symptom that has often assailed her on long runs. She forces down a cup of her special tea concoction, but it tastes so sweet that it makes her gag. She drinks some water, but that sends her hurrying to the bushes to throw up. The medics persuade her to try something she ordinarily shuns—a carbonated soft drink. After a while she begins to feel better, though still weak as a baby bird. Supine and limp beneath a tree, sweating one moment and chilled the next, she watches as runners pass by giving her the same wan smiles she was giving others just two hours earlier. "Yes," she thinks, "matters can deteriorate quickly out here. I was feeling so good only a few miles ago. What went wrong? Somehow fatigue in the lower back seems to lead to nausea, which leads to collapse . . ."

Sitting up, she forces back pain and fatigue. She thinks, "Just get up and keep moving. You've been here before. The worst thing is to sit and feel sorry for yourself." She drags herself to her feet and straps on her fanny pack. Slowly, stiffly, she moves down the trail. Time of pit stop: seventeen minutes.

While nonparticipants marvel at the discipline needed to complete a race like the Western States, Anderson seems to take it for granted. "I never had to go to classes on motivation," she says. "It's come to me naturally. You don't go into math and science without discipline. I recently spoke on this topic at a psychology class. I was on the ticket with a member of the Harlem Globetrotters, who claimed he was motivated by economics. I told the class that wasn't even an issue in ultramarathoning."

Though Anderson earns no money from her sport, she has an entire room in her Oakland home devoted to the impressive number of trophies, plaques, and ribbons she has won over the years. In addition to her dozens of age-group firsts, she has been honored for some of her off-road contributions to the sport. She was the first woman, along with Nina Kuscsik, inducted into the Road Runners Club of America (RRCA) Hall of Fame. She received the Golden Shoe Award from *Runner's World* magazine for her service to the sport. The Long

Ruth Anderson's favorite courses

1. Anything with trails

Distance Running Committee of The Athletics Congress (TAC) honored her with its Woman of the Year award. And countless local running clubs have given her distinguished achievement awards. It's all been very gratifying, but clearly it takes more than gilded shoes to induce someone to run a race as grueling as the Western States.

Laughing her easy, childlike laugh, she agrees: "It helps to receive a ribbon or a plaque, to get some recognition, but in the Western States the main motive is confronting the challenge. Running has been a way for me to test myself. The initial challenge for me was just to be able to run two miles, then six . . . then twenty . . . then a marathon in less than three-thirty. Goals are the perfect motivator."

For many people, the barrier to long-distance running is, in a word, boredom. Anderson, however, says she rarely gets bored, even on the longest runs. "On trails I never get bored. It's too beautiful. I've always been a natural fantasizer, and when I get out there among the flowers I have lovely fantasies. Running the track isn't beautiful, but it's very social and I love that part of it. You have your support crew every quarter-mile . . . friends . . . music, it's great. . . . Still, twenty-four hours on a track is my limit. I prefer the flowers."

Anderson is unusual in her ability and willingness to run both track and trail. In 1982 she captained and ran for a ten-women team in a Masters Women's twenty-four-hour track race, which set a world record of 202.87 miles. (The race finished in driving wind and rain as the tail of Hurricane Eva hit the Sacramento area.) Her first solo twenty-four-hour run was a charity affair at the Santa Rosa Junior College track in which she completed 110.25 miles. She belongs to the World Association of Veteran Athletes (WAVA), which every other year since 1975 has held a world championship in track and field and in cross-country. Anderson has competed in all nine WAVA world championships in distances ranging from eight hundred meters to the marathon, but now plans to confine herself to cross-country and the marathon. "There are medium-distance specialists who just eat me up," she says.

Some researchers believe women have the potential to achieve parity with men at the longer distances. One authority, Dr. Ernst van Aaken, a German physician, biochemist, and sports-medicine writer, says the greatest female advantage in distance running should appear in the fifty- to one hundred-mile range. Dr. Joan Ullyot, an American cardiovascular research physician and runner, agrees: "After the body burns carbohydrates and protein, it is left with fat – the reserve tank. Women carry more fat than men and burn it slower, so that at the twenty-mile mark when men seem to run out of gas, women don't. If you take a man and a woman who have the same time in a ten-mile race and put them in a marathon, the woman will usually win."

Mile 78, 1:00 A.M.. Anderson passes a man bent double beside the trail. Her stomach troubles having abated, she is once again a passer, not a passee. Battling rocky terrain on a moonless night, she is stumbling along at four miles an hour. For just an instant, her mind wanders from her task – "Ah, the scent of pine . . . husband Johnny is sleeping now . . . pain in the right ankle . . . this flashlight is worth the extra weight – " and suddenly she stumbles and nearly falls. The trail at this point is a steep downhill switchback, and a mistake here could kill her. "Better concentrate on the footing," she thinks.

At Rucky Chucky – the American River crossing – an ABC camera crew lies in wait. She smiles at them and thinks, "You just want to see us up to our crotches in ice water."

The water level is high enough to soak her shorts, so on the other side she ducks behind a bush and changes into a pair of long, baggy pants that she has brought to protect her legs from poison oak. Though other runners look askance, it is the right decision. On the move once again, she begins to pass runners, many of whom are tied up with muscle cramps from the wet and cold.

Anderson, a self-described people-watcher, believes that particular habit has contributed greatly to her success. "I love to observe people who are successful," she says. "Watching (high-jumper) Dwight Stones, I could tell he was a visualizer before he became famous for it. He saw himself soaring over the bar before he actually did it. I try to use that same technique – I see the finish line, the cheering crowd, the aid station . . ."

Yet, she insists, she is not obsessively goal oriented. "I don't focus unwaveringly on the finish line. For me, running is not just a means to an end, but an end in itself. On the longest runs, I will set intermediate goals, like trying to reach a particular stretch of the trail when the sun is rising. It's nice to meet your goals, but I guess in my old age I'm getting more philosophical. Even when I'm not going very far or very fast, running is just a joy."

A big part of that joy, she readily admits, has to do with the people she meets. "When I ran in Scotland," she recalls, "I met a man named Duncan McLean who was ninety-two and still running. Known as the Tartan Flash, his specialty was the one hundred and two hundred meters. He used to give demonstrations. He was beautiful.

"That's why I love the international competitions. I've made friends all over the world that I keep bumping into at other racing events. In the Bay Area, I belong to six different running clubs. I even belong to the Lincoln Running Club [of Nebraska], where Johnny and I are from, and I have met some dear friends through those groups."

Does Anderson see herself running when she's in her nineties? "I sure don't see myself quitting," she says. "Hardly any of us quit. Even though I'm not as fast anymore, there are still lots of challenges. What keeps it fresh is the travel and the variety and the people. It's a whole lifestyle. Traveling all over the world to race, I've discovered that there's a common language among the folks involved in this sport. And runners cut across more lines than, say, tennis players. Of my two best running friends, one is a sculptress, the other a plasma physicist. They're total opposites — I love it!"

Mile 95, 8:15 A.M.: For Anderson and her pacer, Marty Maricle (race rules allow a pacer the last forty miles), it's all over but the post-race Rainier Ale. Although she will finish well back of her goal of twenty-four hours, she will finish. And she will break the 30-hour barrier, earning another plaque.

In her mind's eye, she sees the finish line, the cheering crowd, the aid station, and this vision lightens her step. When Maricle, who has won three silver buckles in prior Western States events, tells Ruth that she is having trouble keeping up with her, Anderson grins. She feels almost weightless.

Like an Oscar winner, Anderson has a list of people who she credits for her success. "I couldn't have done all I've done in running without the encouragement of friends and family, particularly my husband, Johnny," she says. "My daughter is my favorite crewperson. Even my dog has contributed. I may have the only running basset hound in the world. His name is Clem Kadiddlehopper and he's addicted to running – a walk won't do. He regularly goes seven miles without stopping. But Johnny is the one. Even after twenty years, he is still so supportive. He crews for me on the big races. He's not an ultrarunner, but he does his twenty miles a week, mostly with me and Clem. I think he gets a little tired of some of the things I do, but a lot of our life still revolves around running. We can hardly plan a trip without directing it toward a race."

Running has given her more than just frequent-flyer miles. "It's made me a healthier person," she says. "I used to drink gin and tonics, but now they just don't taste right. I never used to like beer, but now I have to have my Rainier Ale after the race. My pulse has gone from seventy to forty-two, and my circulation is much better. Since I started my noon runs, I don't get sleepy in the afternoons anymore. One unexpected result: my sense of smell has gotten sharper. If there's a eucalyptus grove up ahead, I can smell it long before I see it."

Anderson can't find anything bad to say about running, for the sport has been so good to her – and for her. She has taken early retirement from her job at the Livermore Radiation Lab, which leaves all the more time for running and running-promotion. She continues to travel all over the planet, pulled here and there by her sport. She has her sights set on the WAVA Championships in Japan in 1993 and hopes someday soon to compete in the world's biggest ultra, the Comrades Marathon, a 56-miler in South Africa (starting field: twelve thousand to thirteen thousand). But even when she's not running, she finds a way to stay close to her sport. She recently returned from Spain, site of the 100-Kilometer International World Cup, where she was manager of the United States women's open team. "We're trying to get IAAF [International Amateur Athletic Federation] sanctioning for the one hundred-K," she says. "We want it to be called a 'Championship,' but right now it's a 'cup,' though a darn big cup – more than five hundred runners from dozens of countries participated. The U.S. women's team finished fourth."

Though Anderson's times have slowed in the past few years – her best marathon time since turning sixty is 3:44 – there are still challenges galore. That is made possible by a combination of what she calls her "insatiable appetite for variation and challenge," good health, and

Ruth Anderson's six remaining running challenges

1. Western States 100 – "to become the second woman ever to finish after age sixty."
2. 10th World Association of Veteran Athletes (WAVA) Championships in Japan in 1993 – "I've competed in the first nine."
3. One of the other 100-milers – "like Vermont or Leadville."
4. The International 100-Kilometer race.
5. Comrades 56-miler in South Africa.
6. Isle of Man 40-miler.

the age-group divisions common to running. She has almost miraculously escaped the lower-limb orthopedic problems that plague as many as 60 percent of endurance runners. On the other hand, she has separated her shoulders four times, all due to falls during races. "The first time was in the Oakland hills," she remembers, "about a year after I started running. I was doing a nine-mile race on a trail. There was a people traffic jam, and in the confusion my foot caught on a stump and I became airborne. The result was a dislocated shoulder; I grabbed it with my free hand and ran on, finishing third among women. After that, I became pretty well known in racing circles. The last time was just a couple of months ago at the Gibson 24-Hour Run. The weather was terrible. I slipped on wet pavement and separated the same shoulder I had injured nine months before. That really is not a good way to drop out of a race – it's too darn painful."

Mile 100, 9:00 A.M.: With a victor's glow, Anderson crosses beneath the red-and-white finish banner at the Placer High School track. The vision that has sustained her for so long is firmly in focus. Though her time of twenty-eight hours is slower than she hoped for, she feels satisfied. She thinks: "Better to have run and finished in twenty-eight hours than not to have run at all." And in the eyes of the people who surround the finish line, the lady downing a Rainier Ale is a sure winner.

Renowned for her effervescence, Anderson is a perennial favorite of the press. She is forever described in terms like "bouncy," "effusive, " and "exuberant." Nearly all the photos taken of her show a dazzling smile. It's enough to make one cry out, "Aren't you ever sad? Depressed? How can you always be so cheerful?"

She would answer that she is cheerful because she is genuinely happy. "I flat-out love running," she says, making believers out of anyone within earshot. "Even my six-mile runs at noon are pure joy!"

The reporters gather around this Pollyanna, firing questions:

"You've finished the Western States twice, will you come back again?"

"Oh yes! But maybe not next year. This rascal is such a commitment, it really takes a whole year of training. Only one woman, Helen Klein, has ever finished the Western States after her sixtieth birthday. I really want to be the second woman to do that."

"What was Helen's time?"

"I don't even know. With the Western States, it's finishing that's the real issue."

"Is your goal of breaking twenty-four hours still alive?"

"I hate to say it, but probably not. Realistically, I'm looking at breaking thirty hours. If everything works out right, maybe around twenty-eight."

"The Western States is not the only ultra you run, is it?"

"No. I've finished forty-three ultras now."

"Isn't there a race named after you?"

"Yes, a one hundred-K race around Lake Merced in San Francisco is now the Ruth Anderson One Hundred. A lot of people are jealous about that, but I thought it was pretty dang nice. Usually, you have to croak to have a race named after you."

"You look a long ways from croaking. Is running a fountain of youth?"

"Well, it sure slows down the aging process. I've been doing it for twenty years and I'm getting younger every year. But seriously, all other things being equal, sixty-year-olds will always run slower than fifty-year-olds. Of course, those other things are rarely equal. They've recently discovered that dedicated runners in their fifties are physically superior to sedentary twenty-five-year-olds."

Still fielding questions, Anderson makes her way to her white 1963 90S Porsche with the personalized license plate SHRODR 1. "Someone beat me to SHROEDER," she explains, "which is what I named the car.

It's after the Peanuts character Shroeder—the one who plays classical music. For years classical music has been my constant companion on those long commutes from Oakland to Livermore. I would turn up the music and have the loveliest fantasies."

As Anderson starts to get into her car, a fellow runner hollers to her, "Hey, Ruth, where are you going?"

"Home," she says. Then breaking into a huge grin, she adds, "The World Veteran Games are next year and I have to get started on my speed work."

STEVEN NEWMAN
Worldwalker

Bethel, Ohio, April 1, 1983. Steven Newman lay in bed nagged by the possibility that he had lost his mind. In other words, he was beginning to believe that everyone else was right. "Walk around the world by myself," he thought. "How could I believe such a thing was possible?"

It was just before sunrise on the morning of his departure, and he was all but consumed by the fear that he would not come back from his worldwalk alive. "I've bitten off more than I can chew this time. There's no way I can walk across an entire planet, with so little knowledge, without dying." Or at least being disgraced. The thought of making it twenty miles down the road and then quitting haunted him, too. And with two million readers of a Midwestern newspaper, *Capper's Weekly*, expecting his stories every couple of weeks, there was no way to keep it a secret. Yes, he could hear the whispers if he failed: there's the guy who tried to walk around the world. He made it all the way to the other side of Ohio . . . har har.

He thought of the risks – from deserts to diseases – and then thought of what he was leaving behind, including his father, who was dying, and his mother, who despite her fears always kept a brave face. Steve felt guilty leaving his family, but by now he had no choice. If he backed down now he'd be the village fool for the rest of his life.

Tumbling out of bed, it hit him how truly weary he was. He had gotten almost no sleep. "Better pull it together," he urged himself.

"Gotta go forty miles today." Whenever he pictured himself walking, really walking, he saw forty-mile days.

Only about a dozen people were on hand for his departure, including family, friends, and the mayor of Bethel, who signed Steve's log book and shook his hand. As the worldwalker hoisted his backpack and took an exaggeratedly ceremonial first step, he thought he might throw up. The sheer immensity of what he was about to attempt nearly overwhelmed him. "It hit me that I would have to take millions and millions of steps to make it. It suddenly felt like I was stepping into quicksand."

At the last minute, while he was still in front of his parents' house, a television camera crew rushed up to him. "Is it true that you're going to walk around the world?" asked a slick-talking man with a microphone.

"Yes."

"Well, how about that. We thought it was an April Fool's joke."

He couldn't blame people for being skeptical. After all, he was not physically imposing. At six-foot-two and 170 pounds, he was rather skinny. With pale skin, reddish-blond hair, and darting, beady eyes, he looked a bit like a chicken. Chickens crossed roads. But walk around the world? Nah.

An hour after his supposed start, Newman had traveled only five hundred feet from his house. The TV crew had taken extensive footage of him waving good-bye and leaving, waving good-bye and leaving, choreographing his every move as though it were a worldwalker commercial. Finally, as an increasingly self-conscious Steven Newman waved good-bye for the last time and turned to walk down the tree-lined sidewalk, the on-the-spot reporter stuck a microphone in the face of a little boy who had watched the whole show. "And what do you think of Steven Newman and his walk around the world?" the broadcaster asked.

The boy's pithy response made the seven o'clock news, no doubt causing thousands of listeners to nod in agreement. "I think he's nuts," the boy said.

By the time Newman had gone only a mile, struggling beneath the weight of his sixty-pound backpack (nicknamed Clinger), he wondered why he was carrying so much crap. It was a cold day, but so inefficient was he that he was sweating profusely beneath long johns, sweater, and jacket.

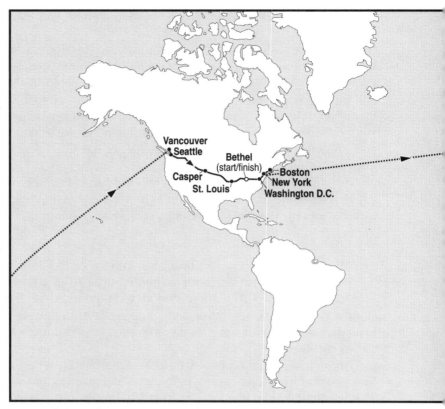

Newman passed through twenty nations during his four-year-long worldwalk.

After two miles, he stopped to rest. It was then he discovered he had forgotten to bring water. "Oh fine," he thought with a mirthless laugh. "I'm walking around the world and forget the water. Some adventurer I am."

At that moment, his mother drove up in the family car. "Just wondered if there was any last thing I could do before we said good-bye," she said with a bittersweet smile.

"Well, as a matter of fact, Mom, I forgot water. And could you take back some of my gear. I've got way too much."

After eight hours of hiking that first day, Newman had covered only thirteen miles. "I knew then I had badly miscalculated," he says. The blow was softened, however, when a factory worker's wife stopped and asked if he needed a place to stay the night.

The first two weeks of the journey brought constant rain, a cold,

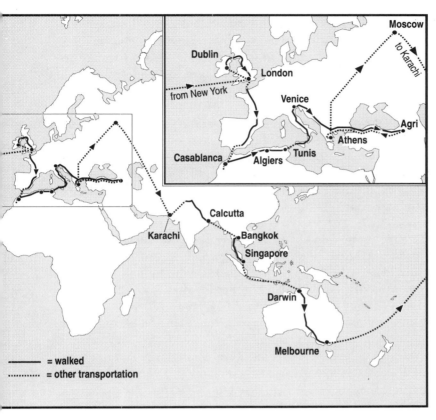

bitter rain that exacerbated the physical hardship of the walk. During that time, Newman averaged about two miles per hour. At twenty-eight, he was in decent shape, but neither his body nor his mind was toughened to the rigors of the road. He suffered from swollen knees, huge blisters, and an almost unrelenting self-pity. "I was the most miserable person alive," he says. "What kept me going at first was the 'fool factor,' the fear that I would be perceived as a fool if I quit. I convinced myself to go as far as West Virginia then quit. At least then it would look like I tried."

Even as a preschooler in the tiny Ohio hamlet of Bethel, near the Kentucky border, Steven Newman sensed that the world around him was a safe place, "a place I could wander freely in," he says. "I was fascinated by fireflies and would follow them at night. Once, when I was five, I followed them all the way across town. I had no idea where

I was. Finally an old lady spotted me and called a cop. I spent what seemed like hours driving around in a patrol car, with him asking me, 'Is that your house? . . . How about that one?' The lesson for me was clear — that wandering about aimlessly could lead to wonderful experiences."

In his sophomore year of high school, Newman joined the cross-country team. "Now I could expand my explorations," he says. "I could go a lot farther and see a lot more. I loved cross-country, but for me it was not so much an athletic event as an exploratory event."

Newman was one of the earliest adherents of the running philosophy now known as Long Slow Distance (LSD). Exceeding the advice of his cross-country coach, he started putting in more than one hundred miles a week. His favorite run was the twenty or so miles to the Ohio River and back, but he also liked just loping along from town to town. Sometimes he would run well past dark, which forced his coach to drive around looking for him. His teammates, who found his love of long distances puzzling, nicknamed him Beebe, after Abebe Bikila, the Olympic marathon gold medalist (1960, 1964) from Ethiopia.

The summer after his sophomore year, Newman and his one close friend, nicknamed Ape Man, decided to hitchhike from Ohio to New England, without telling their parents. They finally called from Pennsylvania and, as Steve remembers it, "By then my folks were so used to my wandering, they weren't even that worried. The trip itself was wonderful. We tried to live off the land for a week in upstate New York, met interesting people, and I guess traveling got in my blood. The next summer, with twenty-five dollars in my pocket, I hitched to San Antonio to see the Alamo."

During adolescence, Steve experienced a highlighting of his three primary loves: traveling, running, and reading. He reveled in the works of Ernest Hemingway and Jack London, and many a night he would fantasize his way onto the pages of *For Whom the Bell Tolls* or *The Call of the Wild*. One evening, when he was nine, he found a stack of dog-eared *National Geographic* magazines in the attic. They sent his imagination soaring. That night he told his mother: "When I grow up I'm going to be a writer and walk around the world."

Bronx, New York, June 12, 1983. Concerned that he was about to leave America with no ability to defend himself, Newman decided to learn how to fight — or at least how to be in a fight. He was staying with a writer in Manhattan, and every night he would take the subway to

Steven Newman's four best places for a worldwalker

1. Ireland – for people
2. France – for lifestyle and food
3. North Africa – for exotic scenery
4. India – for fascination

Harlem or the Bronx and walk the mean streets, actually looking for trouble that would help to prepare him for what lay ahead. Apart from some pushy prostitutes, nobody directly confronted him until the last night of his two-week stay.

He was heading back to the subway when he was suddenly startled by a big, muscular man who stepped out from one of the countless dark alleyways. "Hey!" he said, grabbing Steve's attention. The man wore a black leather jacket dotted with insignias and laden with chains. He spoke from a scarred face: "Didn't anybody ever tell you people like you shouldn't be around here after dark?" he growled.

Newman was so flustered, his mind went to putty. "I'm from Ohio," he stammered, thinking, "God, I sound like an idiot."

That seemed to catch the big man off guard. "Ohio? Where's that?"

"It's in the middle of America."

The man stuck his brutish face in Steve's and said, "You're not a typical tourist, are you? I seen you walking these streets before."

"Y-yes, I'm walking across America." He didn't want to tell him he was walking around the world. It would seem too incredible.

Even America was a stretch. "You walked here all the way from Ohio?" he said, squinting malevolently.

"That's right."

"Prove it."

Prove it? What proof did he have? Then it struck him that although he wasn't collecting souvenirs, he was collecting experiences, so he decided to share one of them. He told the story of an old woman with failing eyesight who had seen him walking and invited him in because she mistook him for an angel. "I got breakfast and helped her go to heaven," he concluded, thinking, "This guy's going to hate this story." But to his surprise, the big man's face showed just the opposite.

In fact, he liked the story so much, he wanted his gang to hear it, too. So he coaxed Newman down an alley to meet the gang members, none of whom looked like an Ohio farmboy. There were about fifteen of them: young, rough, tough black men lounging amid the garbage cans, drinking and smoking joints. For the next hour, Newman bridged a cultural chasm with tales of his travels.

When one of the men suddenly ran off, Newman wondered what that meant. Maybe they just planned to milk him for stories, then kill him. But the man soon came back, carrying a used bowling trophy. They presented it to Newman for being "the bravest American we ever did meet."

"That experience taught me a strategy for dealing with confrontations," he says. "Be yourself and don't show fear. I also learned that people have respect for the heroic, or at least what they perceive to be heroic. That gang gave me a protective escort to the subway, and I left New York with a renewed sense of hope."

Dublin, Ireland, July 27, 1983. It was rainy, foggy, and cold as Newman walked off the ferry into Ireland. As he would write of his first steps on foreign soil: "I knew no one and nothing." He would have to learn by his mistakes, the first of which occurred immediately when he chose to walk north out of Dublin on a main road. Compact cars roared by like racers, an arm's length away. The air was thick with exhaust, and the growl and whine of engines were like hammers to the brain. "How disappointing," he thought. "This is just like America."

Just then an orange Volkswagen sputtered to an involuntary stop in front of him. The driver, an old woman, had a look of desperation on her face. He winced in expectation of a multicar pileup, but the other vehicles deftly slid around her. Newman dropped Clinger and went to push the VW onto the sidewalk. In mid-push, a huge truck roared around the bend and bore down on them. Newman dived back onto the sidewalk. With a screeching of brakes, a grinding of gears, and a shaking of fists by the driver, the truck glided around the stalled car.

After pushing the car out of harm's way, he returned to Clinger, only to find a German shepherd raising its leg over his backpack. "Oh, God! This *is* just like America. Traffic and cities and big trucks and crazy drivers and German shepherds pissing on my gear. This isn't going to be any fun at all."

After graduating from Ohio University in journalism, Newman

moved to Wyoming, where he took a job as a reporter on a Casper newspaper. For a while it was fascinating work that kept him up late at night and brought him into contact with a seedy, sometimes criminal, side of life. His investigative series on the Greek Mafia brought him kudos as well as death threats, the latter causing him to rethink goals and geography. "I've become cynical," he concluded. "What became of the innocence of Ohio? Is that lost forever? What about the brighter side of mankind?"

The answers, he decided, lay elsewhere. It was time to reactivate his childhood dream of walking around the world. First, though, massive preparation was needed. In order to earn money, get in shape, and "confront adverse characters in adverse circumstances," he quit the newspaper and went to work as a roughneck, drilling for oil in Wyoming.

After three and a half years of dangerous, demanding labor, he had money but still didn't feel ready to walk around the world. So he spent the next year camping throughout the West, getting used to solitude, for he believed that the worldwalk would bring huge blocks of time alone. "I needed to strengthen my mental tenacity and spiritualness — as well as my legs. I went back to running, especially through the snow and sand."

The last six months before the start of his walk, he returned to Bethel and refined his training. He intensified his running, added weight training, and did lots of walking. "What I didn't do was walk with weight on my back," he says. "That was a big boo boo."

North Africa, December 10, 1983. On the storm-tossed ship crossing the Strait of Gibraltar, Newman recalled Mark Twain's description of the vessel's destination, Tangier, Morocco. "A rat's nest of thieves and murderers," he had called it. Nothing Newman saw in his first moments on "really foreign" soil convinced him otherwise.

After being detained for several hours on the boat because authorities thought he was a Jew, he was unapologetically released into the night. As he walked into the city from the boat dock, hordes of desperate people scuttled from the shadows of dilapidated buildings. They clawed their way to him, robed, hooded figures, hands out, poking, chanting, making up for limited vocabulary with volume: "Cheap hotel . . . cheap drugs. . . . My friend, you want girl? . . . Come here, my friend. . . . I am your friend, my friend . . ."

This was a far cry from chasing fireflies in Bethel. So alien were the figures that crowded about him, they seemed a different species – a herd of jackals or a frenzied tribe of baboons. As he continued walking toward town, noisy denizens of the night tugged at both him and Clinger until he thought he would lose his mind.

A hooded figure suddenly blocked his path. Peering into the oval-shaped shroud, Newman could make out four or five twisted teeth, a gaunt face with a vertical scar thick as a thumb along his cheek, and one eye. Where the other eye should be – a black hole. Newman shuddered. Had he come face to face with death? As though in response, the figure pulled a switchblade from beneath his robes and hissed, "Why don't you talk? Say something!" Newman stared back, wondering if he would faint or be killed first.

"Give me your money or you die."

Hearing that, something in him snapped. The fear, the disgust, and the revulsion roiling inside of him fused, changing to intense rage. Injustice fortified him. He whipped out his hunting knife, which made the switchblade look like a putty knife, and waved it at the hood. "Me die? Me die? Noooo, you die!" The man's one eye widened in terror. He slowly lowered the knife, then turned and ran.

Newman later wrote, "It worked, but it was all a bluff. If that guy had come at me, I'd have dropped the knife and not known what to do."

Despite that encounter, and despite the continual crush of impoverished humanity in North African cities, he kept himself open to new people and experiences. "I have taken the tack that whatever happens happens. I will not force anything; instead, I will mesh with life's rhythms and trust anyone who appears to befriend me. To do otherwise would be to go around the world a mass of nervous ulcers."

Trust generally served him well. He drank the water everywhere he went and never got sick. He accepted numerous invitations into Arab homes, where guests are treated as royalty. The up side was a cultural education that money can't buy; the down side was a staggering lack of privacy that was exacerbated by the Arab belief that the host family should not leave the guest alone even for a minute. "The hardest custom to get used to was having the men tuck me in bed and kiss me goodnight."

The cities of North Africa offered a crush of people, many of them beggars asking for money, or children asking the same questions over and over: "English? . . . American? . . . Where are you from? . . . Where

Steven Newman's three worst places to walk

1. Eastern Turkey—for danger; last hundred miles before Iran is a no-man's land
2. Australia—for physical hardship
3. Central plains of the United States—for boredom (yet it is the home of the kindest Americans)

---

are you going?" But the rugged countryside of Morocco, Algeria, and Tunisia offered nature in glorious abundance. "The coastline of North Africa is the most beautiful place I've been so far," he wrote. "It is a beautiful place to walk, with rugged peaks and lush valleys."

One memorable night, Newman was crossing the Atlas Mountains in eastern Algeria, moonlight reflecting off newly fallen snow, when he heard a low growl. At first he thought it was his stomach, "because I was always hungry." But a few steps later, he heard it again; then again, this time louder and more ominous. Looking through the pine trees to his left, he saw a low-slung animal, a hideous black creature with upturned tusks, a long snout, and eyes like burning coals—a wild boar.

The boar scuffed once at the dirt with a hoof and charged. Newman, frozen in fear, had time only to think, "God, he's going to kill me!" before the beast stopped about twenty feet away and stared venomously at him. Steve stared back, desperately trying not to show the fear that had his heart pounding and his body twitching.

Finally, not knowing what else to do, he slowly moved on. The pig followed. From the forest came more snorting. Another pig appeared, then another, then another, until there were thirteen pigs following him. He recalled that pigs are omnivorous.

Deciding the balance of power clearly lay with the pigs, he clambered up a pine tree, Clinger on his back, and huddled on a branch. Beneath him the pigs kept sentry, continuing to graze and communicating incessantly through squeaks, chirrups, and grunts. Newman alternated between abject fear and annoyance. Then, sometime during the freezing night, a new voice was heard, one destined to improve his outlook. "What are you afraid of?" the voice asked. "Isn't this what you asked for? Isn't this what you wanted; to live the adventures of

Hemingway and London? You should be thrilled, and thankful. Isn't pain just as necessary as joy? And those pigs will eventually go away."

Although the new voice brought with it new perspective, new patience, it did not immediately protect him from discomfort. After that frigid night imprisoned in a tree, he caught a bad cold – his only illness so far on the whole walk. "It was a small price to pay," he says. "That experience was a turning point. Because of it, I lost my fear of death. I still feel that way. Not that I'll go out of my way to die, just that if I'm told it's going to happen, I can accept it as part of the adventure."

Eastern Turkey, September, 1984. Newman was not looking forward to walking through Turkey. His image of Turkish men was an amalgam of sadistic prison guards from the movie *Midnight Express*. But he knew that other people – Turks included – also stereotyped Americans, usually as larger-than-life figures like Rambo or action-movie star Chuck Norris. Though he was 160 pounds and skinny as a walking stick, he towered over the squat Turks and, in his blue jeans and long-sleeved shirt, bore a superficial resemblance to Norris. He resolved to use that to his advantage.

One chilly September day, while Newman strode a long, flat stretch of road, seven Turkish men rode by on a tractor, taunting him like schoolchildren. They soon passed again, pointing and yelling at him. Newman knew only a few Turkish words, but he recognized a vitriolic tone. It sure wasn't "Welcome to Turkey" they were shouting.

The tractor stopped about a hundred yards ahead. Newman wasn't sure what the men had in mind, but he knew it wasn't good. After eighteen months on the road, he had developed a sixth sense for danger. He walked on, thinking, strategizing. The best way to confront danger, he believed, was to charge into it. Show no fear. That's what a fellow traveler had taught him in Spain. Phillip, who had been all over the world, convinced him that Third-World bullies who prey on travelers are cowards who can be bluffed. And hadn't it worked with Scarface in Tangier?

Still fifty yards from the tractor, Newman began running at the men, shouting, cursing, waving his arms like a madman . . . closer . . . closer . . . until finally the men leapt from the tractor and scattered like rabbits. As he passed their huge machine, knowing the men were watching, he let forth with what he imagined was a karate-like scream and punched a dent in its side. It sent slivers of pain through his hand and wrist, but he was careful not to show it.

Some days later, Newman had a similar experience with a single taunting Turk on a tractor. He was a big man who rolled by, spitting forth remarks about Americans in general and Newman in particular. But this time when Newman shouted and charged at him, the man held his spot, sitting high atop his tractor like a baleful god. Newman stopped his charge, but too late. He bumped into the leg of the scowling Turk, who quickly climbed down from his tractor and curled his sausage-like fingers into fists. Newman was shocked. No one had ever stood up to him before. "Now what do I do?" he thought, forced to confront the awful truth: he still knew absolutely nothing about self defense. He had run from every childhood fight he could, lost every one he couldn't run from. He was ignorant of weapons, karate chops, hand-to-hand combat.

What he did know was talk, cajole, bluff — but then what? Ah, yes, retreat. He turned and walked briskly away, not looking back, hoping the Turk would not follow him. Once again his luck held. "I really am the luckiest person alive," he likes to say. "In this case, I felt lucky to get away with my teeth."

But on the whole, Newman found the Turks to be among the warmest, most hospitable people he encountered anywhere. Many a night he was taken into someone's home, plied with food and drink, and given a place to sleep. Once, during a driving rainstorm, a group of Turkish telephone linemen stopped and asked if he was the guy who was walking around the world. He had no idea how they knew that, but he had a friendly chat with them, after which one of the men asked if he would like a free phone call.

"Of course, I would," he said enthusiastically. He would call his parents.

Before he could say more, the man was climbing a nearby pole. Pelted by a blinding rain, he connected some wires and dropped a phone down to him.

The phone rang three times. He heard a faint, familiar voice.

"Hello, Dad."

"Hello . . . hello . . . is anybody there?"

"Dad. Can you hear me? It's Steve."

"Hello . . . hello? . . ."

"Dad!" He was screaming into the receiver now, desperate to be heard. "Dad! It's me, Steve. Can you hear me?."

A long silence followed. Then ever so tentatively: "Steve? Is that you, son? Steve?" Then he was gone, cut off.

It was the last time he talked to his father, who died a few weeks later while Newman was in India.

Central India, February, 1985. Newman always drew a crowd in India, particularly in remote areas that saw few tourists. Sometimes the crush of onlookers intent on seeing him shave or drink a glass of tea was enough to make him fear suffocation. One time he entered a post office to mail a letter, and the curious throng outside pressed so tightly against the windows that they blocked the sun and the postmaster had to light a lamp. "I can't believe I was worried about being lonely," he wrote.

Despite the American flag unfurled on the back of Clinger, villagers in India tended to assume that he was British. Many Indians loathed the British and would yell epithets and taunt him with rhythmic chants of "Bora, Bora, Bora"—*British* in Hindi.

The most threatening incident occurred in central India, when he passed by what appeared to be a high school for boys. With no warning, teenagers in black uniforms began streaming out of the building. They surrounded him, many brandishing rocks, all of them shouting so loudly that his cries, "I'm an American, I'm an American," could not be heard.

There ensued a tense standoff. Each time he tried to move, the boys would tighten the circle, raising their rocks threateningly. "Where are the teachers?" he wondered. "Had the inmates taken over the asylum?"

Just then two men in a Volkswagen van came through the village. The driver forced the van through the crowd, honking and waving for the kids to move. Drawing abreast of the American, the man in the passenger seat pushed open the sliding door and shouted in English, "Get in!" The buzz of the crowd grew louder. Even amid such tumult, Steve hesitated. He had walked halfway around the world and had never taken a ride; he was reluctant to start now. On the other hand . . ."

Before he could debate the matter further, the man grabbed him by the neck and shoved him halfway into the van, and the driver sped off. The boys, furious at the loss of their prisoner, cut loose with a hail of rocks that broke every window in the van and split the driver's head open.

Newman wrote, "There are times in India when my mere appearance creates danger."

Southern Thailand, May 3, 1985. He had been warned repeatedly not to walk through Thailand. "Gangsters are everywhere," people said, but of course he had heard similar warnings for two years. If he had heeded them all, he never would have left his bedroom. This time, however, there was confirmation. An article in the *Bangkok Post* claimed that four hundred people had been killed by Thai bandits in the past year alone. "Mostly Vietnamese boat people," Newman concluded as he set off toward Malaysia.

Crossing the jungles of Thailand was like hiking through hell. Even when he stayed in the shade of his parasol, the sun tore at his pale skin as though it had claws. In defense, he decided to brave the bandits and walk at night.

He was thirteen miles south of the town of Phet Buri on a star-studded, moonless night when a car went by, only the second he'd seen in the past hour. As his gaze followed the car's headlights, he saw something that made the hair on the back of his neck stand up. Ahead on the left were two human shapes crouching in the weeds below the shoulder of the road. As soon as the car passed, they sprang to their feet and came at him like football linebackers. Terrified, he pointed his umbrella at the men and shouted, "Halt, or I'll shoot!" Sure, it was crazy – no rifle had red, blue, and yellow stripes – but what else could he do?

Well, he could do what he was trained for – run. As he turned and headed back down the dirt road, his heart pounded like a jungle drum and adrenaline poured into his body. But slowed terribly by Clinger, his legs were rubbery. The footsteps behind him grew louder until the bigger of the two men caught him and spun him around. In desperation, Newman went on offense, lashing out frantically with his umbrella, all the while crying, screaming, spitting. Suddenly the other bandit grabbed him from behind, spun him around and swung with his machete. Newman didn't see the blade, but he heard it. *Clang!* The knife, aimed at decapitation, had struck the aluminum frame of his backpack, two inches from his jugular.

His wild gyrations intensified; he fought back with ever greater fury, forcing his umbrella into their faces, taking advantage of his longer arms, trying to delay the inevitable. Suddenly the men retreated, diving back into the jungle just as two headlights came into view. Newman, sobbing, stood in the middle of the narrow track and waved the car down. It was a Datsun pickup truck. He scurried to the back and tried to climb in, but it was filled to overflowing with pineapples. Screaming and gesticulating like a madman, he went around to the passenger side. A farmer, his wife, and two daughters were shoe-horned into the truck's cab. The driver, alarmed by the erratic behavior of this wild-eyed Westerner with the weird contrivance on his back, stomped on the accelerator. Newman, convinced that the bandits were still there and that his life depended on getting into the truck, reached through the open window and latched onto the first thing he could find. Although he didn't yet know it, he had grabbed the woman's breast, causing her to scream in pain and fright, which in turn caused the daughters to join the cacophony. The driver was screaming too, but he kept the truck moving, and Steve was half-dragged, half-carried two miles to a police outpost, all the while locked onto the poor woman's breast and imagining the bandits running up to chop off his legs, which were flopping outside the truck.

That night, as he lay in a room at the rear of the police outpost, he hit emotional bottom. Mosquitoes buzzed outside his netting, a gecko darted across the dimly lighted ceiling, and the swamp sounds outside convinced him that the bandits were coming to finish him off. Sleep was impossible, depression inevitable. "Ooh, I can't do this . . . can't do this," he wailed. "Still six hundred miles of Thailand to go. There must be a million bandits between here and Malaysia. What am I doing? What am I doing?"

It was a desperate monologue and a long, lonely night, but eventually he was visited by the "voice," which provided the answer: "Keep going, but no more walking at night."

After two years and nine thousand miles, he realized that the reasons for continuing the walk had changed. The journey had taken on a life of its own, and in some ways he was just a bit player. All the people who had helped him, who had signed his log book, who were reading his stories in *Capper's Weekly* — he'd be letting them down if he quit. "Mostly, though," he concluded, "I just have to find out what's going to happen next."

Darwin, Australia, July 17, 1985. By the time Newman reached Darwin, he needed a new pair of Rocky boots. Before leaving Bethel, he had written to the Ohio company that makes Rocky boots, explained what he was going to do, and asked for a free pair. Company officials replied that they didn't believe he could walk all the way around the world, Rocky boots or not, but wished him luck and said they would be glad to sell their boots to Newman wholesale. Now, however, with the knowledge that Newman had covered 10,429 miles in two pairs of Rocky boots, they offered him his third pair free.

He would need a good pair of boots and more. He was about to attempt to walk across one of the world's great deserts, a staggeringly large area of aridity that makes up 44 percent of the Australian continent. If he succeeded, it would take him a year to complete the 2,388-mile trek from Darwin to Melbourne across some of the driest, least hospitable topography on earth. Most people didn't believe it could be done; typically, he disagreed.

The biggest concession he made to triple-digit temperatures and sparse settlements was to take Clinger off his back. He rigged a hand-pushed cart—nicknamed Roo—for carrying his gear and plenty of water.

As he headed south from Darwin, he was more prepared for the searing heat than he was for the vicious wildlife of the desert. One afternoon he was awakened from a nap in the only shade for miles by needle-like pains in his neck. He tore at his throat and looked down to see thousands of huge black ants crawling all over his body, boots, and gear. They were Australian bull ants, the biggest and most ill-tempered in the world.

Barefoot and screaming, he ran out onto the hot sand. He tore hundreds of ants, one by one, from his feet and legs. Back in the shade, thousands more, each half as big as his thumb, swarmed over his gear and boots. He knew he had to retrieve his gear or die. He lit a small branch on fire and thrust it at the ants; they attacked it. Finally, able to clear a crude pathway, he dashed in like a firefighter saving a child from a burning building, liberated his boots, and tossed them onto the sand away from the main body of ants. One by one, he killed the ants on his boots. He repeated the process for his water jugs, backpack, and cart. It took hours of panting labor that almost dropped him with dehydration. "It was very, very frightening," he wrote.

As was the entire trek through the outback, where temperatures often exceeded 120 degrees and settlements were so far apart that Newman often had to ration food and water. "Most days I lived on a bowl of muesli and powdered milk for breakfast, nothing else for the rest of the day except sips of warm water, then baked beans for dinner. It shows how tough the body is." His weight dropped to 129 pounds.

After four and a half months, Newman reached the town of

Coober Pedy. It was November, the heart of the Australian summer, in an area so hot and dry that the houses are set underground and residents are limited to one-minute showers. From there, he turned southeast and began walking directly into furnace-like winds. The terrain changed from sand to salt, from brown to a preternatural white. The sun reflected so fiercely off the earth's surface that Newman was forced to don several layers of clothing to protect his pale Irish skin. Ground temperatures regularly exceeded 150 degrees. In two days, the only life he saw was a spider beneath a rock he overturned; death, however, was represented in the form of thousands of dead locusts, encrusted in, and preserved by, the salt. Was that to be his fate, too, he wondered more than once.

Parched and nearly broken, as close to death as he had ever been, he finally came upon a satellite tracking station on the eastern edge of the salt desert. A man emerged from one of the buildings and came running toward him. "Good God, man," he was shouting before he reached Steve. "Did you walk across that?" He gestured in the direction from which Newman had come.

It was all he could do to croak out a syllable. "Yeah."

"Do you know what you just walked across?"

Newman glanced back at the huge expanse of whiteness, like a drunk regarding his vomit. "Desert. But if you tell me it was hell itself, I won't be surprised."

"It's a bombing range, mate. A bloody bombing range!"

"Bombing . . . range?" He tried to make sense of the words. "Saw no signs."

"Of course there are no signs! They never thought anyone would be crazy enough to walk across it, bombing range or no bombing range."

Canadian-U.S. border, June 21, 1986. After more than three years outside the United States (12,767 miles in all), the worldwalker flew from Australia to Vancouver, Canada. He believed that walking across the border would be the more romantic way to reenter the U.S. "I knew it would generate a lot of emotion, and for a writer that's good."

There was emotion, all right, but no fans to cheer him on. He hadn't expected otherwise, of course; he had never gone for the hype. Still, a small part of him was disappointed. "I passed through unnoticed, same as any other traveler," he says. "Except I was the only one on foot."

Newman felt he was ready for America—until he got there. After going for so long on so little, he was shaken by her cornucopia of riches. "It seems that there is a 7-Eleven convenience store every mile . . . and satellite dishes galore, some bigger than the houses. All this after the Australian outback, with outposts every four hundred miles."

Newman did not immediately embrace this ostentatious display of gadgets and gizmos. Part of him was repulsed. "The average income of the hundreds of people I have stayed with has been around two hundred and fifty dollars a year. Now I see these young people driving twenty-thousand-dollar cars and looking so bored. It's disgusting."

Steven Newman covered the last few miles of his worldwalk amid crowds and homecoming hoopla. (Courtesy of Steven Newman)

It wasn't just rich people who alienated him; the common folk spurned him at first. The first American he approached, an old man sitting on the stoop of a ramshackle house in northern Washington, pulled a gun on him. "I asked him for a glass of water; he was drunk. He went inside, got his shotgun, and told me to 'Git!' He was the only person in the whole world to turn me down for a drink of water – and it had to be the first American I saw on my return."

If Americans as a people seemed unprepared for a worldwalker, nature welcomed him as a kindred spirit. Newman was struck anew by the natural beauty his country had to offer, especially in the mornings. "The world is so beautiful in the morning. Dew sits on the leaves and spider webs glisten in the first rays of sun. The birds sing their loudest. The cows are coming out and smells are their most vibrant."

As a confirmed morning person, Newman was usually on the road by daybreak. For the next three hours he would do his steadiest, most aerobic walking. He would average around four miles per hour, though with his long legs and practiced gait he was capable of five and a half. "I usually tried to get in ten miles and then have a good breakfast," he says. "Since twenty miles a day made me feel that I'd done something, that I'd made a dent in the world, I was already halfway to my goal by breakfast. After that, I had the rest of the day to saunter, take pictures, look at nature, watch people, or help someone do something in exchange for lunch.

"Most people back home pictured me sweating, struggling and suffering around the world. Hell, I was floating around the world. Once I got toughened, the walking became secondary – except across the great desert of Australia."

His second most daunting stretch was walking Yellowstone and the Grand Tetons – in the winter. He carried no tent, and during one ten-day period lived on five sandwiches, peanut butter, and crackers. "The human body is far more adaptable that we can ever imagine. Few of us are ever really tested. But I've been right near my limit, and at least now I know where it is."

One night in Yellowstone he was tested by six inches of snow on the ground and a twenty-five-below-zero chill. As he slept fitfully in his arctic sleeping bag, he unthinkingly left his boots outside. Next morning they were two size-twelve blocks of ice. It took hours to thaw them out, which delayed his start until noon. But as day follows night, good follows bad. That afternoon, he came upon a steaming thermal pool in the midst of snow-carpeted, cloud-covered wilderness. Though he was not a highly religious man, he couldn't dodge the feeling that God had seen his solitary suffering and somehow guided him to this hot pool.

He stripped off his clothes and eased into the steam-shrouded pool. Ahhh, just right. The warm water was an analgesic for his aching muscles. He crouched low enough so the water lapped over his shoulders, then took a moment to look around. It was staggeringly beautiful. A craggy granite mountain towered above him; tepid rays of sun filtered through pine boughs, imbuing the snow with the glitter of diamonds. "This is what it's all about," he thought. "You can endure wild pigs or bull ants or frozen boots because you know this is the other side of the coin."

A little bit of a thermal pool goes a long way, however, and after a few minutes he began to feel faint from the heat. Just as he was about to climb out, he heard the foreboding snort of an animal. "Oh no, not more snorting," he thought. Peering through the trees, he was startled to see a huge shaggy hump, then two big horns. It was a bison—or rather, as he soon saw, several bison. He watched in fascinated horror as forty enormous buffalo lumbered toward him and, one by one, plopped down on the snow-free grass around the pool.

Newman didn't know what to do. On the one hand, he had heard that buffalo were the most dangerous animals in Yellowstone, that more people had been killed by buffalo than by grizzly bears; on the other hand, he was about to become Newman Thermidor in the increasingly intense heat of the thermal pool unless he got out soon.

Finally, he forced himself to inch out of the pool and through the herd, his naked body brushing against several of the massive animals. Gritting his teeth, he thought, "They'll never even find my body." But the bison paid him no more attention than they would an insect, though one did rear his head and snort at Steve's genitals, a most peculiar and disconcerting sensation.

Once past the bison, he reached Clinger and hurriedly put on his clothes. As the animals remained passive, he grabbed his camera and took several pictures of the herd. Then, feeling a little drowsy himself, he lay down among the bison and fell asleep.

If the Northwest was nature, the Midwest was people. For nearly four years his stories from around the world had been read by a couple of million heartlanders. By the time he reached Nebraska, word of his walk had spread; it was as though the families of Nebraska and Missouri (where many of *Capper's* readers lived) had adopted him as their favorite son. "Every evening people came out looking for me. I spent the Christmas holidays with farming families who took me into their homes and their hearts. It was a bitterly cold winter, and Nebraska is more than five hundred miles from west to east, but the welcome I received from all the wonderful people made those ungodly stretches a lot warmer."

Bethel, Ohio, April 1, 1987. In contrast to the dozen people who had said good-bye to Newman four years earlier, there were at least a thousand there to say hello. Hundreds of them walked the last few miles with him, waving flags, shouting encouragement as though he was their oldest living pal. "Hi, Steve . . . Good going . . . Welcome back . . ." There were also reporters, helicopters, bodyguards, more flags than the United Nations, and more hoopla than Bethel had ever known.

Though the road into Bethel was flat, Newman traversed steep emotional hills and valleys. He should feel elation. Why then did sadness keep creeping in? For so long the worldwalk had been "the dream that wouldn't go away," but now it was almost over. As soon as he reached that familiar brick house and kissed his mother, he would wake up. "What if my existence never again attains such a larger-than-life status," he wondered. "What if it's all downhill from now on?" Yet he knew there was nothing to be done.

Four years later, the fan mail continues to roll in. Steve Newman still lives in Ohio River country, a land of Baptist churches, tobacco, and corn, and hot, humid, hazy summers. It's Daniel Boone country, Ulysses S. Grant country. Four years after completing the worldwalk, Newman is married, building a house, and still living off his fame. His books *Letters from Steve* and *Worldwalk* have brought him substantial income, which he supplements with speaking engagements. In all, he estimates he has earned more than half a million dollars off the worldwalk.

Organizations still clamor for his slide show, at four hundred dollars a pop. Two or three times a week he travels to a convention of brain surgeons or a session of the ladies' auxiliary of Sidepork, Ohio, to regale and inspire them with tales from around the world. He is an accomplished storyteller, earnest and enthusiastic, with the requisite

Steven Newman's nine skills most needed to walk around the world

1. Trust – in other people and your own fate
2. Patience
3. Ability to find fascination with anything and everything
4. Open-mindedness ("I went one and a half years without a hot shower.")
5. Lack of squeamishness
6. Great instincts – sixth sense for danger
7. High pain threshold
8. Willingness to try anything
9. Lotta luck

level of corn-bred sincerity and an ability to make people feel good about themselves and the world they live in. "There is so much more good in the world than bad," he will say. Or, "Just remember, the people of the world love you." Or, "The four hundred families I stayed with taught me that the best things in life really are free."

He gives walking clinics, exhorting people (before Nike adopted the slogan, he says) to just do it. "Walking is great for the cardiovascular system," he says, "but don't even worry about that. Don't worry about how fast you are walking. Do the act and fall in love with that. It's like kissing a girl – you should want to come back for more.

"At its best, walking is as much mental as physical, a full-rounded experience. Each walk should be an experience unto itself. While I walk, I visualize gliding, floating, rather than plodding. The mental part allows me to suppress the physical pain. On my walk around the world, there was not one minute that I didn't have pain. If it wasn't a sore toe or knee, it was sunburn or indigestion or a canker sore. Yet I never missed a day of walking due to aches and pains.

"The worldwalk was the simplest, most basic world expedition in history," he likes to say. "I conquered the world on nineteen cents a mile. I carried a medicine chest that consisted of ten aspirin and some antiseptic – and never even used the aspirin. My kitchen was an old ravioli can and a teaspoon. For my bedroom, when I wasn't staying with people, I mostly used a blanket I bought off a New York bum for two bucks.

"I saw twenty countries on five continents for four thousand dollars, half of which I spent on postage answering my fan mail. That's as good a way as any of measuring the world's hospitality.

"I took huge risks doing the worldwalk and most people said I was a fool. But I lived to tell about it . . . and tell about it . . . and tell about it. It took six years of preparation and four years to do the walk, but it has been worth it. . . . And it has even given me my greatest treasure, my wife, Susie, who I met at one of my first talks. It's also given me loads of confidence. For you see, I not only discovered the world, I discovered myself."

Newman plans to walk around the perimeter of Ohio in the spring and summer of 1993.

JOAN BENOIT

Crossroads

As little Joanie Benoit ran by a group of boys, someone yelled, "Hey! You run pretty good – for a girl!" "Where did boys get that stuff?" she wondered. "Did they learn it at their father's knee, like girls learned sewing from Mom? Didn't they know it just made girls more determined?"

Benoit, the third of four children in her family and the only girl, had heard that kind of taunting her whole life, much of it from her own brothers. Although her mother provided instruction in the rules of etiquette, her brothers didn't consider Joanie a lady, nor did Joanie herself, so she wasn't given any special privileges. "If I wasn't fast enough to get to the window seat in the car or to the catcher's mitt – too bad for me. And if I struggled carrying my skis off the hill at the end of the day, I was an open target for ribbing. The quickest way to get a rise out of me was to say I did something 'like a girl.'"

When she was growing up in Maine, skiing was the featured sport in the Benoit household. Her father, a World War II ski trooper, was an expert schusser. He had Joanie's mom skiing on their honeymoon and the four kids on skis before they started school. "From the beginning," she says, "I loved skiing for its speed, its sense of freedom. The sport was a great teacher. It taught me about sacrifice, about picking myself up and going on, about striving, about adversity."

Pressed to date the birth of her running career, she cites an annual gymkhana at a country club, the summer after her eighth birthday.

Spurred by her cousins, who wanted to compete, she signed up for five running events and two jumping events. Before her races, she watched the boys' half-mile run with a sharp eye and an inquiring mind. "I was trying to figure out what made the lead runner look so good when a woman behind me said, 'Look at the way Jim carries his arms. You can tell he runs for the high school team.' He had his arms close to his sides, his elbows tucked into his waist. His head and shoulders hardly moved. He saved his energy for powering his legs."

Imitating him as best she could, Joanie won five age-group blue ribbons.

Despite her success, she tended to take running for granted. It was mostly transportation, a means to a greater end, like gathering in a fly ball in a pickup baseball game or swiping some kid's kickball and running away from him on the playground. But the principal of her elementary school believed in educating the "whole child"; accordingly, she decreed a Field Day, a carnival of competition in running, jumping, and throwing.

Benoit vividly remembers the principal awarding her four blue stars for her running victories; just as vividly, she remembers feeling profoundly dissatisfied. "I was obsessed with the thought that I could have done better," she says. "At that point I don't know if I wanted to succeed for myself or to impress others, but the desire was definitely there."

For a time, desire was tempered by social pressure – the lingering viewpoint in the late sixties and early seventies that it wasn't quite proper for a girl to be a jock. "It seemed like almost everything I had ever dreamed of doing with my life had overtones of boyishness," she says. "I guess it bothered me, because when people asked me what I wanted to be when I grew up, I said I wanted to be a teacher. I should have said, 'I want to be a skier, but if I can't I'll be a teacher.'"

While her girlfriends were discovering boys, Joanie remained devoted to skiing, skating, tennis, and baseball. She tested in the ninety-fourth percentile on fitness, as measured by the President's Council on Physical Fitness and Sports. Her teacher said her rating would have been higher if she would only learn to breathe properly. Though that teacher never realized it, her remark was a great motivator, a goad. "Far as I know," she says, "I breathed the same way back then that I did in the Olympics." One senses that a part of her would like to go back and tell her teacher just that.

While she was in high school, a newspaper article appeared that absolved her of the guilt that accompanied her love of sports. According to Dr. Thomas Boslooper of the Episcopal Church, physical fitness was linked closely with emotional health, for both men and women. Consequently, it was time for women to get involved and for men to stop thinking of female athletes as unfeminine. "In 1973 when that article came out, I was running, but always with a little voice that said, 'Girls shouldn't be road runners.' Boslooper silenced that voice forever."

When she was fifteen, Benoit struck a slalom gate while skiing on misnamed Pleasant Mountain and broke her leg. Her body would eventually heal, but the nerve required to heave herself down a slippery mountain slope at breakneck speed never returned. She abandoned her dream, nurtured since she was eight, of skiing in the Olympics.

By the time she entered Bowdoin College (in history and environmental studies), her athletic emphasis was swimming, field hockey, and running. She was not a good swimmer and had to work hard to become competent. Believing the sport was important for fitness, and hating her limitations, she dragged herself to the Bowdoin pool to practice her technique.

In contrast, she was quite a good runner and field-hockey player. She received the Most Valuable Player award in track after her freshman season, in field hockey after her junior season. Success in both sports, though, prevented her from dominating in either. Additionally, the college races were not long enough to truly showcase her talent.

The last few months before college graduation is a time rippling with excitement for young people, but few add the spice to their senior year that Benoit did. She took a break from studying for exams to run the 1979 Boston Marathon, and on a cold, drizzly spring day, she came out of nowhere to win it. Though her time of 2:35:15 seems slow by today's standards, it was a new American and course record for women.

The hoopla that ensued caught her by surprise. "As I crossed the finish line, I entered a whirlwind," she says. "No one expected me to win the race, so it seemed that even the veteran reporters were excited. The press surrounded me, firing question after question as I tried to make my way to the dressing rooms. I don't remember saying anything intelligible."

For weeks thereafter, her mailbox was jammed with missives from agents, promoters, and fans. President Carter called and invited her to dinner at the White House. "If I change as a person," she told family and friends, "be sure to let me know." She even got a call from a talent agent suggesting a movie role. She promised the agent she would send along photos of herself, but when she didn't get around to it fast enough, he called again and screamed at her. After she hung up the phone, she sat on the floor and cried, vowing never to run another marathon. "It just wasn't worth it if I had to deal with people like that."

She found the attention more frightening than flattering. "I worried that I belonged to too many people, that strangers were deciding the course of my life. At first I had trouble saying no to people. As a result, my schedule was jammed all the time. There wasn't enough of me to go around."

It didn't get any better when she won Boston again in 1983, this time in a world-best time of 2:22:43, almost three minutes faster than the record held jointly by Allison Roe and Grete Waitz.

Now the press was beating a path to her door. The *New York Times*, *Sports Illustrated*, *Runner's World*, and countless other periodicals wanted her story. More willing to talk about running then her personal life, she gave it reluctantly, sporadically, if at all.

"How does someone break the marathon record by almost three minutes?" they wanted to know.

"I run how I feel," she would answer. "When I don't feel good, I find a spot in the pack and hang on. Today I felt great and I went for it."

For Christmas 1983, Benoit's parents gave her a diary, inscribed, "May this year be as good to you as the year before . . ." Indeed, as 1983 ended Benoit had every reason to believe that 1984 would be a year to remember. If all went according to plan, she would marry Scott Samuelson and make the Olympic team – maybe even win a medal.

She began the year with a near-maniacal focus: the 1984 U.S. Women's Olympic Marathon Trials, in Olympia, Washington, on May 12. "I just wanted to make the Olympic team," she says. "Anything else would be gravy." In preparation, she lived quietly at home with her parents in bucolic Maine, logging more than one hundred miles of training every week. By March she felt she was approaching the best shape of her life.

On March 17 she felt in fine fettle as she began her Cape Elizabeth twenty-mile loop. She had been running that loop since she first started doing long distances, and it was the best indicator of her fitness. About seventeen miles into the run, she felt a strange sensation in her right leg, like "a spring unraveling in the joint," followed by sharp pain. After hobbling for two miles, she walked the last quarter-mile. It was the first time she had ever failed to finish a training run.

When she got home, she was close to panic. "The most frightening moment in my life," she would call it. "I felt like an artist who had crafted a masterpiece for ten years, only to have it go up in a fire."

She went to see Dr. Robert E. Leach, who injected her knee with cortisone, prescribed anti-inflammatory drugs, and told her to rest. Smiling, he said, "I'm going to be in charge of the Olympic team physicians and I want to see you in L.A. with a medal around your neck." Her return smile was all light and no heat.

For the next few weeks, she incorporated shorter runs and occasional rest into her schedule. During one stretch of two weeks, the knee didn't bother her at all. On April 10 she took a long run in the morning, recording in her diary, "No knee pain." That evening she had a track workout at Harvard, during which she ran three sub-five-minute miles. "I felt terrific," she remembers. But during her cooldown laps, the knee tightened. The next day she had to quit her morning run and walk home.

On April 12, exactly one month before the Olympic Trials, Dr. Leach gave her another cortisone shot. The knee didn't respond. Unable to be both the messenger and recipient of bad news, she stopped writing in her diary. She traveled to Eugene, Oregon, where she saw another elite knee specialist, Dr. Stan James. After examining her knee, he said he would operate, but only if there was no improvement after five days of rest. That meant another agonizing wait. She could feel her fitness slipping away, like lost youth. Sometimes she would break down crying, then feel guilty about it. "It's only running," she tried to convince herself. "It's not like I'm dying of cancer."

She considered retirement. There were, after all, so many reasons to quit the sporting life: family pressures, training time, a down year, lack of money, injuries. But there was one overriding reason not to quite: her visceral hatred of the word "quitter."

On April 25, Dr. James performed arthroscopic surgery. He discovered an inflamed fibrous mass called a plica that was inhibiting the movement of the joint. He removed it, kept Benoit in the hospital overnight, and released her the next day. The Olympic trails were two and a half weeks away.

Dr. James told her to swim and bike but not to run for at least five days. So intent was she on catching up, she might have ignored the doctor's advice except that she once had a roommate who'd had the same surgery. "The doctor had her up and walking the same day," Benoit says, "and she never fully recovered. I remember it so clearly."

On the fourth day after surgery, she jogged a little with no pain. The next day James examined her knee and told her could resume running—"but take it easy." Maybe he should have been more specific; maybe he knew it wouldn't make any difference what he said.

Benoit launched into a daily exercise regimen that began at 6:00 A.M. and ended near 11:00 P.M. It included biking, swimming, running, whirlpool baths, and physical therapy. Five days after surgery, she ran easily for an hour and felt no pain. But in her exuberance to make up for lost time, she ran a second time that day. She pushed so hard and compensated so much that she pulled her left hamstring, making the right knee a secondary problem.

While she was clawing her way back, other people took it for granted she had no chance of making the Olympic team. "No way can she run a marathon just seventeen days after knee surgery," they said, which just made her want to do it that much more. Many fans and fellow runners hoped that an exception would be made to allow her to compete in the Olympics even though she wouldn't be able to run in the trials. One woman wrote, "If I could run as fast as you and qualify, I'd give you my berth." Even knowledgeable people, some of whom knew not only the sport but the tenacity of Joan Benoit, made the assumption that she was down for the count. Her adviser (she says she is self-coached), Bob Sevene, seemed to agree: "This injury is bad not just for Joan but for the country," he announced. "Joan had the best chance of any American woman—even Mary Decker—to win a gold medal in track." Fred Lebow, director of the New York Marathon, appealed to the U.S. men's and women's long-distance committees to allow both Alberto Salazar (the world-record holder, who had been suffering from anemia) and Benoit to compete in the Olympic marathon. Benoit appreciated the sentiment, but she wasn't looking for freebies. She intended to run, though privately she had no idea how well she would do. Publicly she said, "If I don't qualify for the marathon, I think I'll try the three thousand (meters). I have a chance of making the team in the three thousand, but it's not the same. My chances in the Olympic marathon would be pretty good, but in the three thousand I'm just not world class."

In her battle to regain form, she was helped by the fact that she had come back from surgery before. In 1982 both heels had been operated on to correct a chronic Achilles problem. The doctors uncovered scar tissue, degenerated bursa sacs, bone spurs in both heels and a partially ruptured tendon in the left foot. For some it would have been the end of the road. But Benoit left the hospital with casts on both feet and a glint of determination in both eyes. Though she was not immune to the post-operative blues, doubting at times whether all the work was worth it, whether she'd ever really come back, she managed to run roughshod over those doubts. Two days after leaving the hospital she was strapping her casts to the pedals of a stationary bicycle and working out on Nautilus equipment. A month later, when the casts came off, she began swimming; after eight weeks, she was back on the roads. A year later at Boston, she ran what may be the greatest marathon of all time. Yes, she knew about coming back. "The hardest is the mental part," she says. "Fortunately, that's my strongest feature. My body may let me down, but my mind never has." Sevene concurs, calling Benoit "the toughest athlete I've ever seen," and making frequent reference to the "tiger inside the lady."

Eight days before the Olympic trials, she met Jack Scott, who was pushing a new treatment called Minimal electrical neuromuscular stimulation (MENS). Benoit, who had always rejected quirky, new-age therapies, now thought bleakly, "I have nothing to lose." For the next five days, she underwent six to ten hours of MENS treatment a day.

On May 9, three days before the trials, she gave herself a stern talking to: "This is it. If you expect to run in the trials, you have to try to run fifteen miles." She did, finishing but finding no rhythm. That night her fiancé, Scott Samuelson, arrived in Eugene, and Benoit felt an immediate lift. "The next morning we ran together and I felt much better."

Jogging to the starting line of the trials, Benoit didn't know whether she'd be able to finish at all, much less finish within the top three who would qualify for the Olympics. She knew her leg could go at any time. Sevene, too, expressed doubts: "Whether she will finish the last ten kilometers is the question."

From the very first steps, the knee was tight and the damaged hamstring felt like knotted rawhide. She tried to disassociate herself from the pain by pasting a blank expression on her face and "spacing out." She tried to focus on the beautiful scenery, the caressing spring breezes; she imagined that she was home running her favorite Maine course.

At four miles she took the lead with Betty Jo Springs. The two

Joan Benoit's accomplishments have been widely recognized with such awards as the 1984 Amateur Sportswoman of the Year. (Courtesy of Women's Sports Foundation)

runners tossed the lead back and forth before Benoit moved ahead at mile fourteen. The rest of the race could best be described as "hanging on." Doing it on guts, desire, and countless hard twenty-mile runs stashed in her muscle memory, she finished first in 2:31:04, thirty-seven seconds ahead of second-place Julie Brown. As she broke the tape, pent-up emotions poured from her soul. Covering her face, she broke into tears. She was immediately embraced by Sevene, who wore a button that said "Run Joanie, Run." Afterward, he was in no mood to mince words: "She is the greatest athlete in the world!"

Julie Isphording, who finished third and qualified for the Olympic team, said, "I never doubted she would finish. Joan is so tough, she's an animal. She's a step ahead of everyone in the world."

Even Benoit herself was amazed. "I don't know how I did it," she said. "I had nothing left at the end. My cardiovascular system was fine – I wasn't tired – but my legs just wouldn't go. If it had come down to a kick, I wouldn't have had one."

Buoyed by the support of family and friends, she had run what she still considers the race of her life, and she did it at just the right time. She was now on the Olympic team.

Benoit arrived in Los Angeles on July 23 for the Olympics. She went through the opening ceremonies with the team, then retreated to a friend's guest house in Santa Monica, shunning the convivial atmosphere of the Olympic Village for her customary solitary training. But in star-crazed Southern California, there was no such thing as solitary anything, and she was recognized by people every time she went running. She finally flew to Eugene, Oregon to train. Feeling comfortable, she ran 105 miles in the first week, then 70 in the five days before the race. "I intended to taper my mileage," she says, "but tapering never seems to work out for me. I get itchy if I don't run."

On August 3 Benoit caught a return plane from Eugene to Los Angeles. "I wasn't nervous until I got on that plane," she recalls. "When the pilot announced the weather in L.A., I got an upset stomach, which is my companion when I do marathons."

The next day, the last one before the race, dragged slowly, like a hospital vigil. "It was one of the few days in my life in which there were too many hours," she says. That night, in between visits to the bathroom every half hour, she lay in bed with Walkman earphones on, listening over and over to the inspirational theme song from *Chariots of Fire*. Scott wanted to play the song at their wedding, but she had told him, "Only if I do well in L.A." Well, this was L.A.

She slept only about an hour, but that didn't worry her; adrenaline would enable her to transcend a little thing like sleep deprivation.

The start of the first-ever Olympic marathon for women was a bit of a letdown for Joan. Fifty women lined up at the starting line on the track at Santa Monica College, a venue which lacked the glamour of the Los Angeles Memorial Coliseum. And even in the smaller stadium, the stands weren't filled as she had thought they'd be. What wasn't a letdown, however, was the competition. She was part of the strongest field ever assembled for a women's long-distance running event. Besides Grete Waitz of Norway, who had never lost a marathon, there was Rosa Mota of Portugal, Lorraine Moller of New Zealand, and Ingrid Kristiansen, also of Norway.

With a temperature of sixty-eight degrees, the morning was

shrouded in gray. A monochromatic mix of fog and smog hung low, shielding the sun. But the overcast would soon burn off and the course would heat up, which Benoit figured would help her. Rosa Mota was best known for her resistance to heat, but Benoit had just endured one of the hottest, most humid summers in Maine's history. Though she had felt sluggish at times, her splits had continued to improve, and she felt ready for whatever Los Angeles threw at her.

The start was slow, and at three miles the lead pack still included thirty runners. Benoit, at five-foot-three one of the shortest competitors, seemed to be consumed by the pack. With her white painter's hat and her gray, oversized USA singlet hanging loosely on her sinewy frame, she looked like a little kid who had wandered into the wrong race. That is, until you gazed upon her perfect form. She was straight, strong, and steady, with no wasted motion. Her head didn't bob, her arms didn't flail, and each footstrike was a clone of the one before.

At four miles, Benoit broke away. Feeling claustrophobic, she couldn't stride properly in that crowd. And she had long ago decided she was going to run her own race and not wait for someone else to seize the moment. But as she separated herself from the pack, she couldn't help thinking, "I'm going to look like a real showboat if I take the lead now, and then fall off the pace and watch everyone pass me."

Before she could dwell on the negative, she arrived at the first water station. It was decision time. Believing that she had hydrated well in the days before the race and not wanting to get caught in the crowd again, she passed by the aid station without stopping. Most of the others took water as she pulled farther away. Bill Rodgers, broadcasting for American television, told viewers that he thought Joan had made a mistake.

It was a calculated risk. "Yes, I'm going to look like an idiot if the whole pack thunders by me in the last few miles." But she was running 5:40 miles, well within her range, so she increased her pace and her lead grew even more. At five miles, loping down San Vicente Boulevard, she had a thirteen-second lead.

Benoit's lead stretched to thirty, forty, fifty seconds. She resisted the temptation to look around, having always considered it a bad sign when her focus wavered from what lay ahead. People along the route called out the size of her lead, but their estimates varied so wildly as to be useless. She heard everything from one hundred yards to two and a half minutes, but didn't pay much attention.

If she looked straight ahead, she saw the TV truck with Bill Rodgers and Patricia Owens perched on the back doing commentary. Benoit would have liked to talk to them, to ask their advice, but she knew that wasn't proper in the Olympics, so she avoided eye contact with them. Instead, she pasted an impassive look on her face and held form.

About midway in the race, the course presented a three-mile stretch of freeway, which Benoit assumed she would hate. Freeways, after all, were just about antipodal to rural Maine. Today, however, the marathon was queen and no cars or pedestrians were allowed on that freeway. "It was a surprise to find out that the freeway stretch was the only part of the course that reminded me of Maine. I was alone, it was quiet, and if I'd closed my eyes I could have pretended I was in Maine. Next to the finish line, the freeway was my favorite part of the course."

As she left the freeway, she considered the possibility that she might set a world record – she felt that good. But then an inner voice cautioned: "If you really go for it and blow up, you'll never forgive yourself," it said. "Don't take the chance. Win the race."

The temperature rose to the mid-eighties, but Benoit, fluid and smooth, was untroubled. She realized that she hadn't been paying attention to the mileage markers – a good sign. When things were going poorly, she looked for every marker "just to prove to myself that I'm moving forward." No need for that today. She had an eighty-second lead.

Just before stepping onto the ramp that led down into the Coliseum tunnel, Benoit looked up at the building with the bigger-than-life mural of her breaking the tape at the 1983 Boston Marathon. Part of her was embarrassed by the mural, which, along with a similar one of Alberto Salazar, had been commissioned by Nike, her sponsor. But another part of her was thankful. It had been a great motivator, that mural. When she had first come up lame with her plica problem, her first thought was, "On no, that mural will be in L.A. and I won't." When she was on the mend, struggling back, she kept thinking of that mural: "If Nike has that much faith in me, then I've got it in me – somewhere. It would be terrible if I let them down."

Just before entering the tunnel, she heard the anticipatory rumbling of the crowd, which followed Joan's progress on two huge TV screens in the stadium. Inside the tunnel, the noise subsided for a moment, and she became aware of the echoing sound of her own footfalls. She knew it was the lull before the storm. "You think the publicity was bad after winning Boston last year," she thought. "What's this going to be like? Maybe I'll just stay in here and never come out." But she knew that she would come out and that her life would never again be the same.

When she emerged from the dark tunnel into brilliant sunlight beaming on a colorful stadium, 77,000 people rose to their feet, clapping and cheering and urging her on. That was 16,000 more people than lived in Portland, Maine's largest city. For a young woman who did most of her training alone, it was almost overwhelming. "Just look straight ahead," she told herself. "If you don't, you might faint." Her body, showing no signs of fatigue, tingled all over. She couldn't believe how good she felt.

With two hundred yards to go, she took off her cap and waved to the crowd. The cheering grew louder and many people waved back. An American woman winning the first-ever women's Olympic marathon — it was too perfect. Though it had never remotely been a goal of hers, she was, for the moment, America's sweetheart. With her short black hair, her flashing eyes and winning smile, her sweat-soaked singlet strap sliding off her right shoulder, she was the object of a collective crush, an outpouring of affection that transcended national borders.

"I was so charged up that when I broke the tape I could have kept going and run another twenty-six miles," she says.

She finished in 2:24:52, nearly a minute and a half ahead of Grete Waitz, two minutes ahead of Rosa Mota. It was the third fastest that any woman had ever run the distance of 26 miles 385 yards, and the fastest in a women-only marathon. Her time would have won thirteen of the twenty men's Olympic marathons.

During her victory lap, someone handed her an American flag. As she pranced around the track, it struck her how many others had contributed to her victory. She was filled with gratitude for the doctors, physical therapists, friends, and family members who had made it all possible and were, she hoped, sharing this victory with her.

She was further humbled by the knowledge that her timing had been perfect. As a student of history, she saw herself as part of a long process, one that had been playing out for many years. The real trailblazers had preceded her, opening doors through which she could run. She was beholden to, among others, Kathrine Switzer and Roberta Gibb for opening up the Boston Marathon to women; to pioneers like

During her victory lap after the 1984 Olympic marathon, Benoit shared her joy with millions of viewers. (Courtesy of Robert Hagedohm AAF/LPI 1984)

Billie Jean King, who fought for and won equal rights for women on and off the tennis court; to the congressional act of 1972, known as Title IX, which mandated equal access for women athletes to public funding and facilities.

She was deeply indebted to her family, especially her mother, for letting her live life her way. Nancy Benoit had never been enthralled with the sporting life, yet she never prevented her daughter from participating. "Let's say she was supportive but not overly encouraging," says Benoit. Her mom had once sent a picture of Joan crossing the finish line of a marathon in which she looked, not atypically, like death out for a run. In the accompanying note, her mom wrote, "Dear Joanie, if marathons make you look like this, please don't run any more. Love, Mom." Later, describing Joanie's entrance into the Olympic Coliseum, she said her daughter looked like "a little gray mouse skittering out of a hole."

After the Olympics, Benoit returned home to Maine, "paradise on earth," as she calls it. "Maine in August is like a summer camp. We can swim, we can lobster, we can picnic, we can kayak, boardsurf, pick berries, play volleyball."

Of course, there was no time for any of that during the fleeting, hectic days of the summer of '84. The city of Portland threw a parade for her (and the other two Maine Olympians). Her hometown of Free-port honored her with Joan Benoit Day, and she was inducted into the Maine Sports Hall of Fame. In September there was another celebra-tion: she and Scott Samuelson were married in a church ceremony she described as "intimate." There were 500 guests.

All in all, Joan's 1984 turned out even better than her mother had wished in her diary. She should have been on top of the world – and for the most part she was – but being the only woman on earth with an Olympic marathon gold medal was not just a warm fuzzy. The loss of privacy hit her hard, fraying her patience. After Los Angeles, blessed solitude was about as rare as palm trees around the Samuelson house. Joan was inundated with solicitations, everything from charities and job offers to tourists stopping her for an autograph during a training run to strangers asking her to appear at, say, their Uncle Bob's retire-ment dinner. For a woman who appreciated her anonymity, who just liked to take long runs in the country and occasionally test herself against others doing the same, it was a bit much. "I hated the publicity," she once said. "I hated it so much I seriously considered giving up running so I would be left alone. It got worse after the gold medal. I was recognized wherever I went. Cars were beeping and stopping. Of course, I couldn't really blame them." She struggles to be gracious. "I wanted to be able to share my victory with them, but it was so wear-ing. I don't know how really famous people do it."

In one interview, Samuelson told the *New York Times* that she did not expect to run another Olympic marathon. She planned instead to concentrate on the 10,000-meter run at the Seoul Games, assuming it was approved for 1988 competition by the International Olympic Committee.

The women's 10,000 was indeed added to the 1988 Olympic program, but by then Samuelson was in no shape – physically or mentally – to compete at any distance. She was a new mom, having given birth to Abigail, and a burnout on big-time running. "I just wasn't hungry anymore," she says. "I was fried. And part of me was depressed, wondering if I would ever get back into it."

The Samuelsons still live in Maine, in a cozy home right on a cove, away from it all. It's an old house, restored in natural wood colors, with a large stone fireplace, a deck, big windows facing the water, and tons of books. To add to the bucolic scene, there is a barn, a boat, a bird feeder, and a dog named Creosote. Exercise equipment, medals, and trophies are not showcased.

Joan loves where she lives. She loves the Maine countryside and her mostly solitary, contemplative runs through Nature. Her tastes and habits are as incompatible with the big city as those of a Maine moose. Subtract her running and promotion work, and Samuelson's days would closely resemble those of a Pilgrim wife: raising her two children, picking and canning berries, gardening, lobstering, knitting. When she sits in her rocking chair knitting sweaters with pictures of farmhouses on them, she looks more like the cover girl for *Yankee* magazine than for *Runner's World*.

Liz Jackson, a family friend, describes Joan and Scott as "real Mainers. They're devoted to family, real down-to-earth, not at all ostentatious. If you didn't know Joanie was a world-class runner when you met her, you wouldn't pick it up from talking with her." On the other hand, there are some visual clues. "Joanie has so much energy," Jackson adds, "she is busy all the time. She is the most driven person I ever met. When she makes up her mind, there is no dissuading her. She knows what is good for her and she goes for it."

She knows, for example, that she must run, and run, and run. "Every day," she admits, "or I'm not at peace with myself. The day seems incomplete. Oh, I missed a couple of days in January with the flu, but I've run close to three hundred and sixty days in the past year." She laughs ruefully at what she regards as her erratic routine. "I get in sixty to one hundred miles a week. With children, it's hard to be consistent.

"Motherhood is like a marathon that never ends. It's the hardest marathon of all, but the most rewarding. And childbirth makes the pain of a marathon seem minor. In a marathon, you can back off; in childbirth, you don't have that luxury. I got a letter from a woman who said that her husband claimed running a marathon was more painful than giving birth. She disagreed and wondered what I thought. I quickly straightened the husband out on that point."

As dedicated a mother as Samuelson is, it's clear that if she had to work a nine-to-five job, her competitive running days would be over. But she has been on the Nike payroll for more than a decade, doing tests – everything from oxygen uptake to shoe-stress – and displaying the company name and logo on her shoes and apparel. Along with a few other carefully selected promotions, they have more than helped her pay the bills, though time and travel demands seem a lot more intrusive now than they did when she was in her twenties.

A growing part of her would be content to stay home and do her Cape Elizabeth loop. "Running in Maine, I love to watch the progression of the seasons through the color of the grass and trees," she says. "I look for the new baby cows and chickens on the farms along the way. I welcome great blue herons to the cove. At times I go inside my head to write a letter or try to remember the words to a song. Sometimes I play games for extra bursts of energy, like picking a tree down the road and trying to reach it before a car passes me, or pretending it's an opponent I have to catch."

Not for long is she satisfied with imaginary opponents. Prior to the 1992 Barcelona Olympics, Samuelson was again hungry for challenge on a more global stage. At thirty-four, she looked capable of competitive excellence. Her sinewy body appeared to be as fit as it did when she won the gold. Her black hair, cut shorter than in 1984, was silver-streaked; otherwise the clues were subtle that she was eight years older and the mother of two children. Her smile was still dimpled, and her pale-blue eyes danced to life when she was happy or interested. With perfect teeth and chiseled cheekbones, hers was a boyish sort of beauty.

After much soul searching, she decided to pass up the Olympic marathon trials in favor of the 10,000-meter trials. It was a tough call, and Samuelson admits it might have gone the other way if the 1992 Olympics had been in the United States, or even in Britain or Scandinavia, instead of Barcelona. "It's tremendously important that I feel comfortable with my surroundings if I'm going to run a marathon well. I need to feel comfortable with the language, the food,the way of life, because there's just no time to deal with those things when you're running a marathon. I knew in the case of Barcelona that I wouldn't feel comfortable there.

"That's why I don't run well in New York, a big city with all that hustle and bustle. . . . Yes, I now Boston's a big city, too, but it's smaller and in my backyard—I know Boston and Boston knows me." (And Boston loves her, has loved her since 1979 when she won the Boston Marathon wearing a Red Sox hat backward.)

"I run how I feel," she says. "If I feel good nine straight days, I run hard nine straight days. I don't pencil in easy days—they just happen when my body won't cooperate.

"I'm probably stronger now than I've ever been, but I'm bio-mechanically frustrated. One of my legs is slightly longer than the other, which causes knee and back problems. I attribute it to all the miles I've put in [about ninety thousand in the past twenty years] and to my skiing accident when I was a kid. It's all taken its toll. Nike has tried building shoes to help me compensate, but nothing has eliminated the problem. It can surface at any time, as it did in last year's New York Marathon, when there were times my foot wouldn't go where I wanted it to go.

"When I was trying to come back from surgery in 1984, I prayed to God a lot to help me get through it. If he would, I said I'd never ask for another favor. So I guess now I'm on my own.

"I'm in the sport because I love it. I love running and I love challenges, but I'm not obsessive about it. I mean I have to run every day, but there are lots of other things in my life. That balance is important to keep from burning out. I know where to draw the line. When it's time to go out and run, I go out and run. When I'm out there training or racing, I'm all business, but when I walk back through the front door, it's over. Scott and I never talk about running.

"My major professional ambition is to run a sub-two-twenty marathon. It's still alive, but in order to keep it alive I need a PR [personal record] at ten thousand meters. . . . No one is taking me seriously at that distance and that motivates me. If I run a PR, I can make the Olympic team. Of course, it's not going to be easy. The trials are in New Orleans in June, where it's so hot and humid that they scheduled the race at ten-thirty at night. I'm usually in bed by then."

Regardless of what happens in the Olympic 10,000 trials in 1992, Samuelson believes that she can come back for the 1996 Olympic marathon. "It's entirely possible," she says. "My children won't be as needy then and the 1996 Olympics are back in the U.S. I won't be as old then as Francie Larrieu Smith is now." Larrieu Smith, at the age of thirty-nine, made the 1992 Olympic team, her fifth.

What makes Joanie run? She can speak of challenge, of "sharing victories," of loving "the mystery of the marathon," of runner's euphoria, of long, satisfying runs through the Maine countryside, but the evidence is clear: she runs because the fire still rages within her. Clearly she is not in it for the money (she once turned down a fifty thousand dollar offer to run the Chicago Marathon "because I hate to take money if I don't think I can put up a decent fight"), or the awards, or, God forbid, the recognition. She is in it for that transcendent moment, that high she feels, when she is first across the finish line. Though she would put it more graciously — if she admitted it at all — she races to leave the others in her dust.

When asked to imagine the perfect run, she offers this telling example: "It would be a morning run, about twenty-two miles long. The season: either the summer when the water is so blue and the leaves so green, or the winter on hard-packed snow. I'd be with a small group of people who live around here. At first the pace would be comfortable, then someone would take the lead and I would go with him. A few miles later someone else would move into the lead, and after finding my rhythm I would match him stride for stride. With two miles left, I would take the lead for good. And for the rest of the run, everyone else would be back there chasing after me."

Right where they've been all along.

Joan Benoit Samuelson Update. Although she qualified for the 10,000-meter run at the 1992 Olympic Trials, Samuelson chose at the last minute not to compete in New Orleans. Her gaze is now set unwaveringly on the 1996 Olympic Trials.

RESOURCES

Tips to Improve Your Running

GETTING STARTED

- Make a firm commitment to set aside at least thirty minutes every other day for exercise. On a weekly basis, that's about two hours out of every 168, or a mere 1/84th, or 1.2 percent of your time. The other 98.8 percent of your time will be greatly enhanced by that small investment in exercise.
- Make a schedule. Block in your work time, sleep time, eating time, etc. Now fit in those two hours of exercise. Find the time that's best for you; make a date with yourself.

PREPARATION

- Give yourself time to prepare physically and mentally for your walks or runs. Avoid feeling rushed.
- Look forward to having fun. You will enjoy yourself more when you ignore the clock. Exercise by "feel," or do a course of known length and leave your watch at home. According to Jim Fixx, "Stopwatch runners tend to be haunted, driven souls."
- Practice visualizing success. Studies show that the way you imagine an event may shape the way the event plays out. See yourself excelling. See your workout in as much detail as possible – the course, the scenery, the competition; feel the pain, the joy, the weather. Do this regularly and it will become easier. Most successful athletes use visualization to some degree.
- Try these four pre-workout visualization exercises: **1.** Imagine all the tension leaving your legs; now imagine them free and loose. **2.** Imagine your body as a finely tuned, well-oiled machine; that also helps later when dealing with pain. **3.** Picture yourself feathery light on your feet. **4.** If you know your course, see yourself passing several landmarks along the way and feeling great. It might be helpful to repeat a little chant like "I feel so good, I could run forever."
- Stretch regularly. This is a point of controversy, as some accomplished pedestrians like David Horton (chapter 3) skip the stretching and immediately hit the trail, albeit at a slower-than-normal pace.

But I believe there is still a case for light stretching before and after a workout, especially for problem areas like hamstrings, calf muscles, and Achilles tendons. If you do stretch, do it right: **1.** Don't bounce when stretching. **2.** Stretch to the point where it is difficult to go farther, then relax into the stretch. Exhale and hold the stretch ten to twenty seconds. Repeat. **3.** If there is sharp pain with the stretch, back off.

- Sleep regularly and well, but don't worry about it if you don't. In the short run, the amount of sleep you get affects physical performance very little; the biggest impact is psychological. Lying awake worrying about not sleeping can become a self-fulfilling prophesy.

    In the long run, the average person requires eight hours of sleep every twenty-four, and virtually everybody needs between four and ten. How much sleep you need is determined mostly by genetics, but you can improve the *quality* of your sleep. Classic bromides still work: Drink warm milk, take a warm bath before bedtime, avoid regular use of sleeping pills. Also, regular exercise makes you a better sleeper.

- Leave negative emotions in the locker room. A bad day at home or the office can easily spill over, causing a bad day on the road or track. For most people, emotions like guilt and anger interfere with the quality of a workout. Some people, however, effectively fuel their exercise with anger.

- Don't eat a lot right before hitting the road. This is more critical for runners than for walkers, but both would do well to exercise no sooner than two to four hours after eating. Eating just before exercise recruits blood for digestion when it's needed to flush out the lactic acid that builds up in the muscles during a high-intensity workout.

- Set goals. Realistic short- and long-term goals will serve as both a motivational tool and a way of measuring progress.

TRAINING

- Move naturally. Each person has his or her own distinctive natural style and carriage. For example, Jim Ryun, former world-record holder in the mile, was a "head-roller"; four-time Olympic gold medalist Emil Zatopek is said to have "boxed his way through a race."

    Nevertheless, there are some standards to shoot for. In general, you should keep your body erect, your shoulders even, and your head up. Keep your hips, knees and ankles relaxed. Use the arms for balancing and power, but push from the shoulders and don't exaggerate the arm motion. The wrists should be fairly firm, the elbows bent but not held tightly against the chest. The hands should be relaxed C's, not tightened fists, though occasionally shaking tension from the fingertips works.

You should land first on the outside edge of the foot and roll inward, with the rolling action cushioning the impact. Sprinters contact the ground high on the ball of the foot; middle-distance runners hit on the metatarsal arch; long-distance runners, joggers, and walkers strike heel first. If you walk or jog on your toes, you risk shin splints, strained calf muscles, and Achilles tendon problems.

- Breathe naturally. As you move faster, don't be afraid to breathe through your mouth. Gulp in all the air you can.
- Avoid striding too long on uneven ground with the same slant. Banked tracks or roads that tilt near the curb can alter the biomechanics of your gait. If you must use slanted surfaces, change directions after a while to avoid a repetitive imbalance.
- Work for gradual improvement. Don't go too far or too fast in the beginning lest you succumb to injury or burnout. Work up to greater distances.
- Stay with the program. And to help you do this: **1.** Join a walking or running club, or start your own club. **2.** Subscribe to a running or walking magazine; read books about the sport; get jazzed. **3.** Splurge once in a while and buy yourself new workout shoes or togs. **4.** Take a day off every now and then. **5.** Seek variety. Do a different route; do your old course in the opposite direction; explore a new trail through the woods; work out with new people. **6.** Convert others — but be careful not to get obnoxious or self-righteous about it.
- Stay slim. One pound of fat equals thirty-five hundred stored calories. If you are twenty pounds overweight, you have eaten and stored seventy thousand calories as fat. To lose that twenty pounds, you must burn off those excess calories. Since walking or running a mile burns roughly one hundred calories, if you had walked a mere ten minutes a day for four years, you probably wouldn't have gained any of that weight.

That doesn't even factor in the appetite-suppressing nature of vigorous exercise. Dr. Jean Mayer, a nutritionist at Harvard University, demonstrated that rats that exercised moderately ate less than sedentary rats.

George Sheehan's seven tips for a fit and long life

1. Exercise – in work or in play
2. Diet – lots of fruits and vegetables
3. Marriage – (see number 5)
4. Travel and hobbies
5. Contentment
6. Drinking – in moderation
7. Smoking – don't

- Again, practice visualization. **1.** Imagine you're a gazelle, cheetah, or some other fleet animal of your choice; you're tough, strong, graceful, and can go forever. **2.** Imagine crowds of people lining the course cheering you on to greatness; we tend to move faster when others are watching. **3.** Moving uphill, picture yourself suspended from helium balloons. **4.** Moving downhill, picture yourself as liquid, flowing over rocks, roots, or road. **5.** Moving on level ground, picture a giant's gentle hand at your back. **6.** Moving into the wind, imagine you are a bullet or a knife slicing through the heavy air. **7.** Above all, see yourself relaxing. You can't run well unless you are relaxed.
- In the absence of injury, cover the distance you set out to do. If you intend to do two miles, do two miles even if you have to reduce your usual pace. This will help toughen the mind. You will learn to endure the hard runs as well as the easy ones. As Jim Fixx said, "If you quit when training goes badly, you only learn how easy it is to avoid discomfort."
- Do hill work. It can provide the effects of speed work in a more appealing setting than a track. It strengthens the quadriceps and buttocks without the heavy pounding of sprinting.
- Try long slow distance (LSD). Developed by Dr. Ernst van Aaken and popularized by *Runner's World* editor Joe Henderson, LSD conditions the cardiovascular and respiratory systems and hence raises a runner's fitness base. It is also less likely than fast running to injure tendons and muscles. The downside is that it doesn't teach a runner how to relax when functioning at the fast pace needed for racing.
- Walk. The simplest, safest, and least expensive exercise is walking. It is also the one most likely to become a lifelong habit. A study of thousands of Harvard alumni showed that a regimen of walking (an

Dr. Kenneth Cooper's five risk factors diminished by fitness

1. Elevated blood triglyceride levels
2. Elevated blood sugar levels
3. Elevated systolic blood pressure readings
4. Elevated diastolic blood pressure readings
5. Elevated blood cholesterol readings

average of nine miles a week) improved cardiovascular fitness and prolonged life. Walking at a speed of five miles per hour can burn as many calories as moderate jogging, but even strolling can burn sixty to eighty calories per mile. Walking also builds leg muscles, strengthens bones, curbs the appetite, and exercises the back and feet.

Here are some tips to make walking more fun and healthful: **1.** Use the right footwear. Walking shoes should have a rigid arch, as well as some cushioning in the heel and ball of your foot. **2.** Don't ride when you can walk. Get off the bus a few stops earlier and walk to your destination. Skip the elevator and take the stairs. **3.** Put variety in your walking program. Try a different route; take a companion along; alter your pace and terrain. **4.** Dodge the two biggest reasons to stay home: time and weather. Make time; raise exercise from the bottom of your personal priority list. If the weather is severe, walk in a climate-controlled environment. Many malls have walking programs sponsored by the American Heart Association. **5.** If you're inactive but healthy (you can be healthy without being fit, but you can't be fit without being healthy), start with mile-long walks at a pace of three miles per hour five times a week. Gradually increase your distance to three miles at a pace of four miles per hour five times a week. If you can't walk that fast, walk a little farther.

Consider the following twelve-week walking plan to get started and keep going. Walk three days a week for the amount of time shown. At the end of twelve weeks, stay at the level you've reached.

Minutes spent per day walking

Week	Day 1	Day 2	Day 3
1	10	10	10
2	12	12	16
3	15	15	20
4	15	20	25
5	20	25	35
6	30	25	45
7	35	35	50
8	40	40	60
9	45	45	60
10	45	45	70
11	45	45	80
12	45	45	90

Source: *Men's Health* magazine

• Hike. Yes, of course, hiking is walking, but with important differences. Hiking takes place on trails or cross-country, not on roads. It is rambling through the woods or over hill and dale. And it is also a different state of mind: hikers pay more attention to the scenery than they do to their split times.

Hiking is noncompetitive, open to all ages and abilities, and provides a wide range of challenges. You can hike alone or with others. And you can get a first-rate workout. Hiking a rough but level trail expends about 50 percent more energy than walking on a paved road. And hiking uphill adds even more to caloric expenditure and aerobic benefit. Ascending a fourteen-degree slope requires nearly four times the effort of walking on level ground. A 150-pound person hiking at a moderate pace for eight hours over varied terrain will burn about three thousand five hundred calories—a thousand more than a good runner burns doing a marathon. Add a backpack and that total increases.

There are also considerable psychological benefits to hiking. Passing through nature relaxes the mind, stimulates creativity, and helps you shed stress. And force-feeding yourself all that fresh air doesn't hurt either.

- If you must run—and some of us must—hold to moderate mileage. Exercise physiologist David Costill says, "You won't be better off doing one hundred and ten miles a week than you will be doing sixty." Those who go beyond mere fitness (as few as eight to fifteen miles a week, according to Dr. Kenneth Cooper) risk overuse injuries, dehydration, iron-deficiency anemia, insomnia, general fatigue, excessive weight loss, and the overdevelopment of one body part at the expense of another—just to name a few drawbacks.
- Prepare for hot weather. The pedestrian's greatest meteorological misery is heat. Make these summertime adjustments: **1.** Drink water often. **2.** Hit the road at dawn or dusk. **3.** Go shorter and slower. **4.** Stay on the grass. **5.** Increase stretching and icing. **6.** Train indoors. **7.** Break up the routine with a swim or bike ride. **8.** Eat cool, light foods with an emphasis on carbohydrates (which help muscles hydrate). **9.** Visualize cool. **10.** Head north.
- Just do it. Take that first step and take it regularly—ideally every other day for aerobic fitness. Even two weeks of inactivity can measurably reduce your fitness level, an effect called "detraining." If you are sidelined with an injury that prevents you from running, use the stationary bicycle or the stair climber—or something.

EQUIPMENT

- Shoes. A billion people in the world wear no shoes at all, and on average they have fewer foot problems than we do. One reason: bad-fitting shoes. Here are some shopping tips when making that important purchase: **1.** If you have an old pair of running or walking shoes, take them with you when you shop for a new pair. A knowledgeable salesperson can evaluate your form, and hence your needs, by looking at the wear pattern on your old shoes. Remember to take along socks. Don't be afraid to jog or power-walk around the store in the new shoes; what's a few minutes of looking geeky compared with getting the right shoes? **2.** Get the right fit. All size-tens are not the same. There should be one-half inch of space between your longest toe and the tip of the shoe when you put all your weight on that foot. **3.** Compare the left and right shoes. Make sure they are the same length and width. Put the shoes side by side on a flat surface and look at them from behind. The uppers should be perpendicular to the soles; they should not lean to one side. **4.** Hold on to the front and back of the shoe and bend it. It should bend just where your foot bends – at the ball, though walking shoes are more rigid than running shoes. If the shoe bends at the midfoot, it will offer little support. It shouldn't bend too easily or too stiffly. **5.** Hold the heel and try to move the rigid section at the back of the shoe; it shouldn't move from side to side. **6.** If you overpronate – your foot rolls in significantly – look for a shoe with a good arch support, a straight last, and a less flexible sole, especially along the inside edge. If you supinate – your foot rolls outward significantly – look for a shoe with a strong heel counter, a substantial yet somewhat soft midsole, a curved last, and a flexible sole.

No matter how sweet those new running shoes feel in the store, break them in before you take them out for a long run. Purchase new shoes before old ones completely wear out. Wear the new ones on short workouts every two or three days. By the time the old shoes are completely gone, the new ones will be comfortable.

A friend of mine finds athletic shoes hard on his Achilles tendons. Accordingly, he slits his shoes about an inch down the back, relieving pressure on the Achilles without shortening the life of the shoe.

Tests have shown that virtually all running shoes lose about a third of their cushioning after five hundred miles of use. This typically happens before the outer sole or upper shows wear.

Dr. Murray F. Weisenfeld, author of *The Runner's Repair Manual*, believes there are eight important qualities in a running shoe: **1.** Cushioning. Every time your foot strikes level ground, a force equal to three times your weight is sent vibrating through your body. Thus cushioning is vital, especially at the heel and the ball of the foot. **2.** Length. Toes should not touch the front of the shoe. **3.** Width. Shoes should be firm but should not bulge at the side. **4.** Arch. Running shoes should have better arch supports than street shoes. **5.** Counter. This part of the shoe that wraps around the heel should be firm for support. **6.** Heel. It should be flared – that is, wider at the base than at the top of the heel. **7.** Flexibility. The foot flexes 30 to 35 degrees when you push off your toes, so the shoe should bend easily at the ball of the foot to accommodate that movement; this will improve as you wear the shoe. **8.** Comfort. Though a running shoe should be snugger than your street shoe, it should still feel good.

• Hats. Forty percent of lost body heat escapes through your head, and hats keep much of that heat in. Stocking hats are useful in the winter. Consider a visor or baseball cap for summer sun protection.

• Shorts. Nylon shorts, slit up the side, are light and cool and dry quickly. In weather that's chilly but not cold enough for long pants, cotton shorts add a touch of warmth.
• Tights. Nylon or Lycra tights add warmth and an element of support.

PSYCHOLOGY

• Just by doing it – running or walking – you are deriving vast psychological benefits. *Psychology Today* did a study on the effects of running on behavior. It found that people who took up running tended to become more imaginative, self-sufficient, resolute, and emotionally stable.

Dr. Malcolm Carruthers and his British medical team found that men and women who exercised vigorously released greater levels of the hormone epinephrine (adrenaline). According to Dr. Carruthers, this hormone is "the chemical basis for happy feelings." Even ten minutes of strong exercise "doubles the body's level of this hormone, destroying depression – and the effect is long-lasting."

Ian Thompson, a former world-champion long-distance runner, has called the link between happiness and exercise "an unvicious circle: When I am happy, I am running well, and when I am running well, I am happy. It is the platonic idea of knowing thyself. Running is getting to know thyself to an extreme degree."
• Try to look on the bright side – and, yes, there is always a bright side. A couple of examples:
Situation One: The wind is blowing dead in my face.
Dark Side: I'm working hard and still going slow.
Bright Side: It's easy to gulp air; the wind keeps me cool; it's the same for everyone.
Situation Two: I'm ascending a steep hill.
Dark Side: I'm working hard and still going slow.
Bright Side: I'm not going downhill, which is hard on my feet and legs; there's bound to be a top to this hill; maybe it will have a nice view.
• There are striking similarities between the mental states of transcendental meditators and runners. Both activities are simple, free, and allow the participant to "spin out" – that is, to attain an out-of-mind state.

Here are some necessary conditions for "meditative" running: **1.** Give yourself enough time. A half-hour is the minimum. **2.** Run alone. Reduce distractions. **3.** Simplify. Establish a course and a routine that don't demand constant attention. **4.** Go gently. Run at a steady, nonexhausting pace. **5.** Avoid racing. Keep a noncompetitive attitude. **6.** Let your mind go. Don't cling to one idea.

NUTRITION

- Eat breakfast like a king or queen, lunch like a prince or princess, and dinner like a pauper.
- Eat less. Studies of societies whose members live the longest reveal this common characteristic: they eat light meals and almost no meat. Don't be afraid to eat alone. Researchers have also found that meals eaten with other people contain 44 percent more calories than meals eaten solo.
- Cut down on fat. Americans eat way too much fat, with close to 40 percent of calories coming from fat. Try to get your fat tally down below 30 percent by calories.

RECOVERY

- The goal of the recovery stage is to allow your muscles to refuel and rebuild for the next workout. Here are five tips to expedite recovery: **1.** Cool down and allow your heart rate to return to normal. Move right from a run to a brisk walk of three to five minutes. **2.** Drink lots of water before, during, and after a workout. As little as a 6 percent loss of water in the body can damage muscles and slow recovery. **3.** Stretch thoroughly, particularly calves, hamstrings, and Achilles tendons. **4.** Eat enough carbohydrates to restock your glycogen stores. Whether you walk or run a mile, it costs you roughly one hundred calories, which is an extra banana or potato. **5.** Follow hard days with easy days, or rest days. Strength is developed not during racing but during rest, when muscle tissue rebuilds.
- Consider keeping a journal to record your running experiences. Besides distance and time, you might note degree of difficulty, resting heart rate, and other information and comments. A diary allows you to chart development and accomplishments. One potential downside: it can make you compulsive about training every day.
- Recovering from a race? The worst part is often psychological. Clearly, you aren't ready to tackle another race until you've forgotten how bad the last one felt. That may take weeks for a miler, months for a marathoner.

BEST TRAINING TIPS OF THE PAST 25 YEARS

- Training edge. Running is a stress to the body; by training hard but not straining, the body adapts to that stress and eventually performs better.
- Aerobic training for fitness. According to Dr. Kenneth Cooper, prolonged, low-intensity exercise improves physical endurance better than brief, explosive workouts. Train at a running pace that allows you to talk and keeps your heart rate at about three-quarters of maximum. Do this two or three miles a day, three to five times a week.
- Specificity of training. You reap what you sow, so use long runs to increase strength and endurance, and short, fast workouts to increase speed.
- Hill training. Doing hills is another way of doing speedwork. Uphills build the upper-leg muscles, eventually producing speed, while downhills allow you to practice going faster.
- Races as training. The most effective speed training occurs when it is the most compelling to do: in short-distance races.
- Rest as recovery. It used to be that "real runners run every day." Today, influential runner-philosophers preach that less can be more. Don't be afraid to take a day off every so often to allow the body to adapt to the stress of exercise.
- Hard days, easy days. A compromise for the truly driven who are intent on being competitive, alternating hard and easy days permits recovery from the rigors of going hard every day.
- Long slow distance. Another means of recovering from hard workouts, LSD means doing slower miles between more difficult workouts.
- Tapering. To restore life to tired legs, reduce mileage as a race approaches.
- Peaking. This is hard-easy taken to a seasonal level. Because no one can be at their peak all year long, schedule alternate seasons of peak training and relaxed training.
- Listening to your body. According to George Sheehan, perceived exertion is real exertion. The pace that *feels* right is right.
- Stretching. Pedestrians lose flexibility, as their muscles grow tighter and hence more susceptible to injury. Do slow, gentle yogalike stretches.
- Strengthening. Pedestrians also commonly suffer from muscle imbalances. Muscles at the back of the leg overpower those in front;

muscles of the upper body lag in strength behind those of the lower body. To compensate, do exercises for general fitness. Consider cross-training when running or walking seems unappealing.

- Carbo-loading. For maximum energy, carbohydrates are in, fats and proteins are out.
- Hydration. Coaches used to say, "Don't drink before a workout or you'll get a stitch." Not anymore. Today, the best advice is drink before, during, and after a workout.
- Water-training. Injured pedestrians can stay fit by "running" in a swimming pool.
- Walking. Once a dirty word to runners, brisk walking can lengthen workouts and careers.

Special thanks to *Runner's World*, May 1991.

QUESTIONS & ANSWERS

My work often takes me on the road. How do I combine running and traveling?

Follow these guidelines:

1. Prepare for every kind of weather, regardless of where you are going and what the weatherman says.
2. Minimize the effects of jet lag by following the advice of Bill Rodgers: Drink lots of water on the plane to prevent dehydration. Avoid alcohol, coffee, tea, and soft drinks containing caffeine. Eat light meals and avoid salty snack foods. Soon after you arrive, walk or run slowly for about thirty minutes.
3. Upon arrival, reset your watch: eat, sleep, and exercise on local time.
4. Ask where it's unsafe to go.
5. Run or walk to cure travel fatigue.
6. Make time to run.
7. Do out-and-back courses to keep from getting lost.
8. Lighten up. Don't attempt your toughest workout away from home when everything from climate to food is different.
9. Sightsee on the run—it's a great way to explore new places.

I'm returning to running after a layoff of several years. Any advice on how to make my comeback more pleasant?

Here are some tips:

1. Review the reasons you are running—fitness, solitude, competition—and the reasons you quit before.

2. Based on those newly established goals, consider how you can do it better this time.

3. Forget the past and start over. In other words, be patient.

4. Learn to appreciate slow runs. Do the mileage, even if you have to walk some of it. Ease into any speedwork.

5. Pay attention to your age. In other words, be patient.

6. Don't race too soon. In other words, be patient.

7. Keep the faith.

How can I get the most out of running?

You can maximize the running experience by following Joe Henderson's guidelines in his book *The Long Run Solution:*

• Make exercise an everyday habit. It should be an essential part of each day, something you look forward to and miss if it's not there.

• Set aside an hour each day for your activity. Even if that includes dressing for action and warmup and cooldown, you should be left with a minimum of thirty minutes of exercise.

• Pace yourself for the long haul—that is, your whole life. The record books are full of athletes who made it big then retired before their thirtieth birthday.

Henderson, forever the voice of moderation, suggests that you "don't rush it too much or push it too hard. A habit can't take root in a mind that is always harried or a body that is always hurting."

How can I keep from burning out on running?

First, start the run even if you don't feel your best. Reserve judgment on distance and pace, but get started. Any distance you go is better than no distance at all.

Second, leave your watch and your competitive drive at home. Let the pace find itself; stay below the discomfort level.

Third, learn to take pleasure in less than your best, because most of your running will be done at that speed.

According to Joe Henderson, the formula reads thus:

Goal: To keep moving

Means: Stay healthy; stay fresh; stay loose; stay hungry.

Recipe: At least ten parts easy running to one part hard running.

Safety

INJURY PREVENTION

- The first line of defense is the foot, which meets the ground about fifteen hundred times a mile. To avoid foot problems, follow the advice of sports podiatrist and *Runner's World* advisory board member John Pagliano: **1.** Stretch the muscles and tendons of the foot and lower leg before and after exercise. **2.** Pay attention to running form; keep the toes pointing straight ahead. **3.** Wash and dry your feet daily to reduce the risk of athlete's foot. **4.** Trim your toenails regularly, rounding each one to avoid sharp edges. **5.** Choose shoes that fit well, allowing plenty of space between the longest toe and the end of the shoe. **6.** Consider adding a pair of cushioned inserts or soft orthotics to your shoes to compensate for the natural loss of cushioning that comes with aging feet. **7.** Avoid wearing high heels. **8.** Exercise regularly to increase circulation and strengthen foot muscles.
- If you're into racing long and hard, use a lubricant like Vaseline on any area of the body likely to be irritated by friction, including feet, thighs, and nipples. In extreme cold, you can also use it on your face.

TRAINING

- Walking. Walk, or incorporate walking into your long training runs. Walking can help relieve a side stitch or loosen a tight muscle, and it has fitness benefits nearly as great as running.
- The talk test. Except when doing time trials or racing, workouts should be at a comfortable, relaxed pace. If you can't hold a continuous conversation, you are probably moving too fast. Of course, fast and slow are relative terms. For Frank Shorter, who can run five-minute, thirty-second miles straight on till morning, six minutes is an easy, relaxed pace. For most mortals, the answer lies between seven and nine minutes per mile.

• Injuries. For pedestrians, there are three main causes of injuries: **1.** Overuse **2.** Lack of preventive measures **3.** Biomechanical weakness.

Preventive measures include controlling mileage, paying attention to shoe wear, and adequate stretching. Severe biomechanical problems require the attention of a podiatrist or chiropractor.

• Using a track. If you do laps on a track: **1.** Don't count laps—it can drive you crazy. **2.** Don't use the inside lane—the surface there is most worn and the inside of the track is often separated from the infield by a concrete curb, which requires constant vigilance lest you strike it with your foot. **3.** Alternate direction, for variety and biomechanical balance.

• Uphill. Don't gun it. It takes more energy to gain five yards while climbing than it does to gain five yards on the flats. Ground gained in this manner is gained at a high price.

• Downhill. Beware. Contrary to popular belief, downhills are much harder than uphills on the joints and muscles of your legs and feet. As you go downhill, you lengthen your stride and increase your impact with the ground. Jogging on the flats can create a force equal to three times your body weight; going downhill can double that impact. Unless you are racing and seeking the shortest distance between two points, zigzag down steep hills. That moderates the incline, and thus the impact.

• Extreme cold. Follow these tips to avoid frostbite and hypothermia: **1.** Work out during the afternoon; the sun is your winter ally. **2.** Wear several layers of loose-fitting, thin clothing. This helps insulate you by trapping the warm air you generate. It also allows you to remove layers if you get too warm. **3.** Put plastic bags between your T-shirt and your sweatshirt; also between pairs of socks. It will keep body heat from escaping and diminish the bite of the wind. **4.** Use long underwear—polypropylene is best for its ability to wick away moisture—but wear no more than two layers on the legs. **5.** Protect genitals, which can easily freeze (and they hate that). Wear nylon shorts, not cotton. **6.** Wear a hat and gloves. In severe weather, one option is a cap that folds down into a face mask. **7.** Wear the right shoes. Look for good traction and good shock absorption, especially if you will be moving over frozen ground. Winter shoes should have a little extra space inside to trap warm air. **8.** Zip up. Zippers make clothes adaptable. When you get too warm, you can zip down. **9.** Don't overdress.

Dr. Kenneth Cooper's five reasons for runners to have a stress test

1. To provide motivation to exercise
2. To provide your doctor with information on your fitness level
3. To provide a baseline for future reference
4. To help determine whether you have heart disease
5. To predict survival or additional heart problems after a heart attack

Even a moderate workout can make it seem thirty degrees warmer than it is. **10.** Warm up well. It gets the heart pumping and elevates the body temperature. **11.** Drink as much water in cold weather as in warm—before, during, and after a workout. You lose water through sweating and breathing (you must warm and moisten the cold, dry air you breathe), and through increased urine production. **12.** Grow a beard, if you can.

- Pollution. Because you breathe faster and more deeply when you exercise, you also take in more carbon monoxide, sulfur dioxide, and other pollutants. If air pollution is a problem in your area, work out early in the morning or in the evening after rush hour. Consider moving to the country.
- Dogs. If a dog runs at you, barking threateningly: **1.** Stop and face the dog. In most cases, it will stop too. If so, you can usually walk away, still facing it, then carefully begin running again. **2.** If the dog keeps after you, shout something in a loud, stentorian voice like "Halt!" or "Get back!" If further dissuasion is required, raise your arms in a threatening manner, as though you had a rock or stick. If the dog still hasn't gotten the message, throw away the imaginary rock or stick and pick up a real one. **3.** Never turn your back on the dog until it has retreated for good.
- Traffic. When sharing the roads with cars: **1.** Select roads with little traffic and wide shoulders. **2.** Run on the left side of the road, facing traffic. **3.** Wear bright, visible colors. **4.** Pay attention to cars coming from all directions.

• Running or walking at night. Consider these additional safety tips when moving around cars: **1.** Wear fluorescent or reflective material as part of a vest, headband, wrist or ankle bands, belt, or patches. **2.** Use a light. Battery-operated flashing devices are available that clip to belts or strap onto legs. Or you can carry a flashlight. A study by the National Highway Traffic Safety Administration showed that a pedestrian with a flashlight is visible to drivers six hundred feet farther than one wearing reflective material. **3.** Don't look directly at oncoming headlights; they'll temporarily blind you. **4.** Don't wear headphones; you need auditory clues as well as visual ones.

RECOVERY

• Working out too hard? Be alert to the following symptoms of overwork: **1.** Lowered general resistance; chronic sniffles, headache **2.** Apathy **3.** Chronic leg soreness **4.** Poor coordination, clumsiness **5.** Hangover from previous run or walk.
• Heat. Heat cramps, heat exhaustion, and heatstroke are risks in summer. Heatstroke, in particular, requires immediate attention. Doctors in Australia, where it gets blisteringly hot in the summer, have been able to reduce rectal temperatures of 107 to 109 degrees Fahrenheit down to 100 in fifty minutes by applying cold packs over the neck, armpit, and groin areas, and through intravenous rehydration.
• Rest. Rest is vital in building a mileage base. Each workout tears the body down a bit; rest allows it to build back up and get stronger. Without easy days, a runner or walker is likely to improve little or not at all. Worse, the athlete may succumb to injury or illness.

RUNNING SAFETY

The Road Runners Club of America offers these tips:
• Carry identification or write your name, phone number, and blood type on the inside sole of your running shoe. Include any medical information. Do not wear jewelry.
• Carry a quarter for a phone call.
• Run with a partner.
• Write down or leave word of the direction of your run.
• Run in familiar areas. In unfamiliar areas, contact a local Road Runners Club of America or running store. Know where telephones and open businesses are. Alter your route pattern.

- Always stay alert. The more aware you are, the less vulnerable you are.
- Avoid unpopulated areas, deserted streets, and overgrown trails. Avoid unlit areas at night. Run clear of bushes or parked cars.
- Don't wear a headset. Use your ears to be more aware of your surroundings.
- Ignore verbal harassment. Use discretion in acknowledging strangers. Look directly at others and be observant, but keep your distance and keep moving.
- Run against traffic so you can observe approaching automobiles.
- If you must run before dawn or after dark, wear reflective material or carry a light.
- Use your intuition about a person or an area, and avoid if you're unsure.
- Carry a whistle or other noisemaker.
- Call police immediately if something happens to you or someone else.

HEALTH AND SAFETY QUESTIONS AND ANSWERS

When I get a cold, should I work out or rest?

It depends on the severity of the cold. If it's just a slight respiratory infection, it is usually not necessary to restrict exercise or exposure to cold weather. On the other hand, most doctors give different advice if you have a fever, swollen glands, or aching muscles. Some go so far as to recommend at least a week of absolute rest after a bout with the flu or a big-time cold.

Studies show a correlation between mileage and number of colds: if you increase your mileage, you increase the risk of coming down with a cold. Researchers at the University of South Carolina asked more than five hundred runners to keep a yearlong diary of how many miles they ran and how often they got a runny nose, sore throat, or cough. They found that runners who tallied nine to seventeen miles a week had 1.7 times more colds than those who ran fewer than nine miles. Those running between seventeen and twenty-seven miles had 2.6 times more colds. Still, runners as a group average only 1.2 colds per year, half as many as nonrunners.

What are the most common running maladies, and what can I do about them?

Runner's World has taken several polls and consistently found that two-thirds of the respondents were limited by running-related injuries in the preceding year. Many were hurt more than once, and thus the following figures add up to more than 100 percent.

Ten Most Common Injury Sites

Injured Area	Percent of Runners
Knee	25
Achilles	18
Shin	15
Ankle	11
Heel	10
Arch	8
Calf	7
Hip	7
Hamstring	6
Forefoot	6

For care of a sprain or strain in any of these areas, try the PRICE approach to self-help. PRICE is an acronym for protection, rest, ice, compression, and elevation.

Protection and rest. Avoid hazardous terrain or cease the activity altogether if it is causing or aggravating an injury.

Ice. Apply ice for no more than twenty minutes at a time several times a day. You can use manufactured ice packs, but a wet towel in the freezer works just as well. (I favor frozen vegetables in the soft pack.) You can also massage the injured area with ice frozen in a paper cup.

Compression: Carefully wrap the sprained joint or strained muscle with a supporting bandage to reduce swelling. Loosen the wrap if pain increases or if you experience numbness.

Elevation: Whenever possible, elevate the injured area above the level of your heart to reduce swelling.

Continue with the PRICE treatment for as long as it helps your recovery. Moderate sprains and strains generally heal in a week or two. If pain, swelling, or instability persists or increases, see your doctor.

Consider, also, nontraditional therapies. A combination of acupuncture and physical therapy was effective in treating my bad back. And there is persuasive evidence that acupuncture is effective in treating one of the most painful of running injuries, plantar fasciitis.

Why do we get injured?

Lots of reasons:

- Weak feet. Surveys indicate that 35 to 60 percent of all walkers and runners have weak feet. If the feet are weak, then the force exerted upon footstrike causes an abnormal strain on the tendons and muscles of the feet and legs.
- Unequal leg length. Perhaps 15 percent of athletes—including Joan Benoit Samuelson—have this problem. It may cause no symptoms or it may force the shoulders and scapula out of alignment and the spine to curve, causing nerve irritation or causing the pelvis, knees, ankles, and feet to rotate abnormally.
- Poor flexibility. Tight or shortened muscles are more susceptible to injury than stretched muscles.
- Weak anti-gravity muscles. Back and leg muscles become tight and overdeveloped with running. Consequently, doing exercises to strengthen the opposing muscles is essential. Example: strengthening abdominal muscles to ease back pain.
- Stress. We tend to stash tension in our muscles, most commonly in the neck or lower back. Relaxation exercises like yoga, before and after workouts, can help alleviate this problem.
- Overuse. Early symptoms of overexertion are fatigue, chills or fever, insomnia, frequent colds or diarrhea, or localized pain. Listen to your body; cut back to alleviate symptoms.
- Improper training habits. Avoid sudden changes in intensity or duration of exercise. When in doubt, run or walk slower, over shorter distances. Avoid hard, uneven surfaces.
- Poor equipment. Keep your shoes in good shape. Change them at least every five hundred miles.
- Injury rehabilitation. Don't try to do too much too soon.
- Poor advice. Be wary of nonathletic, out-of-shape medicos who favor inactivity and pills as cure-alls.

When I'm hurting, how do I know whether to run (walk) or rest?

The first question you need to ask is, How much does it hurt? There are four general classifications of injuries:

First degree. No limitation of motion, but a low-grade pain at the start of a workout that diminishes as it progresses. Afterward, the pain returns.

Action: Warm up thoroughly before you try anything hard. No other change in routine is required.

Second degree. Pain persists during the workout, but there is little effect on form.

Action: Eliminate the workouts that cause pain to increase; those will usually be the races, steep hills, and long, hard runs.

Third degree. Minor pain on easy workouts; more severe pain on longer or harder ones.

Action: Alternate jogging and walking. Start slowly and don't push it. When you feel the pain coming on, slow to a walk.

Fourth degree. Pain is so intense that it is impossible to move without disturbance of form.

Action: Replace running or walking with another, more benign, aerobic activity, like walking, biking, or swimming.

In general, work gradually toward lesser degrees of pain—from fourth to third to second to first. Be patient.

What's the best way to recover from a workout?

If you're running, keep walking after you finish, which allows your heartbeat to slow gradually. Drink lots of water before, during, and after any workout. Stretch areas of the body that are causing nagging problems. And don't be afraid to take tomorrow off.

How far should I run?

It depends. If you're running for cardiovascular fitness, the consensus is that running fifteen to twenty minutes three times a week is sufficient. To repeat the words of Dr. Kenneth Cooper, "If you're running more than that, you're doing it for reasons other than cardiovascular fitness." On the other hand, if you want to be competitive at marathons and ultras, you will probably have to put in 60 to 120 miles a week.

Will walking make me live longer?

Probably. Cardiovascular diseases are the major causes of death in this country. Heart attacks rank number one, with cancer second, strokes third, and other blood-vessel diseases fourth. The evidence is overwhelming that sustained aerobic exercise will help fight heart disease and stroke. As for cancer, the evidence is murkier, but the exercise won't hurt.

Eleven factors affect your chances of getting heart disease: heredity, stress, diet, fat abnormalities, hypertension, heartbeat abnormalities, diabetes, obesity, smoking, age, and lack of physical activity. Walking, running, or some other aerobic activity improves nine of the eleven – the exceptions being age and heredity.

Studies have shown that people who follow at least six of the following admonitions will live longer, healthier lives than those who follow only one or two.
• Exercise regularly.
• Eat a good breakfast.
• Limit the junk food.
• Maintain your age-25 weight.
• Don't smoke.
• Drink moderately.
• Get a good night's rest.

I just started running, and a friend of mine has told me that it's dangerous. He says, "You only get so many heartbeats, and when you use them up, it's all over." Is he right?

Just say no to that heartbeat theory. Even if it were true, consider this example: If the average person has a resting heart rate of seventy-two beats per minute and a life expectancy of seventy-five years, the heart will beat about 2.8 billion times in a lifetime.

Now consider a runner who trains five times a week for forty minutes a day. Resting pulse in such individuals generally slows from seventy-two to about fifty-five beats per minute, while running pulse increases to around 180. Thus the allotment of 2.8 million heartbeats will not be reached for eighty-three years. That's a win-win gamble.

I'm a woman runner worried about weirdos. What can I do to protect myself?

Joan Ullyot makes these sensible suggestions in *Women's Running:*
• If you hear footsteps, pick up the pace slightly and look back. Don't blithely assume they belong to a friend.
• Try not to run alone.
• If you must run alone, avoid a regular running schedule and dark, lonely places.
• Carry a weapon, like a nail or mace.

And now there is something called the Zapper, a lightweight, hand-held stun gun. It immediately delivers a disabling electrical jolt to an attacker. This unit fits into the palm of your hand and has a belt clip, which makes it perfect for runners. Call 1-800-HOT-STUN.

I like running on roads. How can I best defend myself against cars?
Here are some tips from Joe Henderson's *The Long Run Solution:*
- Run the roads with the least appeal to drivers.
- Use the whole road. Run near the center line, if traffic allows, and be ready to move right or left when a car comes.
- Gently swivel your head right or left, to be able to hear approaching cars over the wind.
- Stay to the outside of blind curves.
- Run defensively.

Running into the Past

Since the dawn of the species, humans have been ardent pedestrians. Walking and running have been central to their lives – mostly for survival, though, not for sport. Only as technology diminished the need for these activities did they become popular recreational pastimes.

Running contests were the ancient Greeks' most revered form of athletic competition. Running was the showcase Olympic Games event, and each Olympiad was named for the champion of the games' footrace. The Greek historian Xenophon wrote that "swiftness of foot . . . is the most esteemed of all contests."

Although the marathon is linked in many people's minds with ancient Greece, the longest running race in the ancient Greek Olympic Games (776 B.C.–A.D. 393) was actually the *dolichos*, twenty-four lengths of the stadium, a mere 2.618 miles. The runners, men only, ran naked and barefoot. The winner of the dolichos was elevated to godlike status, his fame and fortune assured for life.

The first long-distance runners were either messengers or soldiers who got in shape via long marches. The most famous messenger of all was Pheidippides, who supposedly ran about twenty-four miles from the battlefield at Marathon to Athens to announce a Greek victory over the Persians, then dropped dead from exhaustion. The birth of the marathon is often dated from this time, 490 B.C., but did it really happen? Doubtful. The historian Herodotus, a contemporary of the battle of Marathon, said nothing of the feat or demise of the Pheidippides. Instead, it was publicized by Plutarch, 560 years later.

Running has long been important to some societies that never wrote down their history. Consider the Bushmen hunters of the Kalahari Desert in Africa who regularly run after eland for distances of twenty miles or more. Or groups of Hopi Indians who have traditionally run ten miles before dawn to their fields, worked all day, then run ten miles home. Or the isolated Tarahumara Indians of northern Mexico's Sierra Madre, for whom social standing within the tribe depends largely on performance during their customary 75- to 150-mile runs over extremely mountainous terrain.

For the Tarahumara, running is more than a game or a form of exercise; it is a quasi-religious ritual involving purification, shamans, the healing power of special powders and prayers, and special diets. In short, it is a way of life, and an exceedingly healthy one. Physiologists, naturally drawn to this society, have discovered an inordinately healthy people: resting pulse rate of fifty-six to sixty, average cholesterol level of 134, and no obesity.

PEDESTRIANISM

In the late eighteenth century, there was a growing interest in a sport called pedestrianism. Interest was stimulated by betting for or against a pedestrian's claim that he could walk or run a long distance in a given time. Foster Powell walked one hundred miles in twenty-two hours in 1788. In 1806, British captain Robert Barclay covered the same distance in nineteen hours. In 1808, Barclay nailed down his reputation by walking one mile in each of one thousand consecutive hours. Put another way, he walked a mile during each hour of the day and night for forty-two consecutive days. In the last week of the ordeal, the crowds were so thick that the half-mile out-and-back route had to be roped off so that Barclay would have room to walk. The pain in his legs became so intense that he had to be helped to his feet to begin each walk. Barclay's status as a gentleman, and as the premier athlete of the first half of the nineteenth century, greatly added to the popularity of pedestrian sports in England.

In America, sports met with a great deal of resistance. Preachers railed against such sinful activities and mainstream newspapers ignored them. But people still came out in droves to watch and bet on their favorite runner or walker. In New Jersey in 1844, a crowd estimated at thirty thousand watched what was billed as the first international competition in America, an hour-long foot race between American and English runners.

The 1850s saw an explosion of interest in sports, aided and abetted by the appearance in 1853 of a sporting journal, the *New York Clipper*. With the advent of the *Clipper*, the greatest pedestrian stars became household names.

One weird offshoot of the pedestrian craze was an event called

Joe Henderson's ten greatest marathoners (and marathons)

1. Frank Shorter – 1972 Olympic marathon
2. Joan Benoit – 1984 Olympic marathon
3. Buddy Edelen – 2:14:28 marathon in the early sixties
4. Alberto Salazar – 1982 Boston win by two seconds
5. Bill Rodgers – 1975 Boston win under 2:10
6. Clarence DeMar – his seventh Boston win at age 41
7. Johnny Hayes – America's last Olympic marathon gold medalist before Shorter
8. Thomas Hicks – America's first Olympic marathon champ, 1904
9. Miki Gorman – women's champ in 1976 New York City Marathon
10. Johnny Kelley – his sixtieth Boston in 1991 at age eighty-three

"walking the plank." During the 1850s, it became all the rage in the nation's saloons. While participants moved back and forth on an elevated wooden platform fifteen to forty feet in length, raucous onlookers wagered for or against their being able to do it for a specified number of hours.

Distance walking and running achieved a popularity during the 1870s and 1880s that would not be approached for another hundred years. If the glory event now is the marathon, in the nineteenth century it was the six-day race. There were also twenty-four-, forty-eight-, and seventy-two-hour races, as well as twenty-five-, fifty-, and one hundred-milers. Madison Square Garden staged most of the big international matches, but nearly every city and town in the country staged races, some for local pedestrians, some for traveling professionals. The introduction of roller skating about this time provided rinks that could double as pedestrian tracks, but no track was considered too small. While the Madison Square Garden track was an eighth of a mile, some were as short as forty-two laps to a mile.

Interest in six-day races was stoked in 1879 when a British Lord, Sir John D. Astley, established a prize belt for the pedestrian cham-

Verne H. Booth of Johns Hopkins kicked his way to victory in the 10,000-meter run at the 1924 Cambridge finals. (Courtesy of Amateur Athletic Foundation)

pionship of the world. Not to be outdone, a man named Daniel O'Leary offered a silver belt to the long-distance champion of America. Numerous struggles for these belts were staged on indoor tracks, often Madison Square Garden. Contestants walked, ran, slept, and ate for 144 straight hours, and the most mileage won. The greatest distance ever covered in one of those six-day contests was 623¾ miles by George Littlewood at Madison Square Garden in 1888.

Besides capturing a garish belt, winners took home money. When Charles Rowell won the Astley Belt, he pocketed $19,500; the O'Leary Belt was less lucrative, usually providing $2,500 to $5,000 to the winner. The champion could add to his wealth with public appearances.

In his first outdoor race in the United States, the legendary Paavo Nurmi (left) of Finland easily defeated his countryman Vilho "Ville" Ritola in the 3,000-meter event at the 1925 Loyola University Games. (Courtesy of Amateur Athletic Foundation)

Saloons would often pay him just to show up, flex his leg muscles, and say a few words.

Women were also competing at long distances. In 1879 Madame Anderson walked 2,700 quarter-miles in 2,700 hours on a track set up in the Mozart Gardens in Brooklyn. Later in Chicago, Madame Exilde La Chapelle covered 3,000 quarter-miles in 3,000 hours. In six-day races Mae Belle Sherman covered 337 miles to win in San Francisco, and Amy Howard set a record of 393⅛ miles in New York City. Lest one think that equality had been achieved or sexism expunged, Fanny Edwards received a gold medal in the New York event for "neatness and best appearance."

Closeup: Edward Payson Weston

Weston, who began life in Providence, Rhode Island, in 1839, was born to walk. His professional pedestrian career spanned fifty-two years, 1861 to 1913. In 1874, when the hype for six-day races was at a pinnacle, Weston became the first man to walk 500 miles in six days. He achieved this feat on a small indoor track in Newark, New Jersey. The sporting world went mad over this exploit and Weston became the toast of both America and Britain.

In 1879, when Weston was forty years old, he broke the six-day record again: 550 miles. In 1909, at age seventy, he walked a route covering 3,900 miles from New York to San Francisco in 105 days. Disappointed in his time, he walked from Los Angeles back to New York, a distance of 3,600 miles, in 77 days. The *New York Times* carried daily accounts of his progress, and the entire nation was captivated by the old man's spirit.

Weston took his last great walk in 1913, when he was seventy-four years old. Leaving New York City on June 2, he walked 1,500 miles to Minneapolis, where he laid the cornerstone for the Minneapolis Athletic Club on August 2.

Weston died in 1929 at age ninety. According to the obituary in the *New York Times*, ninety years was the goal he had set for himself.

By 1890 ultrarunning was a sport on the decline. The rise of amateurism, the concomitant decline in betting, the growing popularity of bicycle races—with their more dramatic crashes—all combined to bring the curtain down on the glory years of pedestrianism. There would continue to be people like Weston who were willing to test their pedestrian mettle, but fewer and fewer people cared about watching them do it.

OLYMPICS

During preparations for the staging of the first modern Olympic Games at Athens, in 1896, a man named Michel Breal, historian, linguist, and professor at the Sorbonne, suggested to the organizing committee that they include two events that would reflect the glories of ancient Greece. One was the discus throw and the other was an endurance run along the original route supposedly taken by Pheidippides.

So on April 10, 1896, on a hot Sunday afternoon, twenty-five runners started the world's first marathon. The 24.9-mile race went from the bridge at Marathon to the finish line in the Olympic stadium in

Athens, where sixty thousand rabid fans waited. Outside, Greeks lined the course, lustily rooting for a local victory.

The winner was indeed a Greek: Spiridon Louis, a twenty-four-year-old peasant from the nearby village of Marousi, who finished in 2:58:50, giving the host country its only gold medal. In return, his country gave Louis free food, clothing, and barbering for the rest of his life.

Louis's cardiovascular fitness was attributed to his job: as a water carrier, he trotted daily alongside his mule from Marousi to Athens and back, a distance of about fifteen miles. His training regimen? The night before, he went to church and prayed before holy pictures, eating nothing; on the morning of the race he consumed an entire chicken.

Marathon running quickly made the leap across the Atlantic to the United States. In October 1896, thirty New Yorkers raced twenty-five miles through the mud from Stamford, Connecticut, to the Knickerbocker Athletic Club in New York City. Only one-third of the field made it to the finish, led by John J. McDermott in 3:25:55.

Representing the New York Athletic Club, John Simmons won the 5,000-meter run at the 1920 Olympic tryouts in Philadelphia. (Courtesy of Amateur Athletic Foundation)

Many of the members of the United States Olympic team were also members of the Boston Athletic Association. Upon returning home, they urged the association to stage a marathon. The annual Boston Marathon was established in 1897, and is the world's oldest continually run marathon.

The term marathon was used loosely to describe any foot race around forty kilometers in length. Only when the Olympic Games arrived in London in 1908 was the distance standardized at 26 miles 385 yards (42.195 kilometers). The reason: royal convenience. The starting line was placed near the royal lawns of Windsor Castle so the children of the royal family could watch; the finish line was placed opposite the royal box in the Olympic stadium so that Queen Alexandra could see the finish.

Closeup: Abebe Bikila

Born August 7, 1932, Abebe Bikila grew up poor on a farm in Ethiopia. At age 19 he joined Emperor Haile Selassie's imperial body guard. He began running in 1956, and in 1959 came under the tutelage of Onni Niskanen, a Swede who had traveled to Ethiopia in 1947 and stayed to become head of the national board of physical education. He trained Bikila for the Olympic marathon with a combination of long fast runs (up to twenty miles), hill running, and long repetitions (1,500 meters) on the track—all done at altitudes of 5,000 feet or more.

Bikila trained both with and without shoes. But in Rome for the 1960 Olympics, when all the running shoes he tried hurt his feet, he decided to run barefoot. "I will win without shoes," he announced. "I will make some history for Africa." That he did, winning in 2:15:16, a new world record, and ushering in the age of African marathoners. Four years later in Tokyo, the skinny African won the gold again, this time in shoes, beating the closest competition by more than four minutes. His time of 2:12:11 was another world record. Observers noted that even in shoes, his footsteps were nearly inaudible.

In 1969, Bikila was paralyzed from the waist down in an automobile accident. In 1973, at the age of forty-one, he died in Addis Ababa of a brain hemorrhage after suffering a stroke.

WOMEN IN RUNNING

In 1896 in Athens, a Greek woman named Melpomene was denied entry to the modern world's first marathon. Ahead of her time, she decided to run anyway. Without a number and with a friend pedaling a bicycle beside her, she finished in about four and a half hours. For more than seventy years after that, women were officially prevented from running in long-distance races. Organizers cited the usual sexist reasons: women can't hold up; they will get hurt; the pounding will render them sterile.

Roberta Gibb Bingay didn't believe any of it. She loved to run long distances. She planned to run the 1965 Boston Marathon until two sprained ankles put her on the disabled list. Her application for the 1966 Boston was rejected because she was a woman, but like Melpomene she viewed that as a mere technicality. She took a bus from California, donned a hooded blue sweatshirt, put on a pair of size-six boys' running shoes (they did not yet make women's running shoes), and slipped out of some bushes near the start of the race. The first woman ever to run the Boston, she finished in a time of three hours, twenty-one minutes, unofficially placing her 135th in a field of 415.

Race director Will Cloney, speaking to the press after the Boston, was openly disdainful of her performance: "Mrs. Bingay did not compete in the Boston Marathon," he said. "She merely ran along the official route while the race was in progress." Bingay insisted, then and later, that she did not run the Boston to make a feminist statement. "I ran the Boston Marathon out of love. . . . Running expresses my love of nature, my delight in being alive. Yet it was a love that was incomplete until it was shared with others."

Twenty-year-old Kathrine Switzer applied to run the 1967 Boston under the name "K. Switzer." She was accepted and sent number 261 through the mail. Accompanied by her burly boyfriend, Tom Miller, she ran in a hooded gray sweatsuit. Two miles into the race, director Jock Semple, realizing that number 261 was a woman, leapt from the press bus and screamed at her to get out of the race, then ran up behind her and tried to rip the number from her back. Miller, who happened to be a hammer thrower, tossed Semple off the course.

Switzer finished in a leisurely 4:20. (Roberta Gibb – who had divorced and dropped the Bingay from her name – again ran unofficially, this time in 3:27.) Switzer then confronted the press. She too was a reluctant crusader, denying that she had run to further any particular cause, even going so far as to deny knowledge of the prohibition against women in the Boston. "I was so confused. I just wanted to run. I didn't want to prove anything," she said.

Nevertheless, both Gibb and Switzer did prove something. At the very least, they demonstrated that women could go the distance.

Then, in 1967, a fifteen-year-old Canadian girl named Maureen Wilton really rocked the running world. She not only finished a marathon but set a women's world best of 3:15:22. By August 1971, that record had plummeted to 2:46:30. And in 1972 the Amateur Athletic Union (AAU), gave women permission to compete at any distance they wanted, as long as they started separately from the men.

Even this last attempt at segregation did not go unchallenged. At the 1972 New York City Marathon, when the gun went off to start the women's race (ten minutes before the men's start), the women defiantly sat down at the starting line, some brandishing placards with rebellious statements like "Hell, no, we won't go!" The AAU capitulated, although officials petulantly insisted upon adding ten minutes to the women's times.

By 1978 more than one thousand women were running the New York Marathon. In 1979 Grete Waitz broke the 2:30 barrier, improving the women's world best to 2:27:33 and finishing sixty-ninth overall out of 11,404 runners. In 1980, again in New York, she lowered the mark to 2:25:41. Her time would have won the gold medal in any men's Olympic marathon before 1952, yet the International Olympic Committee continued to resist the inclusion of an Olympic marathon for women. In fact, through the 1980 Olympics, women could compete in no race longer than 1500 meters.

A turning point came in 1981 when Ludwig Prokop, an Austrian member of the International Olympic Committee's Medical Commission, reported persuasively to the International Amateur Athletic Federation (IAAF), "The physical performing capacity of women with respect to endurance is absolutely, as well as relatively, equal to that of men. . . . There is no relevant sports medical grounds against marathon running for women."

At the IOC meeting in Los Angeles in February 1981, the committee decided that the case for a women's marathon was convincing. At the 1984 Olympic Games in Los Angeles, eighty-eight years after Melpomene had gate-crashed the original marathon in Athens, women were allowed to compete in an Olympic marathon. (See chapter 8, on Joan Benoit, for the story of that marathon.)

RUNNING BOOM

In the wake of Frank Shorter's victory in the 1972 Olympic marathon, running—and especially the marathon—has been usurped by the masses. One measure of that is the New York City Marathon, which began in 1970 as a circuit in Central Park with 126 runners; in 1980 more than thirty thousand applied to run the race, half of whom had to be turned down. Throughout the land, hundreds of "fun runs" have blossomed. In 1991 the Bay to Breakers, a 7.6-mile run through San Francisco, drew ninety thousand official and unofficial participants.

Meanwhile, as more and more also-rans were going the distance, elite runners continued to improve on world marks. The first marathoner to average less than five minutes per mile was Derek Clayton of Australia, who clocked 2:09:36 in 1967. The women's mark, artificially high from years of discrimination, plunged even faster. At the start of the seventies, the fastest time a woman had ever run a marathon was 3:07:26. Ten years later, Grete Waitz had lowered the mark to 2:27:33. And in 1985, Joan Benoit ran a 2:21:21 in Chicago, breaking Waitz's existing world mark by almost three minutes.

The men dropped the mark to 2:06:50 (Belayneh Densimo), the women to 2:21:06 (Ingrid Kristiansen), and the debate rages on as to just what the limits are to human performance.

BIGGEST RUNNING DEVELOPMENTS SINCE 1967

April 19, 1967. Kathrine Switzer infiltrates the male-only Boston Marathon. Women receive full status in 1972.

August 18, 1968. David Costill, exercise physiologist from Ball State University, does a ground-breaking study on the physiology of long-distance running. His work eventually serves to popularize carbohydrate-loading, and carbo-rich diets in general.

October 20, 1968. Kip Keino of Kenya defeats Jim Ryun for the 1,500-meter Olympic gold medal, fueling African domination in the middle- and long-distance events.

December 11, 1970. Podiatrist Richard Schuster develops orthotic shoe inserts for runners. The custom-made supports are designed to counter biomechanical deviations such as overpronation.

May 16, 1971. Marty Liquori defeats Jim Ryun in the "dream mile." This battle between two guys who broke the four-minute mile in high school captures the attention of the public and helps popularize the sport of running.

June 29 to July 9, 1972. Nike running shoes hit the big time at the U.S. Olympic Track Trials in Eugene, Oregon. Soon after, Oregon coach Bill Bowerman pours rubber into a waffle iron to achieve the waffle sole, the first major advance in the distance running shoe.

September 10, 1972. Frank Shorter becomes the first American in sixty-four years to win the Olympic marathon. His televised triumph is credited with sparking the running boom.

January 3–5, 1975. Dr. Kenneth Cooper and other scientists study nineteen elite distance runners at the Institute for Aerobics Research in Dallas. This ground-breaking research, which measures aerobic capacity, body composition, and psychological health, adds "VO$_2$ Max" to the runner's argot.

April 21, 1975. Bill Rodgers wins the first of his three Boston Marathons in a U.S. record 2:09:55. Baby-faced Rodgers makes it look so easy that millions of Americans are converted to running.

July 30, 1976. Finland's Lasse Viren sweeps the 5,000- and 10,000-meter races at the Montreal Olympics—just as he had four years before in Munich. Many consider this double-sweep the greatest running achievement ever.

October 24, 1976. The New York City Marathon moves from Central Park to the five boroughs, popularizing it beyond all expectations. Urban marathons quickly spread throughout the United States and the world.

February 18, 1978. A new sport, the Ironman Triathlon—a competition that includes swimming, bicycling, and running—is launched in Hawaii with fifteen entrants. Today that event, called the Bud Light Ironman World Triathlon Championship, draws more than fourteen hundred of the heartiest endurance athletes.

April 17 and October 12, 1978. Two running books make the best-seller lists. George Sheehan's *Running & Being* and Jim Fixx's *The Complete Book of Running* both go big time, sweeping more runners into the pack.

October 22, 1978. Grete Waitz, an Oslo schoolteacher who has never run more than twelve miles, wins the New York Marathon by nine minutes. Her time of 2:32:30 breaks the world record and fires up women's running.

January 4, 1980. The United States and sixty other nations boycott the Moscow Olympics. For many athletes the opportunity of a lifetime is lost.

March 18, 1980. Gore-Tex, a breathable fabric, is patented. Today Gore-tex, which allows sweat to escape but keeps rain out, is found in all sorts of sportswear.

October 25, 1981. ABC, with Marty Liquori as commentator, does a live, three-hour telecast of the New York City Marathon.

March 1, 1982. World-class runners begin depositing earnings into a special trust account from which to draw for training-related expenses. This compromise between the athletes and The Athletics Congress (TAC, originally AAU) brings prize and appearance money out from under the table.

August 14, 1983. Mary Decker wins both the 1,500 and 3,000 at the first World Championships of Track and Field. She is named sportswoman of the year by *Sports Illustrated*.

August 5, 1984. Joan Benoit wins the first Olympic marathon for women. She beats Grete Waitz by nearly a minute and a half, capturing the imagination of American viewers and prodding a few million more to hit the roads.

September 24, 1988. Canadian sprinter Ben Johnson is busted for using performance-enhancing drugs immediately after he has apparently set a world record at 100 meters. The consequences are a two-year suspension for Johnson and increased drug testing for athletes.

November 2, 1989. A huge fitness study, tracking thirteen thousand men and women for eight years, shows that even modest exercise can substantially reduce the risk of death from heart attack, cancer, and other ailments. The research, headed by Stephen Blair at the Institute for Aerobics Research and the Cooper Clinic in Dallas, confirms that health is enhanced by a combination of aerobic exercise and dietary restriction of fat and cholesterol.

November 9, 1989. The Berlin Wall comes down, opening up a marathon course that takes runners through both Berlins. The athletic ramifications of the merging of the two Germanys also include less chance of an Olympic boycott, better cooperation and competition between East and West, and expanding commercial opportunities.

November 21, 1989. Smoking is banned on virtually all domestic flights. Runners and other health-minded people cheer their biggest victory yet in the war against ill health.

April 16, 1990. New Zealand's John Campbell, age forty-one, finishes fourth in the Boston Marathon, running a world masters record of 2:11:04. He knocks fifteen seconds off the previous record and in the process helps redefine aging.

Special thanks to *Runner's World*, May 1991.

Pedestrian Oddities

NOVELTY ACTS

- Bill Robinson, tap dancer and entertainer extraordinaire, could run a bit, too. He set records for the 50-yard, 75-yard and 100-yard dashes – backward! His times were 6 seconds, 8.2 seconds, and 13.2 seconds, respectively.
- Plennie L. Wingo walked 8,000 miles – backward! Wearing special glasses so he could see where he was going without turning his head, Wingo began his journey in Santa Monica, California, on April 15, 1931. He arrived at his destination – Istanbul, Turkey – on October 24, 1932. When he turned eighty-one, he celebrated his feat by walking backward from Santa Monica to San Francisco, covering the 452 miles in eighty-five days.
- Noah Young ran a mile in 8:30 carrying a 150-pound man on his back. Young weighed 198 pounds. He accomplished the feat on April 12, 1915 in Melbourne, Australia.
- The record for the three-legged 100-yard dash was set by Lawson Robertson, coach of the University of Pennsylvania and the U.S. Olympic track team, and Harry Hillman, coach at Dartmouth. On April 24, 1909, they ran a three-legged 100-yards in eleven seconds flat.
- John A. Finn of Brooklyn, New York, set the 100-yard sack-race record of 14.2 seconds on April 20, 1941.
- In an unabashed – and successful – attempt to get into the *Guinness Book of World Records*, Dale Lyons ran thirty 8:20 miles – while balancing an egg on a spoon.
- Coloradan Patti Brehler, thirty-five, did a twenty-four-hour stair climb in February 1991. She finished with 68,992 steps, equal to 7.8 vertical miles.
- Blind runner Harry Cordellos of San Francisco recorded his forty

thousandth lifetime running mile—without a sighted guide. Cordellos, who holds the American blind record for the marathon (2:57:42), did it on a Star Trac 2000 treadmill.

- In the 1991 Bay to Breakers, a 7.6-mile fun run across San Francisco, the thirteen-person Reebok Aggie Centipede averaged less than five minutes per mile.

MARATHONING

- Maryetta Boitano started running marathons at age six. She peaked at age ten with a 3:01:15 (under seven minutes per mile). Her brother Mike did a 2:54 marathon at age twelve.
- Doug Kurtis, a thirty-seven-year-old Michigan native, set a record by running twelve sub-2:20 marathons in 1989. Through 1989, Kurtis had run fifty sub-2:20 marathons, second only to Sweden's Kjell-Eric Stahl.
- A twenty-four-year-old ex-Marine, Jay Helgerson from Missouri, became the first person to run a marathon every week for one year, in 1979. He averaged 2:57:05 for the fifty-two events, and had to travel to twenty-one states to find the races.
- Roger Bourbon, a thirty-two-year-old restaurant owner from Los Angeles, claims the title of "world's fastest waiter." He ran marathons dressed in full waiter garb, balancing a full bottle of mineral water on a tray. By his self-imposed rules, he didn't change hands the whole way, nor was the bottle glued to the tray. At the 1982 London Marathon, he finished in 2:47:21, considerably faster than most of the runners who ran without tray. When Bourbon crossed the finish line, he drank the water.
- In March 1987, Albert Lucas completed the Los Angeles Marathon in just over four hours while juggling three balls. He didn't suffer a single dropped ball over the entire 26-mile, 385-yard course.
- At the 1980 New York City Marathon, a runner named Ernest Conner ran the entire distance backward, completing it in five hours, eighteen minutes. At the end, he announced, "I'll never do that again!"
- Two-thirds of the 1991 Honolulu Marathon's 13,260 starters came from Japan.
- An unknown runner, a twenty-six-year-old Cuban-born New Yorker named Rosie Ruiz, was the first woman to cross the finish line of the 1980 Boston Marathon. Her time of 2:31:56 would have been a world's best six months earlier. But there was something suspicious

about Ruiz. She had neither the build nor the style of a world-class runner. And on that sweltering spring day in Boston, she was barely damp from her efforts. Finally, no one remembered seeing her prior to about mile 24. She was eventually disqualified and the race awarded to Canada's Jacqueline Gareau.

- John C. Miles won the 1924 Boston Marathon, beating out four-time winner Clarence DeMar and Olympic gold-medalist Albin Stenroos of Finland. Miles was a nineteen-year-old delivery boy who had never before run more than ten miles. Dressed in white sneakers and swimming trunks, he ran a 2:25:40.
- When Sy Mah died in 1988, he had completed 524 marathons, almost 200 more than his nearest competitor. He accumulated that number in only twenty years, averaging one marathon every two weeks and nearly one a week in the last years of his life.
- John A. Kelley has started sixty-one Boston Marathons in his life, finishing all but four of them. Two of his DNFs were his first two Bostons, in 1928 and 1932, so he is fifty-seven for his last fifty-nine. Back when he was young, John accumulated two Boston victories (1935 and 1945) and a record seven second-place finishes. At the age of sixty-eight, he ran the 1976 Boston Marathon in 3:20 despite hundred-degree heat. The former Olympian is honored at Boston every year with the number one, and his fans cheer him every step of the way.

WALKING

- Anton Haislan walked 15,000 miles over 22 months, pushing a special perambulator containing his wife and daughter. He won two thousand dollars at a Paris exhibition for being the "most durable pedestrian."
- Thomas Patrick Benson of Great Britain walked 314 miles without stopping. For nearly 124 consecutive hours (December 19–25, 1975) Benson remained in motion at Moor Park, Preston, England.
- Steven Newman is not the only person to walk around the world; he is just the only one to have done it solo. John and David Kunst of Waseca, Minnesota, set off on June 10, 1970, to circumnavigate the globe. Attacked by bandits in Afghanistan, John was killed and David seriously hurt. After a lengthy recuperation back in the States, David returned to Afghanistan and completed the trip on October 6, 1974, covering 14,500 miles.
- Try walking rapidly and chances are your pace will be in the neighborhood of four miles per hour. But some people don't hang out in

that neighborhood. Take Robert Rinchard of Belgium, for example, who walked 325 miles (Strasbourg-to-Paris annual event) in 63 hours, 29 minutes, an average of 5.1 miles per hour—for more than two and a half straight days.

- Speaking of walking, consider the world's best racewalkers. To preserve the biomechanical differences between running and walking, racewalkers must maintain unbroken contact with the ground, and the knee of the supporting leg must be straight for at least an instant as it passes directly beneath the body (it prevents walkers from springing off the knee). Given such rigid restrictions, the best times of racewalkers are truly phenomenal. Ralf Kowalsky has racewalked 10,000 meters in 38:55, a 6:25-per-mile pace. And Mikhail Schennikov has covered 5,000 meters in 18:16, a 5:53 pace.

CLIMBING

- Ephraim M'Ikiara, 52, walked barefoot up 17,022-foot Mount Kenya carrying only a thin blanket, a piece of hemp rope, a small package of food, and a Bible. When a party of would-be rescuers offered aid during his descent, M'Ikiara asked, "Was it you who showed me the way here?"
- At the 1990 Mount Washington Road Race, Derek Froude set a record for the 7.6-mile, 4,560-foot climb. His time of 59:17 was made possible by great conditioning and uncharacteristically benign weather: winds of three miles per hour and a temperature of fifty degrees on a summit (6,288 feet above sea level) that has been the site of the highest wind speeds ever recorded on earth.

LONG-DISTANCE RUNNING

- In 1984 Greek ultramarathoner Yiannis Kouros broke the ninety-six-year-old record for the six-day run. On a track in New York's Downing Stadium, Kouros covered 635 miles, breaking the old mark by nearly twelve miles.
- Nineteen-year-old Steve Fonyo, who lost a leg to bone cancer, raised eleven million dollars for cancer research by running across Canada in 1985.
- Rae Clark of California set the U.S. record for running 100 miles, in 1989. Clark's time of 12:12:19 translated into a pace of sub-7:30 miles—for half a day.
- At the 1992 IAAF 100-Kilometer World Cup in Spain, Kostantin San-

talov of Russia finished in six hours, twenty-three minutes, a per-mile average of 6:08.

- After running for almost twenty hours in the 1981 Western States 100 trail race, Jim Howard and Doug Latimer finished in a dead-heat tie for first place."
- The Tarahumara Indians in northern Mexico have a culture built around running. Social standing within the tribe depends largely on individual performance in a 75- to 100-mile run, during which the runners kick a small wooden ball in front of them. They have been known to run day and night through tortuous mountain terrain, sometimes for as long as forty-eight hours straight, averaging up to six miles per hour. Researchers have determined that the energy expenditure necessary to complete such a task exceeds what is humanly possible.

AGELESS WONDERS

- Eula Weaver suffered a near-paralyzing stroke when she was seventy years old. She recovered by jogging three miles every day. Nearing her eightieth birthday, she won a gold medal at the Senior Olympics.
- On March 15, 1987, Frank "Scotty" Carter, seventy, a retired school-teacher, ran an indoor mile in 5:32.4
- On May 3, 1987, Clive Davies, seventy-one, ran the Pittsburgh Marathon in 3:03:05 – a sub-seven-minute pace. Davies also ran 2:42;49 at age sixty-six, and 2:53:42 at age sixty-nine.
- In the summer of 1990, seventy-three-year-old Paul Reese became the oldest person to run across the continental United States. He averaged 26 miles a day for 124 consecutive days, running 3,192 miles in all.
- At age eighty, Marilla Salisbury set a record for her age group in a five-kilometer walk. Her time of forty minutes represented a pace of just under five miles per hour.
- Mall walker Muriel Claeys, seventy-seven, walked more than 2,000 miles in 1991. She put in about four hours a day, six days a week. "The arthritis has left my feet and my heart specialist is very happy with me," she says, adding that "from Penney's to Sears is about two-tenths of a mile."
- Marie Kirk, eighty-five, who has nineteen great-grandchildren, walked 1,479 miles in 1991. She accomplished that feat after a stroke had disabled her for two years.

- In San Francisco, Larry Lewis was running six miles a day and working full time as a hotel waiter—right up until he died at the age of 106.

MISCELLANY

- Kenyans Susan Sirma and Thomas Osano each won red BMW 325i's for their 1991 wins in San Francisco's 7.6-mile Bay to Breakers run. Neither drives a car.
- Henry Rono amazed the track world in 1978 by setting four world records in eighty days: 3,000 meters, 3,000-meter steeplechase, 5,000 meters, and 10,000 meters.
- Olympic marathoner Emil Zapotek used to hold his breath repeatedly until it hurt. He wanted to teach his mind not to panic if his body didn't get enough oxygen.
- An Ohio company—Bonnie Bell, makers of skin-care products—installed a track and exercise room in its headquarters. President Jess Bell offered the incentive of one dollar for every mile his employees ran on company time.

Quotations and Inspirations

I like long walks, especially when they are taken by people who annoy me.

—Fred Allen

Our destiny is to run to the edge of the world and beyond, off into the darkness.

—Thomas Aquinas

I am convinced that anyone interested in winning Olympic medals must select his or her parents very carefully.

—Swedish researcher Per-Olaf Astrand

I can't hear the starting pistol anymore. From now on, I'll concentrate on the longer races. Then I have a chance to watch the others start and still catch up.

—Bill Baker, 83, on retiring from the sprints

I sometimes think that running has given me a glimpse of the greatest freedom a man can ever know, because it results in the simultaneous liberation of both body and mind. . . . The runner does not know how or why he runs. He only knows that he must run. . . . We run, not because we think it is doing us good, but because we enjoy it and cannot help ourselves.

—Roger Bannister

I see no difference between this form of recreation (running) and that bought for a simple fee from the ladies who specialize in chain mail bras, leather panties and a brace of whips.

—Dr. Christiaan Barnard

204

The only reason I would take up jogging is so that I could hear heavy breathing again.

— Erma Bombeck

How you jog is never as important as that you jog. Performance is what counts. It is always more important than technique.

— Bill Bowerman

When running, my body is producing draughts of a hormone called epinephrine, which researchers have linked with feelings of euphoria. This combined with the alpha waves and the repetitive motion of running, which acts as a sort of mantra, makes me higher than is legally possible in any other way.

— David Bradley

Running for me is a time machine. It backs me up and smooths me out. I feel reborn.

— Irene Brown, 64

All I ever managed on those few occasions when I jogged was to concentrate on what a miserable form of self-punishment jogging was.

— William F. Buckley, Jr.

I run because I enjoy it — not always, but most of the time. I run because I have always run — not trained, but run. What do I get? Joy and pain. Good health and injuries. Exhilaration and despair. A feeling of accomplishment and a feeling of waste. The sunrise and the sunset.

— Amby Burfoot, winner of the 1968 Boston Marathon

Applaud us when we run. Console us when we fall.

— Edmund Burke

The great luxury of running is that it disposes of all sorts of junk food, foods that the body would otherwise deposit on conspicuous corners in the form of fat. No serious runner has to worry about weight.

— Noel Carroll

I used to be an eccentric; now I'm an expert. I was once tolerated; now I'm consulted. The oddity I practiced was running. The only wisdom I can now claim is that I continued to run.

— Noel Carroll

Will you walk a little faster? said a whiting to a snail, There's a porpoise close behind us, and he's treading on my tail.

—Lewis Carroll, *Alice's Adventures in Wonderland*

Now, here, you see, it takes all the running you can do, to keep in the same place. If you want to get somewhere else, you must run at least twice as fast as that!

—Lewis Carroll, *Through the Looking Glass*

The average American takes 20 years to get out of condition, and he wants to get back in shape in 20 days. You can't do it. If your heart tolerates it, your legs won't.

—Dr. Kenneth Cooper

People get a relief of tension from running. It's like having your own psychiatrist.

—Ted Corbitt, former U.S. marathon champ

Fitness can't be stored. It must be earned over and over, indefinitely. If a man runs for twenty years and stops completely, it is just a matter of time until he is in the same condition as the fellow who has never done any running.

—Ted Corbitt

Once you cross the finish line at Boston, there isn't anything you can't do.

—Tom Coulter

Running long and hard is an ideal antidepressant, since it's hard to run and feel sorry for yourself at the same time.

—Monte Davis

I feel as good as I ever have in my life. The more I run, the younger I feel.

—Don Dixon, 50ish marathoner

I think the secret of my success is consistency. I run year around and thus have accumulated lots of miles in the bank.

—Don Dixon

The wise, for cure, on exercise depend.

—John Dryden

If you have long legs you can jog slow . . . faster.

—Mary Ann Edenfield

The civilized man has built a coach, but he has lost the use of his feet.

—Ralph Waldo Emerson

Few people know how to take a walk. The qualifications . . . are endurance, plain clothes, old shoes, an eye for nature, good humor, vast curiosity, good speech, good silence and nothing too much.

—Ralph Waldo Emerson

The truth is, there is no runner's high. It's just that everybody else is suffering from non-runner's low.

—Jim Fixx

I find that the three truly great times for thinking thoughts are when I'm standing in the shower, sitting on the john, or walking. And the greatest of these, by far, is walking.

—Colin Fletcher

Two roads diverged in a wood, and I—
I took the one less traveled by,
And that has made all the difference.

—Robert Frost

The mile remains the classic distance because it calls for brains and rare judgment as well as speed, condition and courage.

—Paul Gallico

We are descended from those who ran to stay alive, and this need to run is programmed genetically into our brains.

—Dr. William Glasser, psychiatrist

How do I feel during the race? I hate it. I want to quit over and over. But I love it, too. The challenge of defeating fatigue, of reaching beyond my potential keeps me going forward. When I finish I hate it. I invariably throw up.

—Bob Glover

Far from being an exclusively physical therapy, running provides a solitude where emotional as well as physiological introspection and feedback can occur.

—John Greist, psychiatrist

It was such a primitive country we didn't even see any joggers.

—Hamilton cartoon caption

To run is to live. Everything else is just waiting.

—Mark Hanson

We need to praise running for what it is. There are safer ways to exercise than this, better ways to meditate, quicker ways to get high, truer ways to find religion, easier ways to have fun. I don't deny that running gives some of those things. But praising them too highly hides what we really have here—a sport which like all sports has both pain and joy, risk and reward.

—Joe Henderson, former editor of *Runner's World*

Running is a childish and primitive thing to do. That's its appeal, I think.

—Joe Henderson

Perhaps a marathon is simply a race with great meaning but no purpose.

—Joe Henderson

The difference between the mile and the marathon is the difference between burning your finger with a match and being slowly roasted over hot coals.

—Hal Higdon

Whenever I feel like exercise I lie down until the feeling passes.

—Robert Maynard Hutchins

How much happiness is gained, and how much misery escaped, by frequent and violent agitation of the body.

—Samuel Johnson

Running is a statement to society. It is saying 'no' to always being on call, to sacrificing our daily runs for others' needs, and to the poverty and overwork so many of us face. When we run we are doing something for ourselves, and that is not in society's game plan. We regain control over our bodies and our lives through running.

—Phoebe Jones, who in 1979 helped organize a conference on women's running

Running is just a matter of putting one foot in front of the other, and as long as you remember to alternate feet, you can't run into too much trouble.

—Don Kardong, Olympic marathoner

I run alone. It's a great way to get acquainted with yourself.

—John A. Kelley

The biggest sin is sitting on your ass.

—Florynce Kennedy

He travels the fastest who travels alone.

—Kipling

Running gives you freedom. When you run, you can go at your own speed. You can go where you want to go and think your own thoughts. Nobody has any claim on you.

—Nina Kuscsik, former Boston Marathon winner

Women need a firm bra, not one of the flimsy all-elastic ones. That's especially true if you have large breasts. Otherwise they'll bounce and you'll always be waiting for them to come down before you take the next step.

—Nina Kuscsik

Do you realize how privileged runners are? We discover things about our bodies that most people, even doctors, never learn. We're so much more in touch with ourselves.

—Nina Kuscsik

People who run 10Ks are the kind of people who can put their thumb on a table, hit it real hard, and that's the end of it. Ultras are the type who'll put their thumb in a vice, squeeze real tight, and leave it there for twenty-four hours.

> —Doug Latimere, a ten-time top ten
> finisher in the Western States 100

I don't jog. If I'm going to die, I want to be sick first.

> —Abe Lemons

On long runs, the body has time to give up. Your heart will prevent you from hurting it. But a sprint is like an explosion. Your body doesn't have time to stop you from hurting it.

> —George Leonard

If infantry is the queen of battle, running is the queen of athletics.

> —George Leonard

More than in your legs, the secret of sprinting is in your arms, in your upper body. As long as you do the right thing with your arms, your legs, which are naturally faster, will follow.

> —George Leonard

I walk every day, save in blizzards and cloudbursts, between two and three miles across open wheat fields and through cool, tall woods. I pursue the same path, year after year, and neither I nor the dogs ever tire of it. I watch the deer, and the fox, and the rabbits, and the squirrels, and the skunks, and especially the birds, and I have never seen the same scene twice.

> —James Michener

If I hadn't been a fairly good runner, I'd still enjoy being a fairly bad one.

> —Dave Moorcroft, former 5,000-meter world-record holder

As a nation we are dedicated to keeping fit and parking as close to the stadium as possible.

> —Joe Moore

One of the great joys in life is doing what people say you cannot do.
> —Joe Moore, quote underlined in David Horton's training
> log when he ran the Appalachian Trail

There was larceny in his heart, but his feets was honest.
> —Satchel Paige

Our nature lies in movement, complete calm is death.
> —Pascal

Yea, though I walk through the valley of the shadow of death, I will fear no evil . . .
> —Psalm 23

Our minds are lazier than our bodies.
> —La Rochefoucauld

Even if you're on the right road, you'll get run over if you just sit there.
> —Will Rogers

You lose a lot of speed between 80 and 86.
> —Ruth Rothfarb, 86, on not improving her
> personal best in the marathon.

When I take a day off, I notice it. When I miss two days, the audience notices it.
> —Arthur Rubinstein, pianist

The race is not always to the swift nor the battle to the strong, but that's the way to bet.
> —Damon Runyon

Unhappy businessmen, I am convinced, would increase their happiness more by walking six miles every day than by any conceivable change of philosophy.
> —Bertrand Russell

Walk while ye have light, lest darkness come upon you.
> —St. John, XII:35

Health outweighs all other blessings. . . . Nine-tenths of happiness depends upon health alone.

—Arthur Schopenhauer

The beginning (of exercising) is the most difficult. The rewards are almost nonexistent and the sacrifice required is measurable.

—Fred Schumacher

Then there's life in it. Nay, an you get it, you shall get it by running.

—Shakespeare

Hills make all men brothers.

—Dr. George Sheehan

The jogger has three natural enemies: drivers, dogs and doctors. The first two are easily handled.

—Dr. George Sheehan

Life is just a place to spend time between races.

—Dr. George Sheehan

When I am running, I am the closest I will ever come to who I am, what I believe and what I should do about it.

—Dr. George Sheehan

There are four elements to the running experience: competition, contemplation, conversation and companionship.

—Dr. George Sheehan

For every runner who tours the world running marathons, there are thousands who run to hear the leaves and listen to rain, and look to the day when it is suddenly as easy as a bird in flight. For them, sport is not a test but a therapy, not a trial but a reward, not a question but an answer.

—Dr. George Sheehan

The waste of a mind is a terrible thing. The waste of a soul is worse. But it all begins with the waste of the body.

—Dr. George Sheehan

The intellect must surely harden as fast as the arteries. Trust no thought arrived at sitting down.

— Dr. George Sheehan

Sooner or later he will think about running the marathon again . . . not, perhaps, slumped in the locker room, or on his hands and knees taking a shower . . . But sooner or later. Because the perfect marathon is like the perfect wave, and every marathoner keeps looking for it.

— Dr. George Sheehan

As soon as I got to Borstal they made me a long-distance cross-country runner. I suppose they thought I was just the right build for it because I was long and skinny for my age (and still am) and in any case I didn't mind it much, to tell you the truth, because running had always been made much of in our family, especially running away from the police.

— Alan Sillitoe, *The Loneliness of the Long-Distance Runner*

The older a man grows, the faster he could run as a boy.

— Red Smith

Start slowly, and taper off.

— Aged marathoner Walt Stack, on the secret to longevity in the sport

For my part, I travel not to go anywhere, but to go.

— Stevenson, *Travels with a Donkey*

After twenty miles I make a bargain: "God, if you lift the left foot, I'll take care of the right."

— Kathrine Switzer

We live in strange times, and maybe these runners are right, maybe physical fitness is the last refuge of the liberal instinct. Nothing else has worked, and the ability to run 26 miles at top speed might be a very handy skill to have for the coming ordeal of the eighties.

— Hunter S. Thompson, covering the Honolulu Marathon

An early morning walk is a blessing for the whole day.

— Henry David Thoreau

The moment my legs begin to move, my thoughts begin to flow.
—Henry David Thoreau

Anyone who honestly takes the time to train can finish a marathon.
—Richard Traum, who finished the New York Marathon
with an artificial right leg

I never knew a man to go for an honest day's walk for whatever distance, great or small . . . and not have his reward in the repossession of the soul.
—George Trevelyan, historian

I have two doctors, my left leg and my right.
—George Trevelyan

The best natural runners are young girls who are not biased by football hero-worship and therefore do not try to imitate sprinters.
—Dr. Joan Ullyot

Run as a child runs. Run playfully for 5-10 kilometers (3–6 miles) a day, without pain or fatigue. The plan is the same for everyone from competing athletes to men recovering from heart attacks. Only the pace and the amount of walking varies.
—Dr. Ernst van Aaken

Today I have grown taller from walking with the trees.
—Karle Wilson

I'm willing to accept any kind of pain to win a race.
—Rick Wohlhuter

Whoever wants to win something runs 100 meters. Whoever wants to experience something runs the marathon.
—Emil Zatopek

My creativity went up—running is terrific for problem-solving because it pares you down to the essentials.
—an anoymous man who changed his life through running therapy

I sweat to think.

—Anonymous

I tell my patients that if they don't change their way of life they're going to need a coronary bypass operation. When they start thinking about someone cutting into their heart, they're anxious to take steps to avoid it.

—a cardiologist

Joggers' Brains Similar to Hamsters

—Headline in the San Francisco Examiner

If you pick 'em up, O Lord, I'll put 'em down.

—The Prayer of the Tired Walker

Action absorbs anxiety.

—standard medical axiom

Tell the truth and run.

—Yugoslavian proverb

Walking, biking, and swimming are to running what masturbation is to making love: only a bit better than abstinence.

—a serious runner

Glossary

Achilles' tendon The long tendon connecting the heel bone with the calf muscle in the back of the leg. Even though it is the strongest and thickest tendon in the body, it is a frequent site of sports injuries. Among runners, Achilles-tendon injuries are the second most common complaint (behind knee injuries). Because the blood supply to the Achilles is not particularly good, injuries to that area heal very slowly.

acute mountain sickness (AMS) A condition, characterized by shortness of breath, fatigue, headache, nausea, and other flu-like symptoms. It occurs at high altitudes and is attributed to a shortage of oxygen; most people don't experience symptoms until they reach heights well above 5,000 feet.

addiction The condition runners have when it hurts more not to run than to run.

aerobic exercise A continuous, rhythmic exercise during which the body's oxygen needs are still being met. Aerobic activities include brisk walking, running, swimming, cycling, and cross-country skiing. A conditioned athlete can carry on aerobic exercise for a long time (in contrast to anaerobic exercise).

aerodynamic Having to do with air in motion – specifically the movement of air over, under, and around a runner. Better aerodynamic efficiency means less wind drag, less energy expenditure, and greater speed.

age-group Competition separated by age. Major groupings are junior (19 and under), open (20–39) and Masters (40 and over).

all-comers A meet or race open to everyone, regardless of skill or age.

all-weather track A rubber-asphalt track surface that retains good footing even in pouring rain; often called Tartan, though that is only one brand.

amino acids A group of organic nitrogen compounds found in protein and necessary for metabolism; called the building blocks of life. Of the twenty amino acids, eleven are "essential," meaning they are not produced by the body and must be obtained from foods like meat, cheese, and soy.

anabolic steroids Any of a group of synthetic drugs that stimulate protein-building functions in the body. Steroids are used by athletes to build muscular strength, power, and size that exceeds what is possible with a natural training program. Illegal in the United States.

anaerobic Exercise at an intensity level that exceeds the ability of the body to dispose of the lactic acid produced by the muscles. As a result, this

216

exercise can be sustained for only a short time before exhaustion sets in. Examples of anaerobic exercise include weight lifting, sprinting, and calisthenics.

anaerobic threshold The point in an exercise at which further increase in effort will cause more lactic acid to accumulate than can be readily eliminated. Past this point, the body is working so hard that it is unable to supply enough oxygen for the muscle cells to work efficiently.

anemia A condition characterized by a decreased amount of hemoglobin circulating in the cells. Often attributed to a diet low in iron, it results in reduced number and size of red blood cells, and a general fatigue.

angina pectoris A chest pain, usually short-lived, that indicates the heart is not getting sufficient oxygen. This usually occurs during exertion, then disappears when the activity is stopped. Some angina victims live for years without having a heart attack, but if the narrowing of the arteries continues, the likelihood is high that a clump of debris will eventually produce a blockage. When that happens, the supply of blood (and, therefore, oxygen) to the heart will be cut off.

arm carry The movement of a runner's arms when running. The arms balance the runner and contribute to the rhythm of his or her gait. The left arm should swing forward to balance right leg action, and vice versa.

arteriosclerosis A narrowing of the arteries to the heart by cholesterol and other substances. In arteriosclerosis, the arterial passageways become roughened and narrowed by fatty deposits

that harden into patches along the inner lining of the artery, leaving less room for flowing blood. Exercise can reverse this process.

atherosclerosis Same as arteriosclerosis.

athlete's foot A fungus, usually found between the toes, which can cause blisters, and peeling, raw skin; most often caused by improper foot care, wearing sweat-soaked socks, or tight, airless shoes that create a favorable climate for fungus.

ATP (adenosine triphosphate) A chemical compound produced in the transformation of food to muscular energy. Food is broken down into ATP, which is then stored in muscle cells until needed.

baffles A wall of fabric inside a sleeping bag shell used to limit the shifting of the down fill.

Balke protocol A method of taking a treadmill stress test which utilizes a constant speed and progressive incline, until the twenty-fifth minute.

ballistic stretching Quick, bouncing stretches that force muscles to lengthen. The muscles react by reflexively contracting or shortening, increasing the likelihood of muscle tears and soreness.

Barclay match An exact repetition of Robert Barclay's 1808 athletic feat in which he walked one thousand miles in one thousand successive hours – that is, one mile in each and every hour for forty-two days.

base One's endurance level, which is raised by running many miles at an aerobic level.

bear A metaphorical creature who jumps on your back and drags you down when you've run too far and/or too fast.

belly-breathing The proper abdominal breathing technique in which the belly expands as you breath in and flattens as you breath out. Improper chest breathing is inefficient and can cause a stitch.

beta-blocker Drug used to treat hypertension and other heart-related problems.

biathlon A two-sport event. The summer biathlon features biking and running.

bivouac sack A hooded sleeping bag cover; also known as a bivvy sack.

blood doping Generally, a natural ergogenic aid that is illegal for most competition. Specifically, the act of increasing blood volume – and thus oxygen-carrying capacity – by drawing blood from an athlete well in advance of competition (blood which is replaced by the body's natural processes) and then returning the drawn blood to the athlete's system just before competition.

blood pressure The force of the blood against the walls of the arteries; measured as systolic and diastolic pressure.

blow up To overexert and sap oneself of energy.

bonk, bonks, bonking, getting the bonks The feeling of total physical collapse that accompanies depletion of glycogen in the muscles. It is the point of "no quick return."

Boston The Boston Marathon, granddaddy of all marathons. Dating from 1897, it is the oldest continuous marathon in the world.

bottoming out Compromised shock absorption and support that results from a worn midsole. When the midsole becomes too soft for a runner's weight, it compresses too quickly to offer good cushioning.

Bowerman Bill Bowerman, former track coach at the University of Oregon and one of running's Big Three (along with Dr. Kenneth Cooper and Arthur Lydiard).

bradycardia Abnormally slow heart rate, often found in highly fit endurance runners.

break, breakaway One or more runners who have escaped the main pack.

breathability A fabric's capacity to allow water vapor to pass through it.

Bruce Protocol A method of taking a treadmill stress test that increases speed and incline every three minutes.

burst A sudden increase of speed.

calorie Technically, the amount of heat needed to raise one kilogram of water one degree centigrade; practically, a measure of energy – either how much a certain food provides or how much the body burns when exercising. For example, one apple equals approximately one hundred calories equals approximately one mile of walking.

carbohydrates The sugars and starches in food that provide a valuable source of muscle energy. In their most healthful state, complex carbohydrates are found in grains, potatoes, beans, bread, and pasta; simple carbohydrates are found in fruits and table sugar. "Carbs" are stored as glycogen in the liver. In contemporary nutrition, carbohydrates are "in"; fat and protein are "out."

carbohydrate loading A complicated dietary technique developed by Swedish scientists in the 1970s. Over a period of about a week, a runner depletes the body's glycogen stores by limiting intake of carbohydrates, then, three days before competition, loads up on carbohydrates. The technique has been shown to increase muscle energy but not without a price. The process puts stress on the body and can cause excess water retention in the muscles.

cardiac Related to the heart.

cardiac arrhythmia Irregular heart beat.

cardiovascular Pertaining to the heart and blood vessels.

cartilage Specialized fibrous connective tissue present in and around joints; the only tissue in the body that doesn't have its own blood supply.

centipede racing A specified number of runners competing while linked together by a costume; particularly prevalent in the annual 7.6-mile Bay-to-Breakers fun run in San Francisco, where in 1991 the thirteen-member Reebok Aggies Centipede finished in 37:40, a pace below five minutes per mile.

century A 100-mile (160 kilometer) race.

certified Running course guaranteed to be the distance stated; measured by precise methods established by the governing bodies of the sport.

cholesterol A fatty substance manufactured in the liver and found in all tissues. In foods, only animal products contain cholesterol. It is associated with atherosclerosis, or hardening of the arteries.

chondromalacia A knee injury involving disintegration of cartilage due to improper tracking of the kneecap. Aggravated by overuse, its symptoms include deep knee pain and a crunching sensation during bending. Chondromalacia patella is a roughening of the inner surface of the kneecap. A *Runner's World* survey ranks the knee as the most common problem site for runners.

circuit training A type of exercise designed for both aerobic benefit and strength building. Circuit training utilizes exercise equipment, like pullup bars or incline boards, set up at various stops or stations along a route. The aerobic benefit comes from moving quickly from station to station between sets of exercises.

collapse point The point in a race where the "bear" jumps on and you can go no farther. In distance, it is usually reached at about three times your daily average.

collateral circulation The opening of new blood vessels to offset the effects of atherosclerosis; the remarkable way the cardiovascular system can repair itself. When atherosclerosis begins to close coronary arteries, nearby arteries get bigger and even open up tiny new branches to carry blood to the starving parts of the heart. Collateral circulation is the reason that some people with narrowed arteries never have heart attacks. It also explains some of the seemingly "miraculous" recoveries from such attacks.

collaterals Back-up blood vessels. Exercise causes the heart to increase the density of these blood vessels, or collaterals.

complete protein A protein food (such as meat, milk, eggs, or cheese) that contains all eleven essential amino acids.

congenital Existing from birth, as in congenital heart disease.

cool-down An important final phase of exercise during which the rate of physical exertion, and hence the heart beat, is gradually decreased.

Cooper Dr. Kenneth Cooper, father of aerobics and a leading authority on physical fitness.

coronary arteries Arteries that supply the heart muscle.

coronary arteriography A procedure of inserting a tube into an artery, depositing a dye into the coronary arteries, and then taking an X-ray to determine the degree of clogging. Same as coronary angiography.

coronary occlusion A severe narrowing of a coronary artery to the point that blood can no longer pass through.

coronary thrombosis A coronary occlusion caused by a blood clot (thrombus) that completely blocks the flow of blood to some part of the heart muscle.

corn A callus that often occurs between or on top of the toes.

cramping Painful contraction of muscles due to the loss of potassium and other minerals during the excessive sweating of exercise.

cross-training Regularly performing more than one aerobic activity, which exercises different muscle groups and provides variety. Interspersing running with biking and swimming—as triathletes do—is an example of cross-training.

cross-country Running that is both off-road and off-track.

cushioning The ability of a shoe to absorb shock, which is primarily the function of the midsole. Because a runner impacting level ground generates a force about three times body weight, this is a critical shoe quality.

daypack A medium-sized soft pack, favored by day hikers, for carrying food, water, and other supplies; bigger than a fanny pack, smaller than a backpack.

dehydration A depletion of body fluids that can hinder the body's ability to regulate its own temperature. One can become dehydrated during exercise if the fluids lost through perspiration are not replaced by drinking water. Chronic dehydration lowers an athlete's tolerance to fatigue, reduces his ability to sweat, elevates his rectal temperature, and increases the stress on his circulatory system. In general, a loss of 2 percent or more of one's body weight by sweating affects performance; a loss of 5 to 6 percent affects health.

delayed-onset muscle soreness (DOMS) Pain in the muscles that usually strikes one to two days after performing an exercise to which one is unaccustomed. Believed to be associated with microscopic injury to muscle tissue.

detraining The reduction of fitness level due to inactivity. Studies have found that physical fitness (as measured by endurance, changes in maximum heart rate, and other criteria) declines rapidly in the first twelve days of inactivity and then continues to decline though not as rapidly. However, even after three months of not exercising, these erstwhile athletes were still fitter than people who had never exercised.

depletion run The stage of the process known as carbo-loading in which the athlete runs long and hard to deplete his glycogen stores.

depression insomnia A sleep disorder brought on by overtraining. It is characterized by ease in falling asleep followed by a period of wakefulness in the early morning hours.

devil-take-the-hindmost A track event in which the last-place runner at the end of each lap must drop out; the winner is the last runner left on the track.

diastolic blood pressure The lowest pressure in the arteries that occurs when the heart is resting between beats. Among conditioned people, diastolic pressure remains the same or decreases slightly during exercise; among the unfit, it rises. The diastolic reading is represented by the bottom number in the blood pressure fraction.

DNF Racers' shorthand for "did not finish."

drafting The act of running in the slipstream (quiet air) of a runner ahead, which can dramatically cut wind resistance and reduce the effort needed to run a particular speed. Ideal distances for drafting vary, but generally the closer the better. Drafting is central to the strategy of winning in road and track races but is not usually allowed in ultramarathon racing or triathlons.

electrocardiogram (ECG; EKG) A reading of the electroconductivity of the heart that can detect irregular heartbeats, enlargement of the heart's chambers, mineral imbalances in the blood, and whether someone has had or is having a heart attack. ECGs can be performed while the subject is at rest or while exercising (also called a stress test).

electrolytes Minerals in food and drink; potassium, magnesium, and sodium are the most important for runners because they are sweated away quickly.

endorphins Opiate-like substances produced by the central nervous system that suppress pain. These natural pain relievers seem to be released during vigorous exercise.

endurance The ability to withstand pain, stress, or fatigue and keep going.

ergogenic aid Any stimulant or artificial aid used to improve athletic performance. Just about all are illegal for competition, except the caffeine in coffee.

exercise physiology The study of the workings of the body during activity. The ones doing the studying are called exercise physiologists.

exercise stress test An electrocardiogram taken while you are exercising.

fanny pack A small soft pack worn around the waist, usually by ultra-runners, for holding a few emergency supplies.

fartlek A Swedish term meaning "speed play," it is a type of interval training in which the runner alternates sprinting with relaxed running. A clock is not used; instead the runner sprints for a telephone pole, city-limit sign, sleeping dog, etc. The technique lacks structure in pace and intensity but can be a useful training aid for the disciplined runner.

fast distance Training runs close to maximum effort.

fast-twitch muscle fiber Muscle fiber with two to three times the contraction speed of slow-twitch muscle fiber. A runner strong in fast-twitch muscle fiber is more likely to be a strong sprinter than an endurance runner.

fats The body's most concentrated source of energy. Fats found in foods are either in solid or liquid (oil) form. In the body, fat is part of all cell membranes, where it serves as a stored form of energy, helps cushions organs, and helps create certain hormones.

fell   A hill or mountain. Obscure except in the proper names of hills in the northwest of England.

fell running   An endurance test for both distance runners and mountaineers, deriving its name from the hills of northern England where it is mainly contested. Courses are either out-and-back or circuitous, and may vary in length from two to forty miles.

femur   The thigh bone; the largest bone in the body.

fibula   The smaller of the two bones in the lower leg.

field   The main group of runners; also known as pack.

fill   Sleeping bag insulation, usually either down or polyester.

fitness   Ability to put one's health to work in a dynamic way. One can be healthy without being fit, but not the reverse.

flats   Running shoes designed for roads and cross-country courses; in contrast to spikes.

flexibility   The ability of the joints to move through their full range of motion. Good flexibility is thought to protect the muscles from pulls and tears, as short, tight muscles are more likely to be overstretched.

force the pace   To increase the speed of the race to test the competition.

form   The way a runner or walker moves; also known as style.

fun running   Movement for the pure enjoyment of it, rather than for physical fitness or competition.

glucose   The sugar that results when carbohydrates are converted to glyco-

gen for storage. Because drinks made of glucose solutions require relatively little work to digest, they are commonly used by serious runners.

glycogen   The glucoselike chemical that is the principal carbohydrate storage material in the body.

glycolysis   The process of breaking down glucose into ATP.

gorp   A high-carbohydrate snack food made primarily from nuts and dried fruit; an acronym for "good ol' raisins and peanuts."

Gore-Tex   The trade name of a material for clothing and tents that allows water vapor from the body to escape but will not allow liquid water droplets (rain) to enter. It has high breathability.

half   Short for half-mile, or 880 yards; two times around a standard track.

hamstrings   A group of three muscles that run along the back of the thigh.

hang in   To barely keep contact at the rear of a group of runners.

hang on   To run in the draft of the runner in front without taking a turn; to barely maintain contact with the back of the pack.

hard-easy   Alternating hard exercise days with easy ones to allow the body to recover.

heat cramps   A knotting of muscles – typically calf, arms, and abdomen – usually caused by prolonged exercise in hot weather. To treat cramps, massage the area with ice cubes or hands, and drink a few glasses of cool water with a half-teaspoon of salt dissolved in each.

heat exhaustion   A debilitating ailment, the symptoms of which may include headache, dizziness, nausea, gooseflesh, rubbery legs, fainting, a weak but rapid pulse, muscle cramps, and a hot, flushed feeling around the head and shoulders. Though rarely fatal, it can precede potentially fatal heatstroke.

heatstroke The most severe of the three heat ailments, it causes confusion, loss of neuromuscular control, unconsciousness, and perilously high body temperatures—more than 104 degrees. The best antidote is to lower the victim's body temperature via ice-cube rubs or immersion in cold water.

HDL (high-density lipoprotein) A carrier of cholesterol from the body's tissues to the liver, where it is broken down then excreted. Often called "good cholesterol."

heel counter The rigid section at the back of the shoe that stabilizes the heel.

hemoglobin The coloring pigment of the red blood cells that contains iron. It enables the cells to carry oxygen from the lungs to the tissues of the body.

high-altitude pulmonary edema (HAPE) A potentially life-threatening condition that results from the accumulation of fluid in the lungs; it may occur in individuals who ascend to heights greater than 8,000 feet.

hypoglycemia A dangerous condition characterized by an abnormally low blood glucose level. It can be caused by medications like insulin (taken for diabetes), some illnesses, and severe physical exhaustion.

hypokinetic disease An illness of inactivity.

incomplete protein The protein found in grains and vegetables, lacking one or more of the essential amino acids necessary for good health. The

strictest vegetarian might have trouble obtaining all eleven essential amino acids through diet alone and have to rely on supplements.

indoor Running on tracks that rarely have fewer than eight laps per mile. In the United States, indoor racing season lasts from December through March.

insole The cushioned comfort pad inside a shoe on which the foot rests. Most insoles are removable and replaceable.

interval training A way of exercising that alternates spurts of intense exertion with lower-intensity periods in one exercise session.

Ironman The name of the triathlon held every autumn in Hawaii. It consists of 2.4 miles of ocean swimming, followed by 112 miles of biking, finishing with a marathon of running.

jogging Movement that is in between walking and running. It's debatable exactly where jogging ends and running begins, but Dr. Kenneth Cooper defines jogging as movement that is slower than nine minutes per mile.

joggling Juggling while running. Created by Bill Gudiz, joggling was developed as an antidote to running boredom. But it is much more than that: University of California researchers have determined that joggling raises a joggler's heart rate ten percent higher than does conventional running.

jogamuting Running to and from work. Coined by Boston physician Arthur J. Siegel.

junior An age category in running that includes age 19 and under.

K Abbreviation for kilometer, as in "10-K race."

kick   The acceleration at the end of a run or race.

kilocalorie   One thousand calories.

kilometer   One thousand meters; about 5/8th of a mile.

lace locks   Plastic devices on the upper part of the shoe that maintain tension on the laces.

lactic acid   A byproduct of anaerobic exercise that accumulates in the muscles, causing pain and fatigue.

last   The basic shape of the upper part of a shoe, usually described as either "straight" or "curved."

LDL (low density lipoprotein)   A carrier of cholesterol, LDL delivers cholesterol to tissues in the body; it has been implicated in the accumulation of plaque within the arteries. Often called "bad cholesterol" (as contrasted with HDL or "good cholesterol").

ligaments   Tough bands of elastic-like tissue that join bones together to prevent excessive movement; source of many running injuries.

lightweight trainer   A training shoe that weighs less than ten ounces. It is not as durable or supportive as most training shoes.

loafer's heart   A term coined by Dr. Wilhelm Raab, professor emeritus of the University of Vermont College of Medicine. It describes the weakening of the heart brought on by lack of exercise.

loft   A sleeping bag's thickness or height when it is fully fluffed and lying flat.

long distances   More than 10,000 meters.

LSD   Long Slow Distance; a training technique calling for continuous runs of an hour or more at a steady aerobic rate, usually at about 75 percent of maximum heart rate. The idea is to make running fun. LSD offers the pleasures of walking, but at a pace of seven or eight miles per hour instead of three or four miles per hour.

Lydiard   Arthur Lydiard, famed Olympic running coach from New Zealand, who pioneered a training system that included a base of long-duration, even-paced running and strong speed; the method of training named after him.

marathon   A race of 42.195 kilometers (26 miles 385 yards) over an open course. The name derives from the story/myth of the Greek messenger Pheidippides who in 490 B.C. ran from Marathon to Athens, announced the victory over the Persians, and dropped dead.

Masters   The branch of age-group competition comprised of men 40 and over, women 30 and over.

maximal oxygen consumption (VO$_2$ Max)   A measurement of the maximum amount of oxygen a person can transfer from the lungs to the cardiovascular system in one minute. Though generally predetermined by heredity, improvements can be made by engaging in a serious exercise program. It is a strong indicator of potential performance in aerobic sports.

maximum heart rate (MHR)   The highest heart rate you can achieve during your greatest exercise effort. MHR, computed by subtracting your age from 220, is used to calculate your training heart rate (THR).

MENS   Minimal electrical neuromuscular stimulation; a method of zapping damaged muscles with a mild current to induce repair. Sports therapist Jack Scott is a leading practitioner of MENS; he is credited with contributing to Joan Benoit's stunning recovery from surgery just seventeen days before the 1984 Olympic Marathon Trials, which she won.

metabolism The chemical and physical processes continuously going on in the body. Metabolism is driven by the energy derived from the nutrients in food.

metatarsals Small bones in the forefoot which can be damaged by running.

metric century A 100-kilometer (62.5-mile) run.

middle distances Races that range from 800 to 10,000 meters (roughly a half-mile to six miles).

midsole The material – usually EVA, polyurethane, or a combination of the two – that is sandwiched between the upper part of the shoe and the outsole. It is the most important component of the shoe because it provides most of the cushioning.

Morton's foot A foot problem in which the second toe is longer than the first toe. It distorts the normal weight-bearing tripod in the foot – namely, the heel, the head of the fifth metatarsal, and the head of the first metatarsal. The foot adapts to this deformity by bearing most of the weight on the head of the second metatarsal, often resulting in a stress fracture, or by overpronating (rolling over excessively on the inside of the foot), which can cause all sorts of overuse injuries. Morton's foot is, according to George Sheehan, the most common cause of structural instability in the foot.

muscular endurance The ability to perform repeated muscular contractions in rapid succession; for instance, weight-lifting repetitions.

muscular strength The force a muscle produces in one exertion, such as a jump.

myocardial infarction A condition in which the blood supply to a portion of the heart muscle is blocked, causing that part of the muscle fed by the blocked artery to die; a fancy term for "heart attack."

myoglobin A chemical in muscle tissue that is involved in oxygen transport and storage. The muscle's version of hemoglobin.

obesity A medical term that refers to the storage of excess fat in the body. A person is considered obese when his or her weight is 20 percent greater than what the height-weight tables deem "appropriate."

open Competition that is open to everyone, as are most road races.

orienteering A cross-country event in which competitors, using only a compass and a detailed map, attempt to find the fastest route between a series of flagged checkpoints called controls. The sport has been called everything from "cunning running" to "running a marathon while filling out your income tax."

orthotic A custom-made support worn inside shoes to compensate for arch defects and other biomechanical imbalances in the feet and legs.

osteoporosis A disease, primarily affecting postmenopausal women, in which bones become porous and brittle. Exercise has been shown to ameliorate the symptoms.

out-and-back A course that goes to

a certain point, makes a 180-degree turn, and returns the same way.

overcompensation injury Pain caused by the tendency to favor one part of the body to protect another part of the body.

overdistance Training runs that are longer than the usual racing distance or daily average.

overtraining Any intense training to which the body cannot adapt and that results in physical and mental fatigue not easily overcome.

overuse Doing too much too fast; the cause of most running injuries.

oxygen debt The condition that occurs when the oxygen needs of working muscles exceed the available supply, causing feelings of breathlessness and muscular fatigue. Exercise that results in oxygen debt is called "anaerobic."

oxygen uptake A measurement of the amount of oxygen the body processes during exercise; a good measurement of endurance fitness.

pace Rate of running speed. Distance runners measure it in minutes per mile, as in "five-minute miles," while sprinters are more likely to speak in terms of, say, "sixty-second quarters."

pace-work Practice-running at a pace one wishes to maintain in a race. If your goal is to run six-minute miles, doing quarters in ninety seconds each would be pace-work, while eighty-second quarters would be speed-work.

pack The main group of runners.

patella The kneecap, which protects the front of the knee joint.

peak A period of time when the mind and body are operating at maximum performance level. Some athletes have peak seasons; others peak moments.

peaking Simultaneously reaching a physical and emotional high point.

pedometer A small instrument for measuring the distance walked or run. It is unnecessary to use a pedometer if you have a watch and a sense of how fast you are moving.

pickups Increases in pace – sprints – within longer runs; used for training purposes.

podiatrist A doctor who is a foot specialist; particularly important for walkers and runners who are heavily dependent on the health of their feet.

plantar fascia A thick, padlike band of tissue along the bottom of the foot. Stress to this area from excessive running or jumping can cause plantar fasciitis.

plantar fasciitis An inflammation of the connective tissue that runs from the base of the toes to the heel bone; an overuse injury.

point-to-point A road race that is run from Point A to Point B, covering the course only once.

porosity A fabric's capacity to allow air to pass through it.

power-walking Walking at a pace that rivals slow running, usually between four and five miles per hour. The physical-psychological benefits of this activity are much the same as for running.

PR Personal Record, or the best time for an individual over a particular course. It is the most significant record for most of us, as it allows us to compete against our former selves.

predicted maximum heart rate The maximum number of times a person's heart should beat per minute when running full out, factoring in age and state of fitness. Used in calculating "target heart rate."

preventive medicine Health practices that strive to prevent problems before they show up as symptoms. Based on the principle that it is easier to stay well than it is to get well.

pronation The natural shock-absorbing movement the foot should go through in each stride cycle. Pronation is the natural inward roll of the foot as the arch collapses. If the foot rolls too far inward – overpronation – injuries to tendons or ligaments can result.

pulled muscle A tear in the muscle fiber. Proper warmup is a good defense, as flexible muscles are less likely to tear.

quadriceps The four large muscles at the front of the thigh, the strength of which go a long way in determining a runner's ability to power up a hill. Arguably the strongest muscles in the body (though Trivial Pursuit claims the tongue muscle is strongest). Since they attach to the patella tendon, the "quads" play an important role in recovery from knee injuries; therapy often centers around quad-strengthening exercises.

quality Training that tends to be short and intensive.

quarter One lap around a standard outdoor track, equivalent to 440 yards, or one-quarter mile.

recovery heart rate The goal of the post-exercise cool-down. A leisurely five-minute walk after a run should bring your pulse down below 120 beats per minute, below 110 if you are more than fifty years old. After an additional five minutes of stretching and relaxing exercises, your pulse should be within twenty beats of your pre-exercise resting heart rate.

resistance work Training with

extra "drag," such as in sand or up hills or with extra weight.

repetition Each hard effort in an interval workout.

resting heart rate (RHR) The number of heartbeats per minute while the body is at rest; most accurately measured by taking your pulse before rising in the morning.

retro running Backward running, a term coined by the New York Health & Racquet Club, which sponsors the annual Backwards Mile every April in the Big Apple.

rig Short for "rigor mortis," the progressive stiffening of the muscles that you experience as you near exhaustion.

road race The general term for all races that are not run on a track or cross-country.

road rash The cuts and abrasions received when a tumbling runner meets the ground.

RRC Road Runners Club, an international organization that promotes long-distance competition.

runner's knee A dull pain at the kneecap, which is brought on by repeated stress to the knee. It most commonly affects runners, skiers, and those who do high-impact aerobics.

running therapy A form of adult play which teaches people how to recapture life.

sanction Official approval of an event by one of the sport's governing bodies.

sciatica Inflammation of the longest nerve in the body, running from the lower back down the back of each leg to the foot; structural problems in the back can cause pinching of this nerve and weakness in the legs.

set In interval training, a specific

number of repetitions of an exercise.

sharpening Training with an emphasis on speed, done after a "base" in endurance has been laid down.

shin splints An all-purpose category describing pain in the muscles along the front of the lower leg, usually about coffee-table height.

short distances Another name for the sprints, or 440 yards and shorter.

six-day race A go-as-you-please endurance event popular in the late nineteenth century. Runners or walkers competed for 144 straight hours, or until they dropped, usually on indoor tracks like Madison Square Garden so that the rabid, heavy-betting fans could be up close and personal with the athletes.

slipstream The area of least wind resistance, tight behind another runner. Unless sprinting for the finish line, it is a good place to be.

slow-twitch muscle fiber Muscle fiber that contracts one-third to one-half as fast as fast-twitch fiber. Runners strong in slow-twitch muscle fiber are likely to be better endurance runners than sprinters.

specificity A theory in athletic training that says athletes become proficient at the specific tasks they practice.

speed work Training at a pace faster than you intend to race. Intervals and fartleks are two common types of speed work. Even Ann Trason, who specializes in 50- and 100-mile races, does weekly speed work.

spikes Running shoes with pointed cleats. Used on old-style dirt tracks. On all-weather tracks, and for road racing and cross-country, running shoes are commonly used.

splits A runner's or walker's times for a particular fraction of a race. A miler is most interested in quarter-mile splits, while a marathoner tunes into five-kilometer splits.

sports medicine A burgeoning branch of medicine dealing with the strains, sprains, and sickness incurred by people who recreate vigorously.

sprain An injury that damages a ligament or ligaments, as well as joint capsules. Sprains can be mild, moderate, or severe, the latter meaning one or more ligaments is completely torn.

sprint A short burst of speed by a runner vying for the finish line; also a race of that generic type, such as the 60- 100- and 200-meter dashes.

sprinter's hill A steep hill that is short enough to be climbed quickly, without hindrance from muscular bulk.

stability The ability of a shoe to keep the foot moving in a forward direction, rather than allowing excessive side-to-side movement.

stair climbing Racing up the stairwells of high-rise buildings, first popularized by the 86-flight Empire State Building Run-Up in 1978. Climbs today range from a 25-floor "sprint" in Detroit, to Toronto's CN Tower, a 110-story (1,760-step) ascent that has been tackled by, among others, one person wearing roller skates and two others wearing flippers.

stamina Resistance to fatigue, illness, hardship; staying power.

steady state The dividing line between aerobic (normal breathing) and anaerobic (out-of-breath) running; as fitness improves, the pace at which one can run in a "steady state" increases.

stitch A sharp pain in the side, believed to be a spasm of the diaphragm muscle that separates the lungs from the abdomen. Causes include improper breathing and eating just before exercising. To reduce the problem, try "belly breathing."

strain A stretched or partially torn muscle. Strains often occur when muscles suddenly and powerfully contract. Factors contributing to strains include poor conditioning, fatigue, weakness, and inadequate or improper warmup. The leg, groin, and shoulder are the most common sites for strains.

streaker A runner who runs every day for months and years and keeps track. Someone who runs naked through a public place (archaic).

strength The capacity for resisting stress and strain.

stress What you put your body through when you exercise; the right amount of stress is necessary for improvement, but too much causes the body to break down.

stress fracture A microscopic break in a bone caused by repeated impact. Among runners, it usually affects the foot, shin, or thigh.

stress injury An exercise-related injury, usually caused by the wear and tear of performing a repetitive activity.

stretching Slow, steady exercises that improve the flexibility of tendons, ligaments, and muscles (see **yoga**).

stuff bag A water-repellent or waterproof nylon bag with a drawstring, used for compact storage of sleeping bag, down jacket, etc.

style The way a runner or walker moves; also called form.

supination The opposite of pronation, it is the outward rolling of the forefoot that naturally occurs during the stride cycle at toe-off. Oversupina-

tion—or underpronation—occurs when the foot remains on its outside edge after heel strike instead of pronating as it should to absorb shock. According to podiatrist Joe Ellis, oversupination is quite rare, occurring in less than one percent of the running population.

support crew The staff of people who bring aid and comfort to an ultrarunner. Depending on the length and nature of a race, the crew may supply food, water, clothing, medical aid, moral support, and/or psychological counseling—anything short of physically helping the runner along.

support vehicle The motorcycle, car, van, truck, motor home—or combination thereof—that is staffed by the support crew.

survival shuffle The low-slung style used by runners to get to the finish line when they've gone too far or too fast.

sweats Clothing that runners and walkers use in cold weather or for warming up; that is, sweatshirts and sweat pants.

systolic blood pressure The maximum pressure in the arteries when the heart is contracting. If you're in good shape, systolic pressure will rise during your run, level off, and then drop slightly. It is represented by the top number in the fraction of a blood pressure reading.

tachycardia Fast pulse, usually over ninety. Normal during exercise, abnormal at rest.

tactics Strategy used in racing to gain steps on opponents.

talk test Coined by Bill Bowerman, it is the criterion for determining whether you are moving too fast during a training run. If you can chat while you run, you're okay; if not, you are going too fast.

tapering Cutting back on mileage before an event; racers taper from a day to a week before a big race.

target heart rate The heart rate during exercise in which the greatest training benefit occurs; usually 65 to 85 percent of the predicted maximum heart rate.

tarp A waterproof sheet of material used for protecting exposed objects or people.

tear strength A fabric's capacity to resist further tearing once it has been ripped.

tendinitis An inflammation of a tendon, causing pain and swelling. Most common site in runners: the Achilles tendon above the heel.

tendons The cords of connective tissue that anchor muscles to bones.

tibia The larger of two bones in the lower leg.

tibialis anterior A long muscle in front of the calf that raises the foot.

time trial A simulated race for time over a known distance, usually done alone.

tinman A triathlon in which all three of the sport's events—swimming, biking, running—are shorter than in an Ironman.

track race Any race held on a track; in contrast to road racing and cross-country.

training Working out now for some future reward, like fitness or personal records; the process of applying the proper quantity and quality of stress.

training effect The positive physiological changes that can be brought on by intense, continuous exercise. These include increased number and size of blood vessels, increased lung capacity, increased maximal oxygen consumption (VO_2 Max), reduction of body fat, improved muscle tone, increased blood volume, and lowered resting pulse.

training heart rate (THR) The aerobic heart rate; the rate that provides sufficient training effect for your cardiovascular system. This target zone of safe, beneficial training falls between two numbers, the target rate of 70 percent of your maximum heart rate and the cut-off figure of 85 percent of maximum heart rate.

treadmill A piece of motorized exercise equipment upon which one walks or runs indoors. Many treadmills can be raised at one end to simulate hill work.

treadmill stress test (TMST) A procedure to determine a person's degree of fitness and cardiovascular health. In a properly conducted stress test, the subject walks to exhaustion on a treadmill with a moving, motorized belt.

triathlete One who participates in triathlons.

triathlon A three-sport competition featuring swimming, bicycling, and running.

triggerpoints Local tender spots of degenerated muscle tissue. They can produce severe pain or spasm, and may be caused by faulty running or walking style, structural weakness, muscular imbalance, or tension. In runners and walkers, they are most common in the legs and back.

turnaround On an out-and-back course, the point at which the runners reverse themselves.

ultramarathon A racing distance that exceeds common human limits. Exact distances vary, but the most common are 50- and 100-mile races and 100-kilometer races.

underdistance Training runs shorter than the usual distance that are usually run at near-racing speed.

upper The part of the shoe that is above the midsole.

van Aaken A German doctor and running-for-fitness guru, he is Europe's answer to America's Dr. Kenneth Cooper. Ernst van Aaken's methods center around long endurance runs mixed with very small amounts of faster running.

veteran International term for Masters age group. Includes male runners age forty and up, female runners age thirty-five and up. World Veteran Championships are held every other year.

vital capacity A measurement of the total volume of air expelled after full inspiration. The subject blows into a machine that measures the amount of air intake, output, and residual. Vital capacity and VO_2 Max together indicate how much of the athlete's oxygen is being utilized and how much is residual.

vitamins Biochemical substances essential to good health that help regulate metabolic functions. Contrary to popular belief, vitamins are not sources of energy, but rather play a role in "energy transformation." Contemporary wisdom holds that athletic performance is not enhanced by megavitamin supplements; a well-balanced diet is enough.

VO_2 Max (maximal oxygen consumption) The amount of oxygen that can be utilized during a maximal (all-out) exercise test. Expressed as milliliters of oxygen per kilogram of body weight per minute. Though generally determined by heredity, improvement can be made by engaging in a serious exercise program. It is a strong indicator of potential performance in aerobic sports.

waffle A popular outsole design created by former University of Oregon track coach Bill Bowerman.

walker's heel A group of heel problems that include bone bruises and heel spurs (painful bony growths on the heel). Cause: walking or running on hard surfaces, stepping on hard surfaces with enough impact to cause a bruise, and poorly designed shoes.

wall The invisible but real barrier a runner often hits on a long run that causes an abrupt slowdown. It usually occurs around the twenty-mile mark, which is a reflection of glycogen depletion.

warmup Pre-workout activities, like walking, jogging, stretching, designed to get the body heated up and ready to go.

water-walking Brisk walking in thigh- or waist-deep water that can burn three hundred to five hundred calories per hour. Started as rehabilitation therapy for people whose injuries limit their exercise on land, it is now the latest aerobic craze. The water's resistance helps tone muscles in the legs (and arms, if you swing them through the water). Since the water helps support the body, it is low-impact exercise, putting minimal strain on joints.

weight-bearing exercise Exercise

in which the legs support the body, such as walking, running, and jumping rope.

weight training Lifting barbells and dumbbells to increase strength and correct muscular imbalances.

width sizing The creation of running shoes in multiple widths. Presently, New Balance is the only company offering shoes in several widths. For men: AA to EEEE; for women AA to D.

windchill The cooling of the body that results from wind passing over its surface – especially dramatic if the surface is wet. It is a more useful measurement of meteorological discomfort than is temperature alone.

wind drag (wind resistance) The force a runner encounters trying to move forward through wind. Studies show that middle- and long-distance runners use up 15 to 25 percent of their energy overcoming wind resistance. The simplest way to lower wind resistance is to tuck in close to another runner. From 4 to 9 percent of your energy can be conserved this way.

wind sprints A type of schoolboy torture visited upon track runners in the 1950s, now usually reserved for football players. It consists of sprinting across a field fast and repeating it often. Designed to "build wind" and weed out the weak.

yoga Gentle, slow-motion stretching exercises; ideal for correcting the muscle tightness common to runners.

Organizations

Achilles Track Club (ATC), 9 E. 89th St., New York, NY 10128; 212-967-9300, Founded in 1982 by Dick Traum, a veteran marathoner and an above-the-knee amputee, the ATC trains physically disabled athletes for mainstream races. Thirty U.S. chapters, with offices in seventeen countries.

Amateur Athletic Foundation (AAF), 2141 West Adams Blvd., Los Angeles, CA 90018; 213-730-9696, An institution created by the Los Angeles Olympic Organizing Committee to manage Southern California's endowment from the 1984 Olympic Games. The AAF initiates youth sports programs, including the junior high Run for Fun Program.

American Fitness Association (AFA), 820 Hillside Drive, Long Beach, CA 90815; 310-596-0977, A group of doctors and other health and fitness professionals, as well as corporations and other interested individuals. Promotes interest, involvement, and education in health and fitness. Sponsors seminars, sports clinics, and competitions. Attempts to influence legislation. Publishes, among other periodicals, *Who's Who in Sports and Fitness*.

American Hiking Society (AHS), 1015 31st St. N.W., Washington, DC 20007; 703-385-3252, Group that aims to educate the public on the wonders of walking and foot trails; protects the interests of hikers.

American Medical Athletic Association (AMAA), P.O. Box 4704, North Hollywood, CA 91617; 818-706-2049, Composed of persons in medical or related fields. Encourages and fosters endurance sports among physicians in the United States so that they in turn will encourage the same for their patients. Conducts medical seminars, compiles statistics, sponsors marathons.

American Racewalk Association (ARA), P.O. Box 18323, Boulder, CO 80308; 303-447-0156, Started by Viisha Sedlak, the ARA educates people about the benefits and techniques of racewalking.

American Running and Fitness Association (ARFA), 9310 Old Georgetown Road, Bethesda, MD 20814; 301-897-0197, 800-776-ARFA, The association's mission is to enhance the physical and mental well-being of people through the promotion of running and other aerobic sports. For a twenty-five-dollar membership fee, the organization supplies free FitTips and training advice, medical referrals, motivational programs, and membership discounts. Monthly newsletter, *Running & FitNews*.

American Trails Foundation (ATF), 1446 Glenmoor Way, San Jose, CA 95129; 408-446-4584, Group of individuals interested in the preservation and maintenance of hiking, biking, and riding trails. Financially supports other groups that preserve and maintain trails. Annual publication: *First Aid for Trails*. Formerly American Endurance Ride Conference Trails Foundation.

Appalachian Mountain Club (AMC), 5 Joy St., Boston, MA 02108; 617-523-0636; Fax 617-523-0722, Group dedicated to cultivating public knowledge and enjoyment of the environment in the northeastern United States. Maintains fourteen hundred miles of trails, twenty trail shelters, and an eight-unit alpine hut system. Conducts public service programs in trail maintenance, outdoor leadership, mountain search and rescue efforts, and conservation.

Appalachian Trail Conference (ATC), P.O. Box 807, Harpers Ferry, WV 25425; 304-535-6331; Fax 304-535-2667, Federation of trail and hiking clubs and individuals interested in the Appalachian Trail. Oversees and protects from incompatible land development approximately one hundred thousand acres of federally owned land adjacent to the trail. Maintains museum and archive.

Association of Road Racing Athletes (ARRA), 807 Paulsen Building, Spokane, WA 99201; 509-838-8784, Promotes the development of the sport of long-distance running, especially as it relates to prize money in open competitions.

The Athletics Congress of the U.S.A. (TAC/USA), One Hoosier Dome, Suite 140, Indianapolis, IN 46225; 317-261-0500; Fax 317-261-0481, The national governing body for track and field, long-distance running, and racewalking. Arranges international competition for U.S. athletes, organizes national championships, and provides clinics and training camps.

Big Apple Triathlon Club, P.O. Box 20427, Cherokee Station, New York, NY 10028; 212-289-4113, Founded in 1984, the club promotes physical fitness through safe participation in triathlons. Acts as a clearinghouse for information for triathletes.

Clydesdale Runners Association (CRA), 1809 Gold Mine Road, Brookeville, MD 20833; 301-774-2493, Athletes of medium and large frame (men over 170 pounds; women over 140 pounds). Develops and publicizes information on the relationship between age and weight to performance in endurance events. Advocates the inclusion of age/weight divisions in triathlons and running events.

Continental Divide Trail Society (CDTS), P.O. Box 30002, Bethesda, MD 20824; 301-493-4080, Dedicated to the planning, development, and maintenance of the Continental Divide trail as a "silent trail" – one laid out with appreciation for, and sensitivity to, nature. Serves as a clearinghouse for suggestions from trail users.

DECA (Decathlon Association), Mount St. Marys College, Emmitsburg, MD 21727; 301-447-6122, A group for people who have an abiding love of the decathlon. Maintains files containing results of past decathlon competitions and decathlon training information. Established the Decathlon Roll of Honor.

Federation International Triathlon (FIT), 5966 LaPlace Court, No. 100, Carlsbad, CA 92008; 619-438-8080, International governing body for triathlon activities. Decides and supervises rules for competition. Bestows awards and disseminates information.

Fifty-Plus Runners Association (FPRA), P.O. Box D, Stanford, CA 94309; 415-723-9790, For men and women aged fifty and older who run regularly. Exchanges information and stimulates interest in the sport among the ever-growing contingent of over-fifty runners.

Heptagonal Games Association (HGA), 120 Alexander St., Princeton, NJ 08540; 609-258-6426, Composed of colleges with track-and-field teams. Conducts indoor, outdoor, and cross-country championships.

International Marathon Race Directors Clearing House, International Running Center, Box 881, FDR Station, New York, NY 10150.

International Track and Field Coaches Association (ITFCA), 1705 Evanston St., Kalamazoo, MI 49008; 616-387-2676, Facilitates the exchange of ideas and information among track-and-field coaches worldwide.

Masters Track and Field Committee (MTFC), 5319 Donald St., Eugene, OR 97405; 503-687-8787, A committee of The Athletics Congress of the U.S.A. Sponsors regional and national indoor and outdoor events for the forty-and-over crowd. Also sponsors events for sub-masters, age 30–39.

Melpomene Institute, 1010 University Ave., St. Paul, MN 55104; 612-642-1951, Named for the Greek woman who gate-crashed the first Olympic marathon in 1896, the Melpomene Institute was founded in 1982 to study the health and fitness concerns of physically active women of all ages and abilities. Members receive the Melpomene Report three times a year.

National Indoor Track Meet Directors Association, 187 Marlboro Road, Yardley, PA 19067; 215-295-8804, Sponsors and promotes indoor track competitions.

National Jogging Association, 1910 K. St. N.W., Washington, DC 20006; 202-785-8050, Provides information and advice on the best local running places.

NCAA Division 1 Track Coaches Association, 1705 Evanston, Kalamazoo, MI 49008; 616-349-1008, A division of the National Collegiate Athlete Association, this group represents track coaches from 274 Division 1 universities. Encourages participation in Division 1 track and field. Seeks to improve the division's methods of coaching.

National Women's Health Network, 1325 G St., N.W., Lower Level, Washington, DC 20005, This organization answers questions on a wide variety of women's health issues. Publishes fifty different packets on health subjects from AIDS to menopause.

New York Road Runners Club (NYRRC), 9 E. 89th St., New York, NY 10128; 212-860-4455, Runners united to promote running for fitness and competition. Sponsors about 150 races a year, including the New York Marathon and Triathlon. Affiliated with The Athletics Congress of the U.S.A. and Road Runners Club of America.

North American Network of Women Runners (NANWR), P.O. Box 719, Bala-Cynwyd, PA 19004; 215-668-9886, Group dedicated to maximizing the financial resources for physical fitness, good health, and athletic careers accessible to women internationally. Holds low-cost women's workouts with child care in various sports through community, school, and business facilities.

Road Runners Club of America (RRCA), 629 S. Washington St., Alexandria, VA 22314; 703-836-0558, Encourages road running by sponsoring championships and "fun runs." Originated Run for Your Life, a physical fitness program of fun runs for men, women, and children.

Society of Saunterers, International, 2461 Whitehouse Trail, Gaylord, MI 49735; 517-732-2547, Organization focusing on informing dedicated walkers and inspiring new walkers.

Special Olympics, 1350 New York Ave. N.W., Suite 500, Washington, DC 20005; 202-628-3630, Founded in 1968 by Eunice Kennedy Shriver, the Special Olympics trains mentally retarded children and adults for sports competitions.

Summer Biathlon, P.O. Box 997, Portland, OR 97207, Sanctioning body for the summer biathlon, which combines running and shooting.

Triathlon Federation/USA (TRIFED/USA), 1604 Pikes Peak Ave., P.O. Box 1010, Colorado Springs, CO 80901; 719-630-2255; Fax 719-630-2259, Sanctions safe, well-managed triathlons, coordinates regional, national, and international championships, trains officials, aids in developing youth programs.

U.S. Cross Country Coaches Association, 207 State Gym, Iowa State University, Ames, IA 50011; 515-294-3723, Professional organization of college and university cross-country coaches. Selects the All-American team each year.

U.S. Modern Pentathlon Association (USMPA), P.O. Drawer 8178, San Antonio, TX 78208; 512-246-3000, Develops, selects, and trains the pentathlon teams to represent the United States in the Olympics, Pan American Games, World Championship, and other international competitions.

U.S. Women's Track Coaches Association (USWTCA), Belmont 718, University of Texas, Austin, TX 78712; 512-471-7693, Organization provides information and serves as a forum for track coaches interested in women's track and field.

Women's Distance Committee, 215-4 Sellby Ranch Road, Sacramento, CA 95864; 916-392-5111, Organization for men and women interested in promoting distance running for women; sponsors seminars and clinics, and compiles statistics.

Women's Sports Foundation, 342 Madison Ave., Suite 728, New York, NY 10173; 800-227-3988 (except New York City), 212-972-9170; Fax 212-949-8024, A nonprofit educational organization established by Billie Jean King in 1974 to promote and enhance the sports experience of all girls and women. Provides educational services, opportunity, advocacy; also sponsors the Women's Sports Hall of Fame.

YMCA (Young Men's Christian Association), 101 North Wacker Dr., Chicago, IL 60606; 312-977-0031, Despite its name, this organization is coed. There are thousands of YMCAs located throughout the United States, many with indoor tracks. You don't have to be young, male, or Christian to be welcomed at any YMCA. Some Y's have developed outdoor running paths and will direct you to them.

Bibliography

BOOKS

The Aerobics Way. Dr. Kenneth Cooper, M.D., M.P.H. New York: Bantam, 1978. The book that started it all, by the aerobic guru himself. The fitness point system is appealing.

Beyond Jogging: The Innerspaces of Running. Mike Spino. Millbrae, CA: Celestial Arts, 1976. The director of the Esalen Sports Center discusses the transcendental aspects of running. One of the few running books you would find in a shop carrying incense and candles.

The Boston Marathon. Joe Falls. New York: Macmillan Publishing, 1977. Story of America's greatest foot race and the men and women who have run it. Includes thumbnail sketches of winners from 1897 to 1976; great photos.

The Complete Book of Running. James Fixx. New York: Random House, 1977. Lots and lots of information for all skill and experience levels. He would have been better served by photos than the repetitive line drawings.

The Complete Book of Walking. Charles T. Kuntzleman and editors of Consumer Guide. New York: Pocket Books, 1979. How to start walking and keep going. Well written and full of fascinating facts.

The Complete Marathoner. Editors of *Runner's World.* Mountain View, CA: Anderson World, 1978. This one almost lives up to its title. All you ever wanted to know about 26.2 miles, by a wide range of authors.

The Complete Runner. Editors of *Runner's World.* New York: Avon, 1974. An impressive anthology of articles by everyone who's anyone in the world of running; everything from lifestyle and nutrition to training and competition.

The Complete Walker. Colin Fletcher. New York: Alfred Knopf, 1976. Everything you ever needed to know and what to carry in order to get away from it all.

The Complete Woman Runner. Editors of *Runner's World.* Mountain View, CA: Anderson World, 1980. The female runner's ultimate guide, from beginner to marathon. Includes history, injury prevention, safety, family concerns, and short profiles of fifty U.S. women runners.

The Death Valley 300. Richard Benyo. Forestville, CA: Specific Publications, 1991. The harrowing tale of Richard Benyo and Tom Crawford running from Death Valley to the top of Mount Whitney and back.

Fast Tracks: The History of Distance Running. Raymond Krise and Bill Squires. Brattleboro, VT: Stephen Greene Press, 1982. Everything you could ever want to know about the history of distance running. Fine photos.

Finnish Running Secrets. Matti Hannus. Mountain View, CA: World Publications, 1973. Besides secrets, this booklet contains some memorable action photos. I tend to listen to Finns when it comes to running.

Galloway's Book on Runners. Jeff Galloway. Bolinas, CA: Shelter Publications, 1984. Detailed workout plan and schedule for the serious runner.

Hiking the Backcountry. Jackie Johnson Maughan and Ann Puddicombe. Harrisburg, PA: Stackpole Books, 1981. A do-it-yourself guide to backpacking for the adventurous woman. Everything from equipment and physical fitness to perils and psychology.

Indian Running. Peter Nabokov. Santa Barbara, CA: Capra Press, 1981. All about the ritual running of various Indian tribes; fascinating photos.

Jesse Owens: An American Life. William J. Baker. New York: The Free Press, 1986. The story of the world's greatest sprinter.

Jim Fixx's Second Book of Running. Jim Fixx. New York: Random House, 1980. Fixx confronts the difficult task of following up his first book, which was supposedly "Complete." Some new material, some rehash.

Jog, Run, Race. Joe Henderson. Mountain View, CA: World Publications, 1977. The West Coast editor of *Runner's World* magazine takes the reader through all the sequences of the sport – starting, walking, jogging, running, racing.

The Joy of Running. Thaddeus Kostrubala, M.D. New York: Pocket Books, 1977. The author enthusiastically shares his epiphany with us.

Letters From Steven. Steven Newman. Topeka, KS: Capper's Books, 1987. Stories from the first-ever solo walk around the world, put into letter form.

The Long Run Solution. Joe Henderson. Mountain View, CA: World Publications, 1976. In a field dominated by physiology and the "how-to," this psychological ramble is a refreshing and well-written change of pace.

Lore of Running. Tim Noakes, M.D. Champaign, IL: Human Kinetics Publishers, 1991. The definitive 804-page reference work on the physiology and medical aspects of long-distance running. A must for the serious runner.

The Marathon Made Easier. Cliff Temple. New York: Atheneum, 1982. A safe and simple guide to distance running, including weather, diet, training, how to finish, and records.

The Marathon: What it Takes to Go the Distance. Marc Bloom. New York: Holt, Reinhart, Winston, 1981. The marathon: from history to conditioning.

Marathoning. Bill Rodgers, with Joe Concannon. New York: Simon & Schuster, 1978. Though not brilliantly written, it is full of background and insights on Rodgers's interesting life.

Masters of the Marathon. Richard Benyo. New York: Athenium, 1983. Profiles of thirteen men and one woman, great marathoners all; interesting stuff on the history of the modern marathon.

Masters Running and Racing. Bill Rodgers and Priscilla Welch. Emmaus, PA: Rodale

Press, 1991. A weave of inspirational first-person stories and advice by two world-class runners, both of whom kicked cigarette habits. Lots of charts and tables.

Meditations From the Breakdown Lane. James E. Shapiro. New York: Random House, 1982. The story of the author's eighty-day run across the United States.

Peak Condition. James G. Garrick, M.D., and Peter Radetsky. New York: Crown Publishers, 1986. This covers more than just runners' injuries, but there's plenty of those, too. Handy index and lots of questions and answers.

Personal Best. George Sheehan, M.D. Emmaus, PA: Rodale Press, 1989. A collection of short essays on health and fitness from America's most philosophical runner. A paean for exercise, its joys and benefits.

The Psychic Power of Running. Valerie Andrews. New York: Rawson, Wade Publishers, 1978. The psychological aspects of running, in a nutshell. Well written and illuminating.

Risk! An Exploration into the Lives of Athletes on the Edge. Steve Boga. Berkeley, CA: North Atlantic Books, 1988. Profiles of ten world-class adventure athletes. Includes runners, climbers, skiers, a whitewater canoeist, and others.

Runners & Walkers. John Cumming. Chicago: Regnery Gateway, 1981. A detailed account of pedestrians in the nineteenth century. One of the few histories that includes walkers.

The Runner's Complete Medical Guide. Richard Mangi, M.D., Peter Jokl, M.D., and O. William Dayton, A.T.C. New York: Summit Books, 1979. There's that word again — "complete." In this case, it's pretty accurate — it's far more than I want to know about the physiology of running. Well organized by body parts.

The Runner's Handbook. Bob Glover and Jack Shepherd. New York: Penguin Books, 1978. Well written, well organized, and full of useful information.

The Runners' Repair Manual. Dr. Murray F. Weisenfeld with Barbara Burr. New York: St. Martin's Press, 1980. A cogent explanation for the layman of injuries and what to do about them.

The Runner's Yoga Book. Jean Couch. Berkeley, CA: Rodmell Press, 1990. Yoga instructor Couch argues for specific stretching exercises before running. Simple-to-follow instructions, straightforward prose, and plenty of photos. Also, it is spiral-bound so you can lay the book flat on the floor.

Running A to Z. Joe Henderson. Brattleboro, VT: Stephen Greene Press, 1983. Each chapter begins with a different letter of the alphabet, a technique that is rather contrived, but Henderson writes well enough and his message is worth hearing: run long, slow distances and keep running.

Running After 40. Editors of *Runner's World.* Mountain View, CA: Anderson World, 1980. Training tips for Masters, including stretching, walking, jogging, running, sprinting; records and illustrations.

Running & Being. Dr. George Sheehan. New York: Warner Books, 1978. If you run for contemplation, this book will help direct your thoughts. The man has a command of the language.

The Running Foot Doctor. Steven I. Subotnick. Mountain View, CA: World Publications,

1977. An anecdotal, case-study approach to the subject of running physiology; a refreshing change from the ordinary.

Running Free. Joan L. Ullyot, M.D. New York: G.P. Putnam's Sons, 1980. A book for women runners and their friends by the best-known runner-doctor-author.

Running the Lydiard Way. Arthur Lydiard with Garth Gilmour. Mountain View, CA: World Publications, 1978. How to become a great distance runner by possibly the most respected teacher in the field. Dated in places, but if you want to be competitive, it doesn't get any better than this.

Running Tide. Joan Benoit with Sally Baker. New York: Alfred A. Knopf, 1987. A must if you're interested in one of the great athletic comebacks in history.

Running to Win. Brian Mitchell. Vancouver: David & Charles, 1976. Training and racing for young athletes. Discusses the benefits of running, including the physiological and psychological changes that occur during training; illustrated.

Running Without Fear. Dr. Kenneth Cooper. New York: Bantam Books, 1985. A defense of aerobic exercise in the wake of the dramatic sudden death of Jim Fixx. Science for the layman.

The Self-Coached Runner. Allan Lawrence and Mark Scheid. New York: Little, Brown & Co., 1984. Wanna run a 40-minute 10-K? How about a four-hour marathon? This book has the requisite training schedule outlined, week by week.

Serious Runner's Handbook. Tom Osler. Mountain View, CA: Anderson World, 1978. Offers 255 running questions and their sometimes provocative answers, according to the well-run author.

The Sports Success Book. Karl M. Woods. Austin, TX: Copperfield Press, 1985. Cogent endeavor to answer the question: what are the ingredients of athletic success?

SportsTalent. Dr. Robert Arnot and Charles Gaines. New York: Penguin Books, 1986. Performance requirements and tests for a multitude of sports, including skiing, cycling, running, windsurfing, and tennis. How to measure everything from your body fat to your stride length.

Target 26. John Graham and Skip Brown. New York: Macmillan Publishing Co., 1983. All you want to know about preparing to run a marathon. Some good information, but dated, especially regarding nutrition and warmup exercises.

Training the Lydiard Way. Arthur Lydiard. Basking Ridge, NJ: Lydiard Enterprises and Eugene Brutting's EB Sport International GMBH. This tiny booklet lays out the Lydiard training regime in concise fashion; not pretty, but effective.

The Ultimate Athlete. George Leonard. New York: Viking Press, 1975. This is Leonard's paean to "the new PE." He drifts a bit, but he's a good writer and his chapter on running provides some real insights.

Visual Athletics. Kay Porter, Ph.D., and Judy Foster. Dubuque, IA: William C. Brown Publishers, 1990. Sport psychologists have long advised athletes to visualize ideal performances before competition takes place. This book contains the tips that will help you do just that, not just in running but in other sports as well.

Walking—The Pleasure Exercise. Mort Malkin. Emmaus, PA: Rodale Press, 1986. A sixty-day walking program for fitness and health. Everything from calories to catcalls.

The Wellness Encyclopedia. University of California, Berkeley. Boston: Houghton, Mifflin, 1991. The latest, best information on safeguarding health and preventing illness. Includes sections on longevity, nutrition, exercise, self-care, environment, and safety.

Women, Sports and Performance. Christine Wells, Ph.D. Champaign, IL: Human Kinetics Publishers, 1991. Well researched, this book provides information that pertains both directly and indirectly to women, such as eating disorders, bone health, pregnancy, menopause, and athletic amenorrhea.

Women's Running. Dr. Joan Ullyot. Mountain View, CA: World Publications, 1976. One of the best-written running books by the number-one cheerleader for women runners.

Worldwalk. Steven M. Newman. New York: Avon Books, 1990. A thorough account of the author's four-year walk around the world.

PERIODICALS

Athletics (Ontario Athletics), 1220 Sheppard, E. Willowdale, ON M2K 2X1, Canada, 416-495-4053, Fax 416-495-4052. Medical information, race results and rankings, interviews, editorial, statistics, history, and book reviews.

Boston Marathon Magazine, Boston Phoenix Publishers, 126 Brookline Ave., Boston, MA 02115, 617-536-5390, Fax 617-536-1463. All about the granddaddy of all marathons.

Canadian Runner, 23 Brentcliffe Rd., Suite 308, Toronto, Ontario M4G 4B7, Canada.

Joe Henderson's Running Commentary, 441 Brookside Dr., Eugene, OR 97405, 503-683-2118. For participants in long-distance running; news, comment, practical advice.

Marathon Plus, 1028 Marie-Victorin, Laval PQ H7E 3C1, Canada, 514-661-5586. Features on running (both amateur and professional), physical fitness, health, and nutrition. Published in French.

National Masters News, Box 2372, Van Nuys, CA 91404, 818-785-1895. The definitive periodical covering track and running for people over age thirty.

New York Running News, 9 E. 89th St., New York, NY 10128. America's largest regional running magazine. The official publication of the New York Road Runners Club.

Road Race Management, 1201 S. Eads St., No. 2, Arlington, VA 22202, 703-979-4820. Advice and news for running-race directors, organizers, and sponsors.

Runner's World, Rodale Press, 33 E. Minor St., Emmaus, PA 18098, 215-967-5171. Health, fitness, training, and profiles for runners of all commitments. The dominant consumer publication in the field.

Running Journal, P.O. Box 157, Greenville, TN 37744. Large regional tabloid that covers the sport from Virginia through the deep South.

Running Times, 9171 Wilshire Blvd., No. 300, Beverly Hills, CA 90210, 703-491-2044. Information for both recreational and competitive runners, including training methods and race rankings. A distant second to *Runner's World* in the competition for a national running magazine.

Track, National Federation of State High School Associations, 11724 Plaza Circle, Box 20626, Kansas City, MO 64195. Track and field rules for high school competition.

Track and Field News, 2570 El Camino Real, No. 606, Mountain View, CA 94040, 415-948-8188, Fax 415-948-9445. Covers track and field throughout the world, from high school to the Olympics.

Triathlete, 1415 Third St., No. 303, Santa Monica, CA 90401, 213-394-1321. Publication for triathletes of all intensity levels.

Ultrarunning, 300 N. Main St., P.O. Box 481, Sunderland, MA 01375, 413-665-7573. A national publication covering distances beyond the marathon. Not glossy, but well written.

Walking Magazine, 9–11 Harcourt, Boston, MA 02116, 617-266-3322, Fax 617-266-7373. A national magazine for recreational and fitness walkers.

Shoe Manufacturers

Adidas U.S.A.
15 Independence Blvd.
Warren, NJ 07060

ASICS
10540 Talbert Ave.
West Building
Fountain Valley, CA 92708

Autry Industries
11420 Reeder Road
Box 59149
Dallas, TX 75229-1149

Avia Athletic Footwear
Box 23309
Portland, OR 97223

Brooks
9341 Courtland Drive
Rockford, MI 49351

Converse
1 Fordham Road
North Reading, MA 01864

Diadora U.S.A.
6529 S. 216th, Bldg. E
Kent, WA 98032

Etonic
147 Centre St.
Brockton, MA 02403

Hersey Custom Shoes
Hidden Hills Farm
RFD No. 3, Box 7390
Farmington, ME 04938

Hi-Tec Sports U.S.A.
4400 North Star Way
Modesto, CA 95356

Karhu
1455 Concord St.
Framingham, MA 01701

Lotto U.S.A.
2301 McDaniel Drive
Carrollton, TX 75006

New Balance
38 Everett St.
Boston, MA 02134

Nike
3900 S.W. Murray Blvd.
Beaverton, OR 97005

Pony
Meadow Office Complex
201 Route 17 N.
Rutherford, NJ 07070

Puma U.S.A.
492 Old Connecticut Path
Framingham, MA 01701

Reebok
100 Technology Way
Stoughton, MA 02072

Saucony
13 Centennial Drive
Peabody, MA 01961

Turntec
16542 Milliken Ave.
Irvine, CA 92714

ABOUT THE AUTHOR

Steven Boga has probed the exciting world of adventure sports through dozens of revealing interviews with world-class athletes. Drawing from these studies in excellence, he has written *RISK! An Exploration into the Lives of Athletes on the Edge* and *Cyclists: How the World's Most Daring Riders Train and Compete* (book one of the Adventure Athletes series). Boga has also contributed numerous articles to *Sierra Adventure*, *Pacific Sport*, *Men's Health*, and other magazines.